DATE DUE

DE 1 5 05			

DEMCO 38-296

PLAYING RECORDER SONATAS

Frontispiece Euterpe, the Muse of flute-playing and lyric poetry, by Giovanni Baglione (1573–1644). Baglione painted seven of the nine muses in 1620 for the Gonzaga Ducal Palace at Mantua, whence they were presented in 1624 to Marie de' Medici and displayed in the Salle des Muses in the Luxembourg Palace in Paris. The five which remain are now in the art gallery of the Musée d'Arras. Euterpe, who the inscription implies plays the recorder at special occasions, possesses three tenor recorders (and a sackbut). The recorders are of near-cylindrical Renaissance design, with the narrow 'window' on the underside.

Playing Recorder Sonatas

Interpretation and Technique

ANTHONY ROWLAND-JONES

CLARENDON PRESS · OXFORD
1992

...iversity Press, Walton Street, Oxford OX2 6DP

Oxford New York Toronto
...hi Bombay Calcutta Madras Karachi
...ling Jaya Singapore Hong Kong Tokyo
Nairobi Dar es Salaam Cape Town
Melbourne Auckland
and associated companies in
Berlin Ibadan

Oxford is a trade mark of Oxford University Press

Published in the United States
by Oxford University Press, New York

© Anthony Rowland-Jones 1992

British Library Cataloguing in Publication Data
Data available

Library of Congress Cataloging in Publication Data
Playing recorder sonatas: interpretation and technique
Anthony Rowland-Jones.
Includes bibliographical references and index.
1. Recorder (Musical instrument)—Instruction and study.
2. Sonatas—Interpretation (Phrasing, dynamics, etc.)   I. Title.
MT350.R69   1992   788.3'6183143—dc20   91–36802
ISBN 0–19–879002–3
ISBN 0–19–879001–5 (pbk)

Typeset by Litho Link Limited, Welshpool, Powys
Printed in Great Britain by
St. Edmundsbury Press, Bury St. Edmunds

To Euterpe
(see Frontispiece)
in the hope that she will inspire other recorder-players
to perform sonatas with understanding, imagination, and grace

ACKNOWLEDGEMENTS

MUSIC

I am grateful to Clifford Bartlett of King's Music for letting me use (Ex. 2.1) his facsimile of the 1732 Walsh edition of Handel's G minor recorder sonata. I also wish to make acknowledgement to the following publishers for agreeing to the reproduction of excerpts from sonatas they have published, and to the editors of these sonatas named in the text or notes: Schott and Co., London (Telemann D minor sonata, Handel D minor sonata, 'Furioso' movement, Walter Leigh Sonatina, and excerpts (Handel G minor sonata) from Freda Dinn's *Early Music for Recorders*); Moeck Verlag, Celle (Fontana Sonata Terza); Bärenreiter Verlag, Kassel (Paisible Sonata in F, and incipits of Lœillet, Op. 1 Nos. 2 and 3); Heinrichshofens Verlag–Noetzel Pegasus edition, Wilhelmshaven (Lavigne 'La Persan'); Doblinger, Vienna (Schollum Sonatine excerpts); London Pro Musica Edition, Brighton (Riccio excerpts); and Nova Music, Hove (quotation from Notari's 'Canzona Passaggiata'). I should like to thank Edgar Hunt, for many years editor of *The Recorder Magazine*, for permission to republish my two articles on Baroque trills as Appendix I of this book.

ILLUSTRATIONS

I should like to express my thanks to Annick Notter, Conservateur of the Musée d'Arras, for authority to reproduce the museum's photograph of Baglione's Muse Euterpe, to Werner Helmberger of the Bavarian State Castles Administration for permission to reproduce details of Tiepolo's frescos in the Würzburg Residenz, to Irmgard and Askel H. Mathiesen for the use of their photograph of the Silkeborg recorder, and to Messrs Novello for allowing me to make use of diagrams from their book *Roger North on Music* (ed. John Wilson). Copyright acknowledgement is made for the use of the National Gallery photograph of Watteau's *La Gamme d'Amour*, for the illustration of La Caridad, Seville, from the Conway Collection at the Courtauld Institute of Art, University of London, and for Wim Swaan's photograph of the interior of Wies church. I am especially grateful to Bruce Robertson, of the Media Production Division of the

Anglia Polytechnic, Cambridge, for his skill and patience in photographic work, including making prints from my own negatives.

GENERAL

I am grateful to the staff of Oxford University Press, to Bonnie Blackburn for her meticulous and beneficial copy-editing, and to Sheila Stanton for her patience in some complicated setting of music examples.

Acknowledgements also to Penny Souster of Cambridge University Press, and to the authors themselves, for making available pre-publication copies of books by Peter le Huray and Eve O'Kelly.

Most of all, I should like to thank Jonathan Hellyer Jones, Peter le Huray, and Denise Williamson for reading and commenting on drafts of this book, and I am particularly grateful to Clifford Bartlett, Paul Clark, and David Lasocki, who, as 'author's readers', provided me with very detailed, frank, and perceptive critical commentaries. They have done much to make this a more accurate and useful book. I want, too, to thank my wife Christina for reading several earlier drafts, for her forbearance and support, and for her views on many points of doubt and turns of phrase. Finally, I thank my students who, unwittingly, have constantly kept me on the alert as they encounter new problems and arrive at new solutions and interpretations in their playing of recorder sonatas.

CONTENTS

ILLUSTRATIONS

NOTES ON EDITIONS USED

The Faber edition of the six Handel recorder sonatas (ed. Lasocki and Bergmann; 2nd edn., 1982) is the first to be based on the autograph and copyists' manuscripts as well as the prints; the Schott edition of four of these sonatas (ed. Hunt) gives more interpretational advice, such as suggestions for phrasing.

There are several editions of the Telemann sonatas. This book uses the Schott edition of Hugo Ruf (OFB 104).

The two volumes of six Lavigne sonatas (ed. Hillemann) are in Pegasus Noetzel N3434 and N3449, the latter containing 'La Persan'.

The Herbert Murrill Sonata is published by Oxford University Press.

The Moeck edition of six Fontana sonatas (ed. Braun) is in three volumes; Moeck Ed. 2110 comprises Sonatas Terza and Quarta. The 1989 Amadeus edition (ed. Zumbrunn) contains all six sonatas in one volume (Schott BP 466).

It is hoped that this book has enough quotations from these (and some other) sonatas for it to be self-sufficient, but readers who possess the above sonatas for reference and playing will find that this considerably increases the book's usefulness. This is especially so as, for reasons of space, in most of the examples in this book only the recorder part is quoted. It is essential, however, that the recorder-player should study and hear the continuo bass and keyboard parts in order to achieve a complete understanding and good interpretation of any sonata.

References are made more to the books listed below than to primary sources, as they should be easily available and most are published in paperback editions. Robert Donington's *A Performer's Guide to Baroque Music* (London: Faber, 1973) is not used for reference in this book, but only to avoid confusion. It is as recommendable as his other books. There is a selected bibliography, with comments, of books, articles, etc. of interest to recorder-players on pp. 153–64 of the author's *Recorder Technique* (2nd edn.).

ABBREVIATIONS AND SYMBOLS

Books and journals frequently cited are abbreviated as follows:

Anthony	James R. Anthony, *French Baroque Music from Beaujoyeulx to Rameau* (rev. edn., New York: W. W. Norton, 1981)
AR	*The American Recorder* (New York) (Journal of the American Recorder Society)
Donington, *Baroque*	Robert Donington, *Baroque Music: Style and Performance* (London: Faber, 1982)
Donington, *Interp.*	Robert Donington, *The Interpretation of Early Music* (London: Faber, 1989)
EM	*Early Music* (Oxford)
Hunt	Edgar Hunt, *The Recorder and its Music* (enlarged edn., London: Faber, 1977)
le Huray	Peter le Huray, *Authenticity in Performance: Eighteenth-Century Case Studies* (Cambridge: Cambridge University Press, 1990)
New Grove	*The New Grove Dictionary of Music and Musicians*, ed. Stanley Sadie, 20 vols. (London: Macmillan, 1980)
Newman	William S. Newman, *The Sonata in the Baroque Era* (4th edn., New York: W. W. Norton, 1983)
North	Roger North, *Roger North on Music*, ed. John Wilson (London: Novello, 1959)
O'Kelly	Eve O'Kelly, *The Recorder Today* (Cambridge: Cambridge University Press, 1990)
PB	Anthony Rowland-Jones, *A Practice Book for the Treble Recorder* (Oxford: Oxford University Press, 1962)
Quantz	Johann Joachim Quantz, *On Playing the Flute*, tr. Edward R. Reilly (2nd edn., London: Faber, 1985)

RMM	*The Recorder and Music Magazine* (as of 1990, *The Recorder Magazine*) (London)
RT	Anthony Rowland-Jones, *Recorder Technique: Intermediate to Advanced* (2nd edn., Oxford: Oxford University Press, 1986)

Fingerings (as in *RT*)

0 123 4567: thumb and all fingers on (treble F)

– –– ––––: all off

∅: thumb-hole partly open, or 'thumbed' (not 'pinched'!)

7̷, 6̷ etc.: half-holed

(3), etc.: third finger optional (depending on how the recorder is tuned, for example)

3ˣ: trill with third finger

X at the end of a fingering: covering of the bell-hole

In music examples ˣ over a note suggests the use of a non-standard fingering if this is musically and/or technically advantageous. When there are two important non-standard fingerings they may be differentiated by ˣ̇, e.g. ˣ is 'closed G'' - 123 4567, ˣ̇ is thumbed G' ∅ 123 4567̷ (*RT* 77–8).

Pitch-names

To avoid the proliferation of primes inherent in the Helmholtz system when applied to high-pitched instruments, lower octave notes are represented by e.g. F (lowest treble recorder note), C (lowest descant note), second octave notes by e.g. F', C', and third octave notes by e.g. F'', C'', as in *RT*.

Symbols

√̸ end of section or subsection, or take big breath, or (usually) both

√ breath

(√) breath if needed, otherwise . . .

, . . . phrase, breath probably not needed

(,) possible phrase-point

⌐—⌐ closely relate these notes, though not actually slurring

∿∿ vibrato, of changing amplitude and wave-length in this example

Throughout this book the masculine pronoun presupposes the feminine.

INTRODUCTION

THIS book concentrates on the sonata repertoire for treble (or sometimes descant) recorder with keyboard or thorough-bass. It is intended for players who may have embarked upon this repertoire and who wish to extend their understanding and enjoyment of a wide range of accompanied solo sonatas from Handel and Telemann to eighteenth-century French compositions, then forward to twentieth-century sonatas and sonatinas, and back to early seventeenth-century Italian sonatas and canzonas.

Although reference, often in depth, is made to other sonatas, five pieces have been selected for special attention. Each of these pieces is used to illustrate a particular aspect of interpretation. The pieces are Handel's Sonata in G minor, Op. 1 No. 2, Telemann's Sonata in D minor from *Essercizii Musici*, Lavigne's Sonata 'La Persan', Op. 2 No. 5, Murrill's Sonata, and Fontana's Sonata Terza.

After some general points on playing baroque sonatas (Ch. 1), five broad aspects of interpretation and technique are considered in Chs. 2–6. These are sound and expression (exemplified in the Handel sonata), dynamics and Italian style (Telemann sonata), French style and inequality (Lavigne), articulation and slurs (Murrill), and ornamentation and improvisation (Fontana). As all these aspects of interpretation apply generally, there is considerable overlap between chapters, and reference is made to other sonatas: for example, baroque articulation is illustrated by the Furioso movement of Handel's D minor recorder sonata. Some passages or movements of the five sonatas which seem especially illustrative of certain points of interpretation and technique are dealt with in much greater detail than other parts of the same sonata. No attempt is made to offer a complete interpretative guide to any of the five sonatas.

Further aspects of performance are discussed in Ch. 7, mainly in relation to the five selected sonatas. The final chapter (8) refers to interpretative or technical points in ten other sonatas, and these pieces also exemplify the range of solo sonata-type music which may be played on the recorder. There is no specific consideration of other recorder chamber music such as trio sonatas, ensemble sonatas, cantatas, duets, concertos, or consort music, but a person who can play solo sonatas with confidence and musicianly understanding will be better fitted to enjoy recorder-playing in all its forms.

Written words, however, can never adequately demonstrate how music should, or might, sound. Aspiring soloists must miss no opportunity to hear live or recorded performances of recorder sonatas. Moreover, a book cannot replace a good teacher who knows how to develop each pupil's insights so that every performance becomes an exciting new experience. It may, however, give both teachers and players fresh ideas about how to approach a piece of music, how to recognize and respond to its language and substance, and how to resolve its complexities.

A sonata involves collaboration between a composer and a performer, the perceptions and personalities of both contributing to its fulfilment. This book therefore seeks to help players to appreciate the style and quality of a composer's invention and imagination within the conventions and circumstances of his time, and to stimulate understanding, skill, and enthusiasm in recommunicating the composer's thoughts and ideas in an ever-changing environment. It is this continuing process that makes sonata-playing so challenging and so rewarding.

1

The Approach to Playing Baroque Sonatas
Some General Points

Sonate, que me veux-tu?
(remark attributed to Fontenelle *c*.1740; see Newman, 353)

THE performance of a piece of music is likely to be of more significance, and probably more effective, if the player knows what the music 'wants of him', what it is intended to communicate, what its purpose is. In his analysis of the meaning and use of the sonata in the Baroque era,[1] Newman cites many contemporary opinions, all saying that the purpose of music is to please and move an audience, the delectation of the player not being a prime consideration.[2] More specifically, instrumental music dissociated from a church or dramatic context is 'for the refreshment of the ear at entertainments and assemblies'.[3]

Baroque sonatas, however, even those that are light-hearted and gay, are normally conceived as serious entertainments, not just amusing trifles. A succession of short pieces in a concert can become tiresome, and the essence of a sonata is that it is an extended composition.[4] It therefore needs to possess coherence over a span of time, by its key relationships, by its dominant mood or 'affect', and (possibly) by thematic integration. Within this unity, it should have sufficient variety and contrast to sustain an audience's attention. Music associated with words can derive its extent,[5] form, substance, and mood from the meaning of those words. An extended form of music that is sounded on instruments (whence the derivation of the word 'sonata'[6]) must therefore, unlike sung music ('cantata'), evolve its own structures and compositional devices. Various conventions developed in the process of resolving this problem. Even so, writing a sonata posed special demands on its composer. It is not surprising that several Baroque composers, arriving at the stage of first publishing their work, displayed their quality in the form of a set of carefully-wrought sonatas,[7] an Opus 1 consisting of six or twelve 'solos'.[8] In performing recorder sonatas, the player should be aware of the compositional problems they had presented.

Through this awareness, he should try to communicate to his audience how the composer has attained coherence and variety, and in doing so he should share the composer's sense of achievement. The player needs from the outset to feel and convey the form and span of the sonata in its entirety.

Quantz repeatedly insists that the performer should 'divine the intentions of the composer'.[9] Although written in 1752, after the Baroque era and therefore applying more immediately to the *galant* sonata, much of Quantz's advice is relevant to the period of his own musical education during the earlier decades of the eighteenth century, when recorder sonatas were at their most fashionable.[10] Earlier tutors[11] offer some similar advice, but far less comprehensively. Quantz's chapters on 'Good Execution' (ch. 11) and on tonguing (ch. 6) are vital reading for recorder-sonata players.[12] His advice for good execution is that it should be 'true' (i.e. in tune) 'and distinct', 'rounded and complete', 'easy and flowing', 'varied' (in colour and dynamic), and, most important of all, 'expressive and appropriate to each passion that one encounters'.

Baroque and earlier[13] writers and musicians, in their belief that 'the true aim of music is to move the feelings' (Heinichen, 1728),[14] held that the vibrational patterns of concords and discords worked through the body upon the mind and the soul, the outcome varying somewhat from one person to another according to his own blend of the four temperaments, phlegmatic, sanguine, choleric, and melancholic. In vocal and dramatic music, the 'affect', an ideal emotional or moral state such as sorrow, valour, or tranquillity, is usually clear from the words and the dramatic situation;[15] instrumental music must similarly move an audience, but without the support of words. To do this, Baroque sonatas contain forms of expression and symbolism ('figures') derived from affective situations in vocal or dramatic music. A recorder-player needs to recognize compositional practices and patterns of notes that recur in Baroque sonatas, and try to arrive at conclusions about their affective connotations. We are by no means lacking in advice on this process from Quantz and his predecessors.

First, different keys were associated by many Baroque composers with different affects. It may be argued, and it occasionally was argued, that such ideas are invalidated by the variety of pitches prevailing in the Baroque period, especially the pitches of organs, and by the widespread practice of transposing one's own or another composer's music to form part of a different composition or to fit a different instrument. Key-colour, however, derives largely from the differences in tone-quality of notes on different instruments, and from tuning temperaments. Charpentier (1692) and Mattheson (1713) provide lists with interesting similarities and differences, and Rameau (1722) also gives guide-lines.[16] 'Generally a major key is used for the expression of what is gay, bold, serious or sublime, and a minor one for the expression of the flattering, melancholy and tender' (Quantz, 125). Thus, for Mattheson C major is, among other words, 'bold' (Charpentier 'gay and warlike'), F major is 'beautiful' (but Charpentier says 'furious', and Rameau agrees), A minor is calm (Charpentier 'tender') and D minor is 'religious' (Charpentier 'grave and pious').

Secondly, the word at the beginning of the piece, such as Spiritoso, Affettuoso, or Mesto (gloomy), further indicates the dominant sentiment of the piece (Quantz, 126). Telemann uses words such as Cunando, cradling, or Ondeggiando, undulating.[17]

Thirdly, 'The passions may be perceived from the dissonances . . . they always produce a variety of different effects' (Quantz, 126).[18] Affects may also

be discerned by whether the intervals between the notes are great or small, and whether the notes themselves ought to be slurred or articulated. Flattery, melancholy and tenderness are expressed by slurred and close intervals, gaiety and boldness by brief articulated notes, or those forming distant leaps . . . Dotted and sustained notes express the serious and the pathetic; long notes, such as semibreves or minims, intermingled with quick ones [as in a French overture] express the majestic and sublime (Quantz, 125–6).[19]

The player, having recognized an affect, should then 'seek to enter into the principal and related passions that he is to express' (Quantz, 124–5). He must 'take on the feeling which the composer intended in writing it'. C. P. E. Bach said (1753) that 'A musician cannot move others without himself being moved.'[20] And Mattheson proclaimed that music without affect 'can be considered nothing, does nothing, and means nothing'.[21]

It is essential that the recorder-sonata player should apply himself to recognizing and appreciating the purposes of the conventions through which musical communication took place in the Baroque period. Some familiarity with Baroque vocal and dramatic music, especially that of J. S. Bach and Handel, can make recorder sonatas more meaningful. Handel's A minor recorder sonata can be seen as a veritable operatic *scena*.[22] The first movement is melancholic and weary, with its drooping bass which thrice lapses into silence while the recorder sorrowfully meanders on.[23] The second movement faces the situation with operatic determination (an anger aria), but in the following Adagio, where the melody hardly manages to lift itself into expected lyricism, there is a feeling of defeat, with frequent falling short phrases,[24] as in bars 3–4 (Ex. 1.1).

The last movement bursts into fury. In this interpretation, to play the third movement serenely would miss the point. Its ornamentation should

EX. 1.1. Handel, Sonata in A minor

be restricted, to express the affect of resignation.[25] It is always worthwhile before playing a Baroque sonata (or having played it through once in an exploratory way) to 'let your imaginative forces work' and to think of descriptive words or phrases which will characterize each movement,[26] or even the whole sonata if it seems that the composer has aimed at a unity of affect. The player should then endeavour through his dynamics, his phrasing, his choice of speeds, his articulation, his ornamentation, and even his appearance, to put across what he thinks and feels about the music to his audience.

Baroque music should therefore be communicated to its audience in an outgoing and persuasive manner. If no audience is present during the playing of a sonata, it must be imagined as a kind of *alter ego*. The player should address this real or imagined audience like a prima donna coming forward to express her feelings, point of view, or state of mind while the action of the plot (told in recitative) is suspended; or like an orator pleasing, moving, and convincing his audience by the cogency, variety, commitment, and skill of his eloquence. Renaissance and Baroque writers[27] equate the disciplines of rhetoric with those of music, painting, acting, dancing, and other arts.[28] Music 'differs from rhetoric only in its medium' (Mattheson).[29] Baroque composers such as Monteverdi, Schütz, J. S. Bach,[30] and Telemann[31] drew upon their knowledge of rhetoric for musical forms and expressive devices, both particularly needful in unworded instrumental music. Recorder sonatas must be approached with a certain rhetorical deliberation, and an awareness of their craftsmanship. The music must flow, but each phrase, down to the relationship between pairs of notes, can have significance. No piece of music should be played in a matter-of-fact, unconsidered manner, least of all Baroque music that is so carefully crafted and empassioned. The parallel with the discourse of an orator persuading his audience must never be lost sight of. An orator should be audible, clear, and distinct, with pleasing variety, and 'he must express each sentiment with an appropriate vocal inflexion, and in general adapt himself to the place where he speaks, to the listeners before him, and to the content of the discourse he delivers' (Quantz, 119).

PL. 1.   East frontage of the Old Schools, Cambridge, between King's College Chapel and the Senate House (designed by Stephen Wright and built in 1754–8). Consider the following features of this Baroque façade:

1. Its entity, its good order and clearly defined sections, and its symmetry both laterally with the matching recessed bays and at different levels with the two complementing balustrades.

2. Its theatrical appearance, like a stage set, with mysterious dark central openings, and, above, with swags festooned beneath the cornice, draped at their ends like curtains.

3. The firmness of the lower part with its 'rusticated' arcade, the middle opening faced as if the hewn rock had just come out of the ground—a *basso fundamento*, or ground bass.

4. Its dominant design statements—equivalent to the melody and its development and resolution—at an upper level, and with a further round-arched window seen through the climactic central window—a touch of fancy and surprise.

5. And, above that, its discreet, harmonious, well-balanced, yet varied decoration of swags and symbolic faces of the four seasons, with stone vases ornamenting and punctuating the top line of the building.

The discipline of rhetoric calls for order and proportion. In the eighteenth century, balance, symmetry, and 'just proportion' were cultivated as much by composers as by architects. A section of a sonata movement may thus be seen as equivalent to the bay of a Baroque façade (see Pl. 1 and the caption, which shows how this analogy can be developed), or to the stanza of an ode, or the paragraph of an essay.[32] Similarly, a complete musical phrase is equivalent to a sentence, and the groupings of two or more notes (= syllables) within it are equivalent to the words that make up that sentence.[33] 'Hence you must strive to learn to see clearly and grasp what constitutes a good musical phrase, and what must therefore hang together . . . You must be attentive not to link passages that contain more than one phrase, and hence must be divided' (Quantz, 90).

Baroque music is close to poetry in this respect. In reading poetry aloud, the end of a line, and any natural break or 'caesura' within the line, is conveyed by a slight 'give' in delivery. This does not, however, disturb either the recurring metrical pulse of strong and weak syllables or the sense and rhythm of the words. The frequent cadences of Baroque music express phrase- and line-endings within the flow of the music. Each phrase resembles a single group of figures in a picture separated from other groups but related to them by similarity, significance, or subtle contrast, as are the receding groups in Watteau's *Love's Gamut* (see Pl. 3). Every phrase has its rhetorical climax followed by the relaxation of its cadence. The art of the Baroque-sonata performer is to combine a full awareness of, and identification with, the affects of the piece and a close perception of its complete rhetorical pattern of paragraphs, sentences, and phrases, with an impression of spontaneity as if he had just composed the piece himself. 'Everything in music that is done without reflection and deliberation . . . is without profit' (Quantz, 19).[34]

Poetry and music come closest in lyric verse and song. The commonest form of a lyrical or ballad stanza is the four-line quatrain. There are many implied quatrains in Baroque sonatas, and the shape of sections of sonata movements is often disclosed by a realization of their presence. This may be illustrated by the first movement of J.-B. Lœillet's Sonata in G minor, Op. 3 No. 3 of 1715 (ed. Block, Musica Rara): the 'lines' of the quatrain in bars 3–11 are shown by breath-marks, the caesuras by commas (see Ex. 1.2). The first line of the quatrain (starting at the up-beat to bar 4) has a certain firmness as it is founded upon the G minor tonality of the piece. The opening notes, which lift off from an up-beat dominant to a down-beat tonic, call for a deliberate poised beauty, auguring what is to follow. The upward movement of the first five notes needs to be balanced by the

EX. 1.2. Lœillet, Sonata in G minor.

Phrase-marks are given only for bars 3–11 because (1) recognition of the quatrain
and its phrase-structure determines the interpretation of the whole movement, and
(2) the bass part would also need to be shown for a full working-out of the phrasing.

downward movement of the next five notes, like inhaling then exhaling. In
comparison with the first line, the second line, which rests on four ledges,

E♭', B♭', F♯', and D, as it makes its way down, is more plaintive with its falling sighs, but, lacking a caesura, it has more impetus. The third line, fragmented and bolder, strengthens the opening statement by eschewing the lilt of the dotted figure, providing a rhythmic contrast which is used with effect later in the movement (e.g. bars 31–4); it has one, perhaps two, caesuras. The last line of the quatrain gently arrives at its cadence after what would have been its caesura. Having dispelled the slight melancholy of the second line by skipping down from D' to D (the first and last notes of the second line) with only G' in between, the fourth line comes straight to its conclusion with a holding back of the pulse to show that the full stop has been reached. This 'give', and a slight prolongation of the final note, enable the shorter last line of the quatrain to be kept in balance with its second line.

One can almost hear words in playing this music. Indeed the movement as a whole gives the impression that a story is being told. The story starts with two bars of introduction[35] ('Once upon a time . . .'). After the statement of the quatrain the story continues, but clouds soon appear (bar 16) and the music becomes more dramatic until it reaches a climax in bars 34–6, where the bass inverts the motive stated by the soloist in bars 31–4 (a motive derived from the third line of the quatrain) against the soloist's reiterated A's. After this complexity, all ends peacefully and happily ever after in the da capo.

Lœillet's choice of key accords with Mattheson's depiction of G minor as having an affect of 'quiet beauty, moderated between pain and pleasure'. Much more could be said about this movement: how short are the semiquavers? are the slurs to be slightly articulated or not? how fast does it go? what about dynamic levels, and ornamentation?[36] In considering all these matters, it should not be overlooked that this movement, like many opera arias of the time, derives from a dance form, the siciliana.

The greater rhythmic attack and sprightliness of instruments as compared with voices makes them ideal to accompany dancing, and this function has resulted in a profound association between dance-forms and sonatas. The *sonata da camera* ('chamber' or 'court') is made up of named dance movements that are close to the style and structure of the original dances, and even the supposedly more serious *sonata da chiesa*—though one does not usually expect to associate dancing with churches—frequently has movements derived from dance-forms, or rhythms which only achieve the right lilt when played in the manner of a dance, like the Lœillet movement above. A recorder-player who has had the experience of playing for a courtly- or country-dance group (e.g. Praetorius or Playford)—or of taking part as a dancer—will feel the exhilaration of the up-beat lift that characterizes much dance music. Knowing the style of each dance,[37] its purpose, figures, and steps, will enable him to feel the right pace and lift of dance-based movements in recorder sonatas. He would not, however, play most sonata dance movements as if they were real dances, for in a sonata the dance is often transmuted into a more flexible and sophisticated art-form.[38] A sonata gigue is normally vivacious and springy, but the music is far more contrived and elaborate than that of, say, a morris dance.

A varied sequence of dances, even if unified by tonality, does not constitute a sonata, though it could bear the title of 'suite'. Sonatas usually have more coherence, deliberateness, and sense of occasion. In a *sonata da camera*, or a French suite worked out in a similar manner, the overture, prelude, or other opening movement will often provide the gravity and theatrical splendour which acts as a setting for the following group of dances: it should be 'played big'. The composer will then usually place the more serious dances first, for example an allemande, a courante and a sarabande.[39] The player should never lose the characteristic rhythm of each dance: the four-square, almost military, style of the 'learned' allemande, the running courante swaying between two and three beats in the bar, the sinuous yet grave and expressive sarabande with its first beat lifted and its second firmed down. These dances generally need to be played in a concentrated, searching manner, so long as this does not destroy by over-expressivity the rhythmic character and drive of the dance-form. Then the player may relax a little in the lighter dances that follow. Some of these, such as the minuet, are so short that they need to be paired in ABA form, probably without change of speed,[40] though some composers suggest that a 'B' dance in a minor key might be played a little more slowly than the 'A' dance. Many French-style suites, and an occasional sonata, end with a magnificent chaconne, where the use of a ground bass gives length and coherence. Despite being so stylized and predictable, chaconnes are deeply satisfying, with their long unfolding, the pathos of the minor episode, and the sweep to the close.

Two points made earlier in this chapter apply particularly to dance movements. First, to match the steps of a dance, its music has to be regular in form, most typically with four phrases of four bars each. This structure demands the same kind of internal balance as the verse quatrain.[41] The constraints of the regularity of dance-forms place a special responsibility upon the sonata performer, who, while sustaining a supple and steady rhythm, should cultivate variety in presentation, with the light and shade ('chiaroscuro'[42]) of contrasts of dynamics and articulation, little expressive subtleties, and graceful or exhilarating ornamentation at repeats. Secondly, dance-movement performance should in all ways be subservient to the affect of the music. Unless ridicule was intended, a dramatic or symbolic personage in a masque or opera-ballet would perform dances which were appropriate to his or her character. 'Every dance should convey some affection of the soul.'[43] Mattheson identified the courante with 'sweet hopefulness', the sarabande with 'ambition', the passepied with 'frivolity'.[44] Such affects should be conveyed through the devices of oratory. Denis Gaultier (1603–72) called his dance suites 'La Rhétorique des Dieux'.

Beyond the association of affects with dances, various metres and rhythms had affective connotations, down to the rhythms of particular ornaments. Lasocki and Legêne[45] show how Handel uses the insistent rhythm of inverted mordents placed on nine successive crotchets in order to convey aggression. These affective forms and rhetorical devices constituted a means whereby a Baroque composer could convey an affect or emotion to an audience who would have been accustomed to responding to symbolic representation in all forms of art.

The image of the orator, or of the operatic prima donna supported by the powerful symbolism of Baroque stage-effects ('machines'), of sumptuous and exotic costumes, and of rhetorical gestures, poses the question of the display element in the Baroque sonata. An orator must command attention, and if the hearers' minds wander, the sonata becomes as nothing. The early association of the sonata with the violin and with the increasing virtuosity of its exponents—their ever-higher finger positions and more astounding double-stops—caused some seventeenth-century writers to regard the sonata as an occasion for display, calling for rich sonority, great dynamic contrasts, many changes of speed, florid ornamentation at protracted cadences, and rhythmic exuberance.[46]

Quantz advocated modesty in flautists (pp. 203–4), but it is not immodest for a player to want to share with others his pleasure in the capabilities and qualities of his instrument, nor even to revel in his own achievement in mastering technical difficulties. Sensationalism for its own sake, however, is self-defeating, as yesterday's dazzling brilliance becomes today's expected commonplace. Many sonatas contain passages designed to surprise and delight, and Italian sonatas in particular have an element of swagger, often frowned upon by both French and German writers.[47] This fire and passion does not make them any less serious in intent. Couperin declared that 'in all good faith I am more pleased with what moves me than what astonishes me' (Donington, *Baroque*, 2); yet, despite his nationality, which prized elegance, refinement, and restraint above Italian effusiveness, he held in high regard the robust and showy (though finely crafted) sonatas of Corelli, to the extent of apotheosizing him.[48] Even ostentation, for example in one's style of ornamentation, may be justified, if that, or arrogance, or vanity, or aggression, is believed to be the intended affect of the music. Fast and difficult passages in sonatas are less likely to be challenges to the performer's technical prowess than expressions of fury, bombast, or jubilation, although in some concerto-like sonatas the composer himself may have intended display in performance as a kind of rhetorical effect.

A player's enjoyment and understanding of a sonata is likely to be enhanced if he considers the process of creation of the music, participating vicariously in the composer's invention and craftsmanship. What did the composer have in mind when, possibly pressed by patron or penury, he surveyed the empty page before him? Accepted sonata structures gave him an excellent start. The slow-fast-slow-fast four-movement structure of the standard *sonata da chiesa* assured rhetorical effectiveness—a beguiling beginning to capture the attention of the audience, a more demanding Allegro, a contemplative Adagio, and a lively ending to revive flagging spirits and send the audience away happy.[49] Composers and performers alike worked within conventional forms for the movements of a sonata—for example, the gentle French rondeau and its more boisterous English cousin the 'Round-O', the fugal forms developed from the polyphonic ricercar (= 'research'), the walking andante bass, the pompous French overture, the dance-like air—each, along with many dance-forms, requiring a different attitude of mind and feeling on the part of the player. He must get to know the significance of the 'time-word' (as much an 'affect-word', for speed was also indicated by the time signature[50]) usually given by the composer for each movement, remembering that it varied by period and country. Purcell's Largo was not slow (Donington, *Interp.* 388), and for Telemann 'vivace' meant 'lively' rather than 'quickly'. The speed of a movement depends on its affect, on the exigencies of good phrasing, and on a balancing of speeds within the sonata as a whole (see Ch. 7). Although Baroque music encompasses a wide variety of tempos, it is rarely extremely fast or extremely slow.

The performer should also be aware of compositional methods used to enlarge and develop a subject (Newman, 68), such as sequence (see Ex. 1.3);[51] he must respond to the affective implications of the harmonic progression of a movement; he must sense the need for dynamic changes, including echo-effects; and he must be ever susceptible to the rise and fall, the tension and repose, of short, quickly cadencing phrases set in apposition to each other, a process at the heart of Baroque composing. Many Baroque sonata movements are conceived as a duet or dialogue between the soloist and the supporting bass, and within the solo part itself a kind of urbane conversation may develop. Consider the excerpt from the second movement of Handel's F major recorder sonata (bars 20–4) given in Ex. 1.3—one can imagine two characters conversing, almost in repartee. Do they both slur?[52]

EX. 1.3. Handel, Sonata in F major

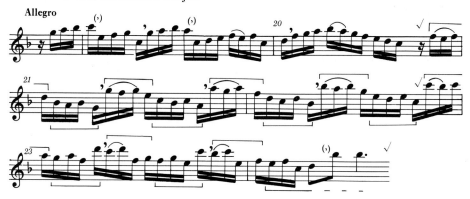

The extract also exemplifies sequential composition (between the breath-marks in bars 20 and 22 the eight-semiquaver figure is played four times, rising by one note of the scale on each repetition), and the use of passage-work to elaborate and sustain a harmonic progression. In late Renaissance solo ricercars (e.g. by Bassano or Virgiliano) there are long passages of continuous quavers, challenging the performer to shape the music in relation to its harmonic and melodic implications through his phrasing, dynamics, articulation, and slight speed-changes within the prevailing pulse. There are similar challenges in Baroque sonatas, especially during long lines of passage-work semiquavers which must discourse and have an objective.

Although Baroque musical conventions provided accepted modes of communication between a musician and his cultivated audience, musicians were expected to exercise a freshness and novelty of invention and imagination—'What oft was thought, but ne'er so well expressed' (Pope, *Essay on Criticism*). Fancy and surprise are an essential part of Baroque music.[53] French harpsichord-players saw no contradiction between the formalities of restrained good taste and the liberties allowed by unmeasured preludes without barlines (Donington, *Interp.* 426 and Anthony, 252). The best performers displayed a freedom and intensity of expression that transcended regularity, yet without eccentricity or crudeness. Being dull was a greater sin than being unconventional, but Baroque artistry avoided both.

In his enjoyable discovery of Baroque sonatas the recorder-player needs to supplement much playing—and much listening[54]—with constant reference to books on Baroque performance practice.[55] Donington emphasizes 'the great baroque principle of flexible interpretation' (Donington, *Interp.* 670), and he distils the characteristics of Baroque sound into the words 'transparent sonority and incisive articulation' (*Baroque*, 167–71). Clarity and flexibility of interpretation can only be achieved, however, if the performer has carefully considered what he believes the music wants him to say, and how best he should say it.

Sound and Expression: Handel's Sonata in G minor

THE recorder, or 'flûte douce', cannot be regarded as an instrument ideally suited to playing sonatas. Because of its plangent articulation, and its intense yet pure and ethereal sound, the recorder was associated with scenes of 'soft delight',[1] pastoral or garden settings, and other-worldly contexts. Except for the second and fourth Brandenburg Concertos, the Handel sonatas, and some of Telemann's sonatas, trio sonatas, and other chamber music, the best Baroque music specifically written for the recorder is found within a literary or vocal milieu, such as episodes in Purcell's Odes and theatre music and in Bach cantatas and Handel operas, where the sound of two recorders contrasts wonderfully with the presence of other instruments and voices. These are on the whole short passages and special occasions. The paucity of harmonic upper partials in the make-up of recorder sound, which gives it this ethereal, disembodied quality becomes something of a disadvantage in playing sonatas. Mattheson commented that recorder tone ('soft and insidious'[2]) tired the ear more rapidly than that of more harmonically complex instruments. It is therefore a special challenge to the performer of a recorder sonata to show that his instrument can transcend its Baroque theatrical symbolism (as well as its present-day educational associations) and to play his instrument with sufficient variety of expression to command the unflagging attention of his audience. Across an entire recital, however, the recorder-player does have the advantage that he can choose pieces that call for different types and sizes of recorders, thus providing tonal contrast.

The problem is exacerbated in that most Baroque sonatas, already conceived as extended pieces of up to about fifteen minutes' duration,[3] derive from Italian models, where qualities not especially associated with recorder sound predominate—passion, energy, fire, and a wide variety of tone and dynamics—qualities with which the violin, the prime instrument of Italian sonatas, is well endowed. The Italian-style sonata was also associated in the seventeenth century with the trumpet, and in the eighteenth with the expressive flute, with its suave timbre and its ability to express rapidly changing affections. It behoves a recorder-player to be prepared to use the whole range of capabilities of his instrument, however limited they may be at first seem to be. Otherwise his performance may sound pedestrian or monotonous.

The sonata-performer needs first to consider the sound-qualities of the different recorders available to him in relation to the music he wishes to play. The tonal range of recorders of different sizes, pitches, and designs is extraordinarily wide, yet they all produce a recognizable and characteristic recorder sound. The large recorders have depth and richness of sound but lack definition and volume; the smaller recorders have great penetration (e.g. the sopranino in a Vivaldi concerto) but can be shrill and lack body. The compromise is probably at its best with a low-pitched treble recorder at $a' = 415$. The warm-toned voice-flute (a 'tenor' recorder in D) projects less easily than the treble and needs to be pushed in its lowest register to be on terms with most continuo instruments. The tenor itself, in C, does not have enough bite and power to command an audience as the main instrument in a sonata recital, although its soft and velvety sound is gravely beautiful with a guitar or lute continuo. The descant, an octave higher, commands attention through its pitch and agility, but its expressive limitations and lack of tonal weight become apparent in slow movements; nevertheless it balances well with the harpsichord, and suits music which is not too intense—certain French suites, for example. The descant, or better still the sixth-flute in D a tone higher, is very effective in short concertos[4] where some element of piccolo-like display is a feature. Though descant or even tenor recorders may sound well in some sonatas, and are useful for programme contrast, the treble in F was the main recorder for playing sonatas and chamber music in the high Baroque period. It has been conjectured that the voice-flute in D, which continued to be made later in the eighteenth century, would have played music written for the eighteenth-century transverse flute, which had much the same range as the voice-flute.[5]

The tone-quality of a recorder of a given size depends on a complex interrelated series of design factors, of which the material with which it is made is but one (see *RT* 7–8). Sound-quality is affected by the bore—wide or narrow, cylindrical or tapering (or both, or flaring), thickness of walls, etc., by the spacing, size, obliqueness (if any), and undercutting of the holes (i.e. their being wider at the bore than on the exterior surface), by the position of the labium edge in relation to the windway exit (low-set or high-set, distance away), and by the profile and dimensions of the windway and the crucial chamferings at its exit (*RT* 6–7). For example, a Baroque recorder has a wide curved windway tapering to a shallow exit. The windway may possibly be slightly arched within its length. Makers design recorders to give of their best when played at a particular level of breath-pressure, with particular modes of articulation or tonguing, and with particular fingerings, and the player must realize and master the playing characteristics of each recorder. Medieval-model recorders (*RT* 15–16) are designed with a narrow elongated window and play at their best with very high breath-pressure and firm tonguing, giving an 'open' (i.e. unreedy) but penetrating sound. They were thus well suited to be used out-of-doors or at entertainments in large (and probably draughty) halls. Some present-day recorder manufacturers may design one model to sound at its best with a gentle tone at lowish breath-pressure in consorts and recorder ensembles, and another, more penetrating and fuller in tone, to meet the requirements of the soloist. For confident sonata-playing, one needs a recorder which produces a firm, clear, out-going tone at a medium to high breath-pressure, and sounds satisfyingly beautiful to the audience. The player himself should revel in the beauty of his instrument. In the same way that a violinist conveys his feel of the springiness of a taut vibrating string, the recorder-player should experience the rich resonance and supple response of the wood of his instrument, animated by his breath.

Over the centuries, recorders have changed to meet the changing requirements of the music, the performance conditions, and the taste of each succeeding period. Even before sonatas were written, evidence from woodcuts by Virdung (1511), Agricola (1528), and Praetorius (1619) (Hunt, 17–18, 21, and 30), and from high-note fingerings 'discovered' by Ganassi[6] (1535) show recorder design moving from a wide, roughly cylindrical bore with a range of little over one and a half octaves to a conical bore with flared foot, as in the example of a seventeenth-century recorder shown in Pl. 2.

The 'high Baroque' recorder, designed (by the Hotteterres and other French makers of the mid-seventeenth century) in three sections, thus facilitating bore-reaming, is at its best in instruments by makers such as Bressan and the Stanesbys. In comparison with its late Renaissance predecessor, the Baroque recorder has a more elegant, reedy, 'bottled' tone (like a mature claret), softer, but still robust. Such recorders have a carrying power resulting from their lack of coarse, breathy 'undertones'. All the air put in the windway seems to be translated into pure note and the player has the impression that his sound is focused forward upon the audience. As a result of the resistance created by the shallow tapering wind-channel, the Baroque recorder is more dynamically flexible, as variations in breath-pressure do not have such a marked effect upon intonation. Sonata-players should exploit to the full this inbuilt expressivity of the Baroque recorder.

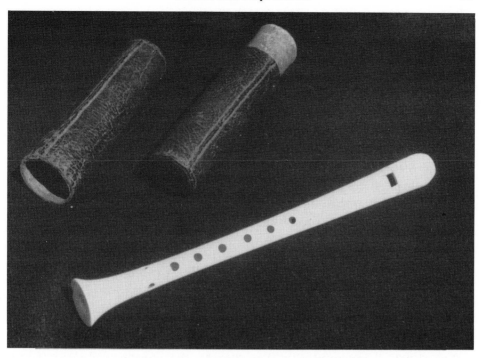

PL. 2. Edgar Hunt's book contains many photographs of sixteenth-, eighteenth-, and twentieth-century recorders, but few from the seventeenth century. The ivory descant recorder shown in Pl. 2, a 'descant' in E♭, was found in the mid-80s (after Hunt's book was written), together with its apparently original leather case shown in the picture, near Silkeborg in Denmark. Mathiesen and Waldbaum, Historical Woodwind Instruments, Jyderup, Denmark, who make copies of this and other recorders, date it from about 1630–40. This recorder, and one in the Edinburgh University Collection of Historical Musical Instruments (No. 1037) an early recorder by Richard Haka (1645–1709), who later changed his style, indicate that the seventeenth-century recorder before Hotteterre (Hunt, 38–41) was already of a markedly conical bore, with equally spaced and sized finger-holes, and a flared bell. Recorders of this type appear in seventeenth-century and even some eighteenth-century paintings. The Van Eyck-type Hand-Fluit illustrated here plays, with fingerings of the period, a full two octaves or more, and is quick-speaking and clear and penetrating in tone—ideal for the variations Van Eyck piped in the churchyard at Utrecht. The Haka recorder has the same range but speaks less nimbly and has a richer, stronger, more ardent quality—a good instrument for early Italian sonatas.

The bore design, which is cylindrical at the head, then conical in body, with many subtle differentiations in cross-section, but straightening at the foot, favours the upper octave. Low notes on many Baroque recorders may have to be nurtured, particularly bottom A♭, though this does not seem to have been the case with the English instruments which Handel knew. Handel did not employ the very highest notes, possibly because their tone-quality on these recorders was uneven or their production or intonation a little uncertain. Later Baroque German makers such as Oberlender made recorders with a more narrow conical bore which produced reliable high notes into the third octave with a sweet, expressive, and silvery sound, suiting the high tessitura of Bach and Telemann recorder parts, but—inevitably, for no recorder can do everything well—at the expense of the lower notes, which lack power and sound rather nasal. An experienced recorder-player who has a recorder put into his hands which is of a design contemporary with the music of a particular period will, having adapted himself to its playing characteristics, find that he identifies much more closely with that music, realizing its merits, and gaining fresh insights and understanding. But the resource implications of owning five different recorders to play the sonatas represented by those in Chs. 2–6 of this book are daunting.

The situation is confused still further by the question of pitch. Until recently, widely varying pitches were in use from place to place at the same time, and even in the same place for different functions. On average, however, Renaissance pitch was higher than modern pitch. Our present usual $a' = 440$ may represent a rough mean of the wide range of pitches used in the early seventeenth century. In the high Baroque period, pitches in general were much lower, though today's makers of 'Baroque' instruments mostly seem content to compromise at $a' = 415$, an exact semitone below 440, rather than 409 or lower.[7] Some recorders are constructed to take interchangeable bodies to play at either 440 or 415, and some harpsichords have a shift-mechanism to achieve the same result, but this produces intonational side-effects, so that the harpsichord needs to be reset for temperament (the work of only a few minutes), and the recorder may need modified fingerings.

Recorders purporting to be copied from those of Baroque makers should in principle use Baroque fingerings, with the holes so spaced that bottom B♭ is (usually) without the little finger and top B♭' is with half 6. Upper C♯' is then likely to be so flat with the normal ∅ 12– 4––– fingering that awkward refingering problems arise, for the alternative C♯' ∅ 12– –5–– is often difficult to articulate. Several makers assert, however, and playing experience bears this out, that only a Baroque-fingered low-pitch Baroque-design recorder, without half-holes for bottom F♯ and G♯,[8] can emulate the supreme tonal qualities of an original Stanesby or Bressan recorder.

Although derived from a Baroque original,[9] Dolmetsch recorders in the late 1930s onwards were constructed with a deeper windway and a larger bore. They adopted improved fingerings to give a more even tone in chromatic passages, and a better high C♯'. They were made at modern pitch. These 'modern' recorders have, compared with their originals, a bigger, if slightly coarser, less reedy sound, designed to be loud enough to hold their own, hopefully, with pianos, large harpsichords, and even, with effort, modern orchestral instruments.[10] There is a fine repertoire of twentieth-century music composed with such recorders in mind, which even the most enthusiastic early-music devotee should not forgo.

Pressures to play the Baroque repertoire at low pitch have now become almost overwhelming. Some colleges of music require entrants to possess treble recorders at $a' = 415$. Low-pitch trebles do on the whole sound more mellow and expressive, without loss of sparkle, than trebles at $a' = 440$, although some makers, sometimes using very un-Baroque computer technology, are finding ways of reproducing the tone-quality of low-pitch treble recorders in instruments pitched at 440. Plastic recorders, often of excellent quality, are now modelled, at least in windway design, closer to Baroque originals, though no machine-made recorder will emulate a hand-crafted recorder in its individual response to the wood used, and in nuances of bore dimensions, undercutting of holes, and voicing.

Although pitch is less of an issue, recorder-players are now increasingly expected to play Renaissance music on wide-bore instruments, certainly in professional performances. The early Italian solo-sonata/canzona repertoire is small but very attractive. It should in principle be played with the eager sound of the late Renaissance or early Baroque recorder. This music does not sound at all right on a soft and elegant low-pitch high-Baroque recorder, and only slightly better on the louder, more open-toned, modern recorder. Iconographical evidence, unreliable as it is, suggests that recorders with wide and only slightly tapering bores were used well into the seventeenth century (see Frontispiece caption), and any instrument labelled by its maker as 'Renaissance' should be suitable for the early sonata repertoire, provided it has an adequate and reliable compass. The use of a Renaissance-type descant recorder for the Fontana sonata is assumed in the comments on technique in Ch. 6. Recorder-players of that time would have been accustomed to Renaissance instruments with a strong, open-toned lower octave, an almost percusssive 'chiff' to strong tonguings that so well suits the dance-like tripla ritornelli in these sonatas, and a response to complex soft double-tonguings ('di ri li ri') that brings out the prized quality of *squisitezza* (exquisiteness) in Italian music. They would also have been practised in controlling intonation, especially at different dynamic levels, by partial covering of the large finger-holes of Renaissance recorders.[11]

Whatever may be the recipe for an ideal sound for particular sonatas, and however the winds of pitch-change may blow, the foregoing should not deter the possessor of a good plastic recorder from attempting any recorder sonata composed from 1600 to the present time. It is still possible, however, to obtain good hand-made wooden recorders at no more than about five times the cost of the plastic equivalent. Ganassi comments on the variety of recorders used in the sixteenth century. Similar anarchy probably prevailed in the Baroque period. Unless the player feels that his instrument is producing an inadequate and not very enjoyable sound, or if it is too much of a struggle to play it in tune, he should be able to give an acceptable performance of, say, a Handel sonata, on an inexpensive recorder. Understanding and enthusiasm for the music, an empathy with the composer and his intentions, and—following the precepts of this and other books—putting into practice a sound knowledge of Baroque performance style: all these ultimately matter more in the playing of a sonata than considerations of an ideal or authentic sound. In any case, few audiences could say with assurance whether the piece they had just heard was at $a' = 440$ or $a' = 415$. They do, however, appreciate beautiful sound[12] and expression, lively and graceful articulation, good ensemble, and variety in dynamics and ornamentation. To achieve this, the recorder-player must first study closely the basic tonal characteristics of his instrument, and its potential for dynamic and expressive variety.

On each of his recorders, a player should start by discovering at what general level of breath-pressure the instrument sounds best for sonata-playing. He will need to experiment with each note of his instrument, working out what small differences of breath-pressure he has to remember to make to achieve good tone and intonation. A pitch-meter is a very salutary companion in this process. He will need, for example, to hold back on dominating G's and to cream up low F♯s and G♯s (see *RT* 101–3). Some notes, possibly low G or even C, may have an unwanted natural oscillation or 'burble' (the recorder-makers' nightmare) at stronger breath-pressures, and one has to blow under the burble-point. If that does not work, send the instrument back to the maker for correction. Fingering modifications should be learnt at the same time; for example, how much of finger 6 does C♯ need, and does upper C', B♮', or even A' need a touch of little-finger shading? Good phrase-shaping in sonata-playing cannot be achieved until the player has examined the tone-qualities and intonation of each note of his instrument under varying breath-pressures, and compared notes one against another.

A way of tackling this process methodically is to make a chart of all the notes of the recorder with headings for 'breath-pressure', 'intonation' (i.e. the tendency of a note to be sharp or flat in normal playing), 'special fingerings needed', and 'comments' (interesting tonal characteristics, etc.). Start this voyage of discovery on treble C in the bottom octave,[13] and blow with increasing breath-pressure so that the note goes very sharp and finally breaks upwards with a rasp into the next register. Call this point—on the verge of breaking—breath-pressure 9. Then decrease breath-pressure so that the note goes very flat and becomes so wispy and attenuated in tone that it threatens not to be a musical sound at all. Call this 1. Concentrating hard, try to find the middle point between these extremes, breath-pressure 5. This will probably give the purest tone-quality. Check its intonation, with a pitch-meter if available, in order to establish a starting-point against which other notes can be tuned. The tone-quality of this note may well turn out to be that most satisfactory for an *mf* passage in consort music. Now, moving up this 'Beaufort scale', try C at breath-pressure 7, half-way between mid-pressure and the break-point, and listen very intently for the additional harmonics or overtones which have been excited by this breath-pressure increase. The note should sound enriched, less pure, with more 'edge' and penetration, and it will of course be slightly sharper. This tone-quality is probably that best suited to the *mf* of sonata-playing. When played hard at higher breath-pressures some recorders may take on a not unpleasant strident quality as a result of the activation of more upper partials. Even the 'flûte douce' can retaliate a little when challenged by louder instruments.

Because instruments, and people, differ, there is a lot of 'hit and miss' about the breath-control method described here. By carrying out the process for every note, however, including the common alternative fingerings,[14] the player will be introduced to the qualities, strengths, and weaknesses of his own recorder. This process will systematize his investigation into the sounds most suited to sonata-playing. It is assumed in all this that his instrument is clean and well maintained, and warmed before playing (*RT* 22–5), and that he has acquired good breathing and breath-control techniques (*RT* 28–9).[15] Assuming a sympathetic continuo, the general level of sound-quality for sonata-playing that should be arrived at through these investigative processes is the richest, warmest and most focused, the most beautiful, and the most characterful that each recorder is capable of.

Although such a sound should be the norm of sonata-playing, expressivity cannot be achieved without variety of sound. With the help of a tape recorder, or a willing and critical listener, extemporize a minimalist piece of music consisting of one note at constant pitch, but with every possible variety of articulation, volume, and, above all, tone colour. Disregard pulse and rhythm so that the interest of the music arises only from changes in tonguing, vibrato (all types—*RT* 106–8—as well as speed, amplitude, and wavelength variations), and, especially, fingering changes (see *RT*, ch. VIII, 'Tone'). After a while, change to another note. Then do this exercise with a group of notes (e.g. a 'five-finger exercise' repeated with many tonal variations). Finally, try playing a recorder sonata slow movement with each phrase demonstrating a different tone-quality.[16] Some recorder tone-qualities, though common in avant-garde music[17] (such as flutter-tonguing, or sung or hummed sound), are not suitable for Baroque recorder sonatas, but far more variety of sound is admissible than many players employ, especially in movements or passages played at a low dynamic level, where an affect can be communicated through the use of imaginative fingerings, tonguings, or breath-delivery.

In solo-playing, a recorder-player should experience a sense of pride in his instrument, and in his command of its tonal capabilities; otherwise he may fail to captivate his audience. It is often overlooked that a recorder has qualities not possessed by some other instruments. For example, a piano, harpsichord, or Baroque organ (with no swell pedal) cannot enlarge or colour a note after it has started. The recorder can, and it shares this ability with the human voice, and with string and wind instruments; but the recorder is far more agile than the human voice, able to negotiate wide leaps accurately, cleanly, and quickly. With skilful thumbing and tonguing it can manage to play high notes softly (*RT*, ch. VI) and low notes louder. Above all, and in this respect no instrument is its superior, the recorder can articulate sounds quickly and distinctly, with all the variety of speech, as, unlike other wind-instruments, it operates at a low breath-pressure, allowing the tongue to move as freely and naturally as it does in talking.[18] The recorder's adeptness in imitating the rhythms of speech applies equally to the lilting rhythms of dancing.[19] Robert Donington's words about the ideal Baroque sound, 'transparent sonority and incisive articulation' (see the end of Ch. 1 above), describe the qualities of recorder sound perfectly. It is by such criteria that recorders should be judged, rather than by the standards of nineteenth- and twentieth-century orchestral wind-instruments, with their bigger dynamic and greater tonal variety.[20]

Except for Telemann, who exploits the recorder's agility and its high notes in his sonatas (he played the instrument himself), Baroque sonata-composers did not write for the recorder in an idiom that differed from their writing for other wind-instruments. Recorder sonatas were written only during periods when the instrument was fashionable and there was a ready market for expensive publications of sets of sonatas, as in Britain with its many gentlemen amateurs from about 1680 to 1740. Even then publishers would not wish to restrict sales only to recorder-players. Many French publications of solo sonatas and suites were for 'dessus', meaning any upper melody instrument.[21] In the Renaissance, excepting keyboard, lute, and gamba compositions, the choice of what instruments, or voices, were to be used had depended on availability and on the choice of the performers themselves, though style and range might have suggested some instruments as more suitable than others.[22] A certain freedom of instrumentation persisted throughout the Baroque period. A recorder-player need not feel that the characteristic sound of his instrument makes it unsuitable for playing sonatas conceived for other instruments, so long as their style and range makes them acceptable as recorder sonatas.

Woodwind instruments were tuned to produce their best sounds in keys close to the home key: F for treble recorder, D for the flute. Recorder sonatas were usually written in key signatures ranging from no more than four flats to no more than two sharps, while flute sonatas tended to be in sharp keys. This is noticeable in Handel's Op. 1 sonatas, where particular instruments are specified—none of the recorder sonatas has a key signature with a sharp.[23] As Handel does not use a high tessitura in writing for the recorder, the general sound-quality for playing his sonatas should be full-throated, with the tongue in mid-position, rather than high up against the upper palate (which favours the high notes; *RT* 85 and 103–4). This 'er' to 'oo' position is excellent for producing a singing tone, well suited to Handel as the supreme Baroque melodist. All Handel's sonatas should sing, even the dance-style movements and fugues.

The infrequency of high notes makes the Handel sonatas easier to play than those of Telemann, and the G minor sonata, which only goes up to E♭', is probably the easiest—at least for the soloist. That is one reason for choosing it for this chapter; another is that there is a commentary on it in Freda Dinn's *Early Music for Recorders* (London: Schott, 1974, pp. 37–50), which the points made in this book are intended both to complement and to supplement. Dinn considers the whole sonata rather than, as here, selected illustrative aspects of it. A facsimile of the complete sonata from the Walsh 1732 edition is given as Ex. 2.1. This is used, despite its errors (the second beat of bar 6 of the Andante, for instance, should read ♫♪ ,

EX. 2.1. Handel, Sonata in G minor, Op. 1 No. 2 (Walsh, 1732)

Flauto Solo

not ♩♩ , and should show slurring), as an example of a facsimile of early printed music. Most eighteenth-century recorder-players would have experienced Handel's sonatas from such an edition, although in this case Handel himself wrote out an unusually legible and accurate fair copy.[24]

Some players, enthused at having a new piece of music put before them, will want to play it through at once. This exploratory run-through can, however, all too easily fix certain presentation styles, speeds, and phrasings in one's mind which are then difficult to eradicate later. It is probably best to think about a sonata before starting to play any of it—its 'affect', the speed of movements, thematic relationships, the character of the bass line, dynamics, and so on. With experienced players of Baroque sonatas, this methodical process of first thinking about a sonata may only take a minute or so, but it should not be skimped. Some detailed points of special interest or beauty in a sonata will nevertheless only reveal themselves in the course of actually playing the music. Indeed, a good sonata by a great composer tells you more about itself with each playing over the years as new subtleties emerge.

Handel's G minor sonata has four movements, with Italian tempo indications and no apparent dance-movements. It conforms to the Italian-style *sonata da chiesa* model, calling for a certain *gravitas* (perhaps it would sound well with a chamber-organ continuo). But one should not assume that *da chiesa* is never jolly and *da camera* never serious,[25] for this distinction is more one of form than of mood. Mood, or affect, is more likely to be suggested by the key. This sonata rarely strays from its G minor tonality. It will be seen that there are no long modulating semiquaver passage-work sections, and that there are few motives based on leaps—the melodies mostly go gently up and down from note to note in conjunct motion, with the expected exception of the last movement. This lack of excitement matches the G minor affect of 'serene earnestness mixed with happy loveliness', to quote further from Mattheson's concept of this key. The sonata breathes contentment: it is coffee-house music—port and urbane conversation—neither melancholic nor bucolic.

While this affect accounts for the second movement not being an Allegro, nor in complex fugal form (for such hard work would disturb the serenity), the marking 'presto' for the last movement is a puzzle until one realizes two things. The first is that the feeling of 'presto' belongs more to the bass part and is the outcome of continuous quavers without rests where phrasing-points, which do not coincide with the recorder's phrasing, have to be expressed very quickly. In preparing the sonata, the soloist should if possible try out the bass part on a bass recorder, with carefully considered phrasing, in order to arrive at a lively but practicable speed which then determines how fast the melody line should go.

The second point is that this movement *is* a dance, in fact a gavotte with the barlines deliberately in the wrong place—try playing the melody line with all the barlines in the first section moved back by two crotchets.[26] Contrary to expectation, the harmony in the middle of the bar is frequently in root position (no bass figure marked), whereas the chord at the beginning of the bar is often not (6 or other figures marked in the bass part). This bar-marking gives a slightly askew feeling to the whole movement. Despite this angularity, the gavotte tune needs to sound graceful and not too fast.[27] The pulse will probably be in a lifted two-time, rather than four crotchets to the bar. An expressive way of counting this minim beat is 'one (and) two'. This sets up delicious little rhythmic twists as the movement progresses—for example, the gavotte 'hemiola' to slow into the cadence at bar 19. The bass part may be played as a kind of decorative division; this is more evident in Handel's organ concerto reworking of the movement. Delicate ornamentation to touch up the rhythmic subtlety is called for at repeats; Dinn offers a choice of various ideas.

In Ch. 6 below, Freda Dinn's suggestions are given for the complete ornamentation of the Adagio (see Ex. 6.7). They catch the contemplative spirit of the movement well, but not all players will agree with every detail. Note how many of the phrases start on the second beat of the bar, linking this Adagio with the previous Andante, which shares this characteristic.

The activity of the bass in the last movement, while the recorder nonchalantly plays its gavotte (in the first section the bass plays 105 notes to the recorder's 59), is also a characteristic shared with the second movement, where the bass has many more notes than the recorder as a result of its gruff semiquaver comments on the recorder's rhapsodizing. Moreover, the recorder again has an implied barline shift, creating interesting rhythms against the unyielding, rather masculine, bass, for the melody seems to want to dance a sarabande with its stress on the second beat of a three-crotchet bar. Twenty-four of the thirty bars in the recorder part call for this gentle second-beat stress. This suggests that the opening crotchet D should be taken lightly, in order to prepare the listener for the pattern of sequences that begins in bar 5. Here the movement is given new impetus by the displacement of the sarabande rhythm one crotchet forward. To maintain the calm affect of the sonata, the sarabande-style secondary stresses, now across the bar (Walsh has omitted the ties at bars 9 and 11) should not be roughly articulated. They should come more from a slight increase in breath-pressure just after the note has sounded, rather than from strong tonguing (see Pl. 5 in Ch. 5). The second beat of the bar needs to be firm enough to carry the next repeated note across the bar on the rebound (bar 5 onwards), and, as Dinn points out, it has to be accurately placed against the bass's semiquavers. In the second long sequential episode, starting in bar 16 where the bass subsides petulantly into mere crotchets and gives the recorder its full freedom, it is essential to maintain the calm flow by respecting Handel's slurs.[28]

The second movement, Andante in place of the expected Allegro, needs to be taken at a speed significantly faster than the opening Larghetto, otherwise the whole sonata drags. Dinn suggests ♩ = 100. For the first movement, she suggests ♪ = 92 for the 𝄵 time of Larghetto. Although this Larghetto has a 'walking bass' in quavers, to count the solo part in eight quavers can make it too rigid. A crotchet count is better, imagined as flexible strong-weak pairs to give a slow beat (e.g. ♩ = 48), which contrasts effectively with the more deliberate, faster, three-crotchet stride of the second movement. The difference in movement between the Larghetto and the Andante is thus considerably greater than Dinn's metronome marks imply. Moreover, there is a slight emphasis on the first and fifth quavers of each bar in the Larghetto, and it is possible to feel a slowly recurring pulse in long-reaching minims, underlying the actual beat in crotchets or quavers. The feel of a slow pulse arching over several beats gives music greater expressive flexibility; a more closely spaced pulse gives stability and drive.[29]

As with other movements, the player should examine the structure of the Larghetto by first marking off—in soft pencil or just in his mind's eye[30]— the ends of the subsections with large breath-marks (see p. xiv). This applies at the subsectional cadences at bars 5, 11, and 18. There is a short coda of 2½ bars, slowing to 'adagio' (an invitation to ornament), before the close of the movement. Note the irregular lengths of the three main subsections: 5 bars (counting the bass's link figure), 5½ bars, and 7 bars. The movement seems to stretch, almost languorously, as it develops, and this calm expansiveness should permeate one's playing.

Remembering Mattheson's dictum about the importance of a good start, let us look closely at the first subsection of 4½ bars as far as the bass's link figure in bar 5. It will be seen that the bass plays twenty-two quavers before it reaches a rest. Assume, for the moment, that no more than four of these quavers may be played consecutively without interrupting the flow of the music, and then derive a pattern which will roughly accord with the treble melody. It will be found that the bass quavers fall into groups as follows: the first 3 (underpinning the recorder's dotted crotchet), 4 (under the recorder's next mini-phrase), 2 + 2, 4 (this phrase needs to be carried forward up to the F♯), then 2 + 2 + 3. The recorder's opening phrase as far as its quaver rest in bar 2 consists of four (or five) balancing mini-phrases. The first note, G′, establishes with its continuo chord the sonata's key of G minor. It is firmly articulated, but self-contained, perhaps with a slight crescendo to prepare the way for the more singing nature of the second mini-phrase (three notes), which starts with a gentle downwards semiquaver sigh. The third mini-phrase, a tone higher, seems about to reiterate sequentially the second phrase but is cut short as the unexpected asymmetry of the note-grouping begins to take effect. It will be seen from the Lasocki–Bergmann edition that Handel in his autograph slurred the first pair of semiquavers in bar 1, and the editors then slur the next two, but that neither Handel nor the editors have slurred the two semiquavers starting the fourth mini-phrase (three notes), as they need to be differentiated from the two previous sighing semiquaver pairs. The F♯′ at the end of the fourth mini-phrase is a strong note as it pulls the melody down from its climbing propensity and precipitates a cadence—it is shown trilled in the Walsh edition but not in Handel's autograph, which has equal quavers F♯′ and G′ at this point. The final three-note mini-phrase, which ought perhaps to be regarded as a continuation of the fourth mini-phrase, peters out in a feminine ending (i.e. a strong-weak pairing of notes at a phrase-end) of a falling fifth, while the bass firmly strides on upwards one extra quaver to its F♯. This both counterbalances the strong F♯ of the recorder melody, and also provides continuity across the recorder's rest. This last three-note phrase in the recorder part tails away somewhat from the strong F♯′ at the end of the fourth mini-phrase. It sounds more effective if each note is accorded a declining strength of articulation, for example 'daa ti re'. The recorder's rest in bar 2 is then used, as Dinn puts it, as 'a silence through which the music gathers intensity', in this case revitalizing the recorder to sing its way to the B flat cadence at its D in bar 3. Here the flow of bass quavers flags, and the recorder abruptly sets up a brief interchange of ideas with the bass. Then, having reached serenely upwards to the B♭′ in bar 5, the music relaxes to its cadence in this key, with a short cadential trill required on the C (to which the preceding D acts as a cadential appoggiatura) to round off this 4½-bar subsection.

The dotted crotchet C′ in bar 12 of the Larghetto presents a particular phrasing problem, for it may be seen as a 'Janus note', facing both backwards and forwards. In the backwards direction it completes a cadence from its preceding leading-note B♮′; in the forwards direction it starts the sequential phrase which corresponds to the phrase announced by the dotted crotchet D′ in bar 11. The cadential function of the C′ prevents a breath or phrase-point being taken before it. In its phrase-starting role it ought to match in length and emphasis the D′ of the previous phrase, so its cadential function has to be momentary—it fulfils its cadential purpose simply by being arrived at. Then, as soon as possible, it should plunge forward with a tiny impetus of increased breath, with finger 7 being ready to shade its half-hole sufficiently to compensate for any resultant sharpness. A touch of vibrato helps to show in which direction Janus is now peering most intently (see *PB*, Ex. 7). Enough breath needs to be taken at the rest in bar 11 to last until the second B♭ of bar 13. This note ends the second of the two sequential phrases, following which a new mini-phrase of a rising fourth opens a discussion between the recorder and the bass, which goes on up to the beginning of bar 15.

There is, however, another interpretation of the subsection at bars 11–13 which does not cause the dotted crotchet C′ in bar 12 to become a 'Janus note'. This is to make a slight separation between the opening note of the passage, the dotted crotchet D′ in bar 11, and the following group of six notes, a phrasing somewhat similar to that suggested above for the opening notes of this whole Larghetto movement. This places a phrase-point after the dotted crotchet C′ in bar 12, according it only a cadential role. The following group of six quavers, cadencing on to the second B♭′ in bar 13, then constitutes the last element of the sequence. The cadential emphasis of this interpretation may be enhanced by decorating the penultimate note of each of the six-note sequential groups, i.e. the B♮′ in bar 12 and the A′ in bar 13, with a short turned trill. Each player needs to decide which of these two and other possible interpretations of this thirteen-note subsection he prefers.

Sections in sonatas are usually marked by double bars, and the clear cadencing of Baroque music with its contours of tension and repose makes finding the end of subsections within these sections relatively easy. The essential patterning of notes into smaller groups in order to form phrases and mini-phrases,[31] and especially to locate places where breaths can be taken without prejudicing the logic and flow of the music, is more difficult. Several principles and generalities apply, however, which assist the performer. One is that if the opening subject starts from an up-beat to a down-beat (and remember that the opening subject may follow a first, isolated note intended to signal commencement and tonality), then the majority of phrases in the movement will conform to the same pattern, non-conforming phrases being for purposes of contrast. The first movement of the Handel G minor sonata is mainly in the common up-beat metre, weak to strong, or iambic. The melody line of the Presto gavotte (but not the bass line) has a prevailing down-beat pattern of two-beat phrases, which end at barlines—in the first section the main phrases begin at bars 3, 5, 7, 9, and 12, and only bar 9 has a quaver up-beat. From the start the phrasing quickly establishes itself in two-bar modules. Note how brilliantly Handel contrives to extend the section to thirteen bars. In the Andante, phrase-seeking is assisted by the profusion of sequential elements—the same melodic contour repeated at a different level of pitch. This can be a boring device, but Handel artfully avoids dullness through his handling of the bass line.

Symmetry is so ingrained in Baroque craftsmanship that, when the performer is in doubt about phrasing, he may find that phrase-points emerge by looking for them at or near the half-way point of a passage (though occasionally a passage may divide into three parts). Correspondingly, phrasing may often be resolved, both in Baroque and in Renaissance music, by identifying related groups of four notes, four beats, or four mini-phrases—again, the quatrain principle. Rests are usually, but not always, good guides to phrasing. A wide leap in the melodic line after a passage where notes have moved stepwise in conjunct motion is another possible phrasing indicator, as are melodic images—groups of notes that repeat or almost repeat a preceding group, or which end on the same note. Such patterns can often be elucidated by comparing similar passages in different sections of a movement, both in the solo and the bass lines. Harmonic progression in relation to the continuo part is another excellent indicator of phrasing structure, as sometimes an apparently self-contained melodic phrase is found to be unviable when one examines its harmonic context. A good way of trying out phrasing is to play the music very slowly so that one physically needs more breaths (or breathe out before playing the music). Another is for the recorder and the continuo to break off completely at what looks like a phrase-point, sustaining the final note to hear how it sounds with its underlying harmony. There are rights and wrongs about phrasing, but often various alternatives are equally valid. One has to make one's choice, know the reasons for making it, and finally play the chosen phrasing with complete assurance.[32] Different players, for example, will have different ideas about the phrasing in bar 15 of the Larghetto, where the lush succession of first-inversion chords figured by the 6s in the bass provides no harmonic help towards choice of phrasing. Are these thirteen quavers taken 4 + 4 + 5 or 5 + 4 + 4?

Coming in ever closer to the music, the player, having decided where to breathe and phrase, should then consider, always with the affect of the music in mind, how to shape each phrase, how to establish its coherence. In

the performance of sonatas, the moulding of phrases, as in poetry, needs to
be upon the framework of an established metre, that being a prerequisite
for good ensemble playing. One must therefore first consider the means at a
recorder-player's disposal to establish the music's metre.

Metre in mensural music is the outcome of a regular recurrence of a
pattern of stressed and unstressed notes. A melody-instrument such as a
recorder establishes this pattern primarily by comparative note-length,
articulation, and volume, three factors which make their effect either
independently, or, more usually, in association with each other. Imagine
first a series of equal-length, absolutely regular sounds at the same pitch,
with no differentiation in volume or articulation, like the bleeps of a
cooker-timer or the ticks of a metronome. Twelve such sounds could be
imagined as four threes, three fours, or, say, 5 + 4 + 3. The establishment
of a metrical pattern removes such options, and organizes the notes into a
regular series of bars by the creation of a recurrent system of emphasis, e.g.
1 (strongest) 2 (weakest) 3 (less strong than 1) 4 (weakest), as in the first bar
of the hymn 'All things bright and | beautiful'. The four different note-
weights involved in this example, and in many marching songs, could be
expressed as $\frac{9}{10}$, $\frac{5}{10}$, $\frac{7}{10}$, and $\frac{3}{10}$ of a full-value crotchet. Omitting the
denominator, an allemande dance-pattern might then be expressed as 5 2 3 1,
a minuet 5 3 1, and so on.[33] Metre can also be established entirely by
variations in strength and lightness of tonguing, with all the notes exactly
the same length and volume, or alternatively it can be established entirely
by slight volume differentiations, with equal-length notes and undifferenti-
ated articulation. On a series of single crotchets on the same note and each
of exactly the same length, a harpsichord (or an organ) cannot
communicate metre, as a recorder can, by differentiating articulation or
volume. It can, however, very effectively communicate metre, and
changing rhythms within a metre, not only (as a recorder can) by varied
note-lengths, but also (as a recorder cannot) by chord changes and by
volume changes effected by varying the number of notes in each chord.
Thus the two instruments complement each other in sonata-playing, the
continuo taking the chief responsibility for maintaining the harmonic
rhythm, thereby allowing the recorder more expressive melodic freedom.

An excellent preliminary for learning to control nuances of expression is
for the recorder-player, using crotchets on one note, first to reproduce a
uniformly unstressed line of bleeps; then, determinedly avoiding changes in
tonguing and dynamic, to establish a metre by differentiated note-length
alone. Next he should go back to the uniform line of bleeps and then
establish metre on a series of $\frac{5}{10}$ crotchets by tonguing alone, for example

'D t dh r';[34] and finally by volume differentiation alone—not too much or it becomes blustery.[35] In practice, metre in music is usually maintained with a mixture of any two of these three components, or by all of them working together. Certainly two of them must be used together in a chaconne or sarabande, where the second of three crotchets is longer than the first, but with the first, which identifies the placing of the bar, necessarily being more strongly articulated, possibly tongued 'De ther ti' (see *RT* 46). It is this rhythm, in varying guises, that pervades the Andante of Handel's G minor sonata (see above).

The ongoing bass quavers in the Larghetto provide, as in many Baroque sonatas, a regular beat which must be phrased sensitively yet stay firmly in step, expressing 'steddyness of mind' (Roger North (1726), 195). As North goes on to say, this 'humours' the cantabile upper voice 'most exquisitely'; 'one may fancy a rider singing finely while his horse trotts the time.' To sing, one needs to imagine the presence of words. Such words will obviously not all start on the same consonant (and some will start on vowels), so the recorder-player, exploiting his instrument's response to nuances of tonguing, should vary his articulation, as a singer has to in enunciating words. The words, identified by the mini-phrases, should almost be perceived.[36] In enunciating words and communicating their significance, and in building up the music's longer lines of sentences and paragraphs, a singer, unless he is a very dull person, will use, half-deliberately (for his mind is more on meaning than technique), a whole range of expressive devices, many of which are also available to the recorder-player. Here are some of them:

1. Dynamic rise and fall to match the undulations of the music, and the periodicity of its sentence-structure. Normally, as notes rise in a melody they get slightly louder (which suits the recorder admirably), and become softer as they fall, especially when relaxing into a cadence. This is not always the case, and the reverse process can be very effective—Quantz gives many examples. Such dynamic changes must be contained within the overall dynamic (e.g. *p*, or *mf*) of the section or subsection. One can differentiate between expressive dynamics and structural dynamics (see Ch. 3).

2. Dynamic rise and fall on one (long) note.

3. Varied lengths of notes, from the shortest staccato up to the point of $^{10}/_{10}$, where a note becomes attached to, or slurred to, the following note. The silences between unslurred notes are as important as spaces in architecture. Because down-beats often have to carry metrical stress, their contribution to expressivity is slightly less than that of up-beats, which, with

their greater flexibility in variety of length and of articulation, elicit the finer nuances of phrasing.[37] Take, for example, the A′ quaver up-beat at the end of the second bar of the Larghetto of Handel's G minor sonata—*exactly* how long should it be? Should it extend itself towards its following B♭′? Or should it be more reticent, so enabling the following B♭′ to be more independently defined? Should there, as Quantz suggests (pp. 73–4), be slight silences of articulation before appoggiaturas, for example before the D in bar 42 of the Andante?

4. Variety of articulation. There are two kinds of variability, strength (the range from strongest to lightest tonguing) and duration (from the quickest-speaking tonguing to the slowest-speaking tonguing). See Ch. 5.

5. Note-placing, the harpsichord-player's chief expressive device.[38] A down-beat note placed just before the exact moment of the regular pulse sounds eager and gives the music an impetuous forward drive. One placed fractionally after a beat gives a *frisson* of pleasurable surprise, a little moment of drama. Over-indulgence will romanticize Baroque music, but restrained use of this device in carefully chosen contexts is the mark of a good musical orator. How exactly does one place the dramatic high D′ in bar 11 of the Larghetto? Quite apart from the question of its length, where should one place the quaver A′ referred to in para. 3 above? Should it align exactly with the bass quaver D, or should it sound fractionally after it? As an up-beat, it is particularly sensitive to expressive note-placing. In the first four bars of the Andante, should the quavers align exactly with the notes in the bass, or should the soloist assert his independence with a touch of overdotting and inequality? The bass cannot exercise such freedom as it must keep to the beat with steady regularity. Would such playfulness be in accord with the mood of this movement?

6. Slight slowing down and speeding up—rubato, usually within a bar, or within a slow pulse. The feel of a slow, rolling pulse, such as the minim pulse suggested for the Larghetto, gives room for the expressive freedom of rubato. *Tempo rubato* is mentioned by Quantz (p. 174). Pulse itself can, within narrow limits, be slightly pushed forward and held back without destroying its momentum. Bars 15–16 of the Larghetto, for example, might be pushed forward a little and balance re-established by slowing down to compensate at bars 17–18.[39]

7. Slowing down, or speeding up, usually at the composer's request (*rit.*, *rall.*, etc.), so that the established regular speed of a pulse is changed, its former measure lost, though it might afterwards be regained. This may be associated with a marked pause (fermata), or used for dramatic silences, or for the drawing out of cadenzas. Thus Handel's 'adagio' marking of the

coda at the end of the Larghetto is open to an infinite variety of interpretations, even discounting the effects of ornamentation.

8. Changing the written value of pairs of notes within a pulse—'inequality' (see Ch. 4). Dinn suggests that the semiquavers in the Larghetto should be unequal to enhance expressiveness (see Ex. 4.7). Some inequality of semiquavers—not too much, as this could spoil the flow and unduly slow the pulse—is almost certainly desirable in this movement, with its pairs of falling conjunct strong/weak semiquavers. The fact that in his autograph Handel marked slurs over several semiquaver pairs (not indicated in the Walsh edition) reinforces this interpretation.[40] It then becomes important to distinguish with slight overdotting those semiquaver pairs which are actually marked dotted at the close of the Larghetto, and in bar 5 of the bass (and, in the autographs, in bar 7, though not, inconsistently, in bar 11). It is also necessary to identify up-beats to phrases which need to be assimilated into the rhythm of the phrase; for example, in the Andante the quaver A′ at bar 24 and the quaver G′ at bar 28 should be shortened to semiquavers in order to bring the up-beat into the rhythm of the ensuing phrase.

9. Changing the pitch of a note, such as sharpening a leading-note to bring it closer to its tonic.

10. Changing the tone-quality of a note or series of notes by breath-pressure variation or by fingering. The right fingering needs to be chosen to suit the expressive requirements of the music (see *RT* 161). Ex. 2.2 shows the recorder's opening phrase in J.-B. Lœillet's A minor sonata, Op. 1 No. 1.

EX. 2.2.

G♯′ fingered – –23 456– is usually a powerful, slightly coarse note. To use it here spoils the balance of the phrase as it is too prominent for its context. A better fingering for G♯′ in a tonic A′–G♯′–A′ context is the thumbed alternative Ø 123 456– which gives a more remote-sounding, less aggressive, and also slightly sharper leading-note.[41] It is also easier to play, as the thumb need not move.

11. Refingering a passage so that the more complex physical movements of the fingers come before a note which needs a slight expressive accentuation.[42] Consider the two slurs in Ex. 2.3. The most complex finger-

EX. 2.3.

movement in this six-note slur across the recorder's lower register-break is between G′ and A′ with normal fingering. This suits slur (*a*), as the stress then falls where it is needed, on to the A′. In slur (*b*) the stress is required on the G′, so it is better to use alternative G′ - 123 4567 (provided it is in tune[43]) in order that the greatest finger-movement, crossing the register-break, takes place between F′ and G′. This also places the strong-toned closed G′ on to the down-beat.

12. Adding intensity to notes by vibrato. There is conflicting evidence about the use of vibrato by singers and instrumentalists during the seventeenth and eighteenth centuries. It is probably wisest to reserve it for special occasions, treating it as an ornament. Its use would then be restricted to climactic notes in a phrase (e.g. the B♭′ in bar 7 of the Larghetto), and it should not therefore usually be used on the last note of a cadence.[44]

13. Ornamentation. One of the chief purposes of ornamentation is to enhance expression (see Ch. 6).

In the same way that articulation can be quick-speaking or slow-speaking (see Ch. 5 and *RT* 40–2), so an actual beat of music can be of fast or slow duration. Think of looking from the window of a train travelling at a constant speed first passing four equidistant telegraph-poles (like four dots) then going under four equidistant road-bridges (like four dashes). The actual time taken by the impulse of the beat has an immense effect, as every conductor knows, on the tautness or expressive breadth of the music. To communicate the music as he wishes, the soloist must therefore generate in his mind before the music starts not only the speed of the beat but also the character of this beat and of any underlying pulse. This should be derived from his conception of the affect of the music, and he must convey this concept to the continuo-players. Upon the nature of the pulse much expressiveness depends.

Although performers of Baroque sonatas will benefit from attempting to cultivate an affinity with the composer's apparent intentions and an appreciation of his craftsmanship, their eloquence on the composer's behalf must not be overstated, for it could become mannered. Some passages may even be played in rather a matter-of-fact way (e.g. bar 6 of the Larghetto) to enhance what follows. The most thought-out phrasing should ultimately sound the most natural.

For references to further commentary on Handel's Sonata in G minor and to other Handel sonatas, see the Index.

Dynamics, and Italian Style
Telemann's Sonata in D Minor

Most Baroque recorder sonatas have Italian origins. The earliest instrumental ensemble pieces entitled 'sonata' were those of Giovanni Gabrieli (Newman, 95–101) published in Venice in 1597. About thirty-six of Gabrieli's polychoral or other multivoice instrumental pieces were termed 'canzona' and seven 'sonata', but there is no great difference between them. Praetorius (1618–19; Newman, 23) thought that the sonatas were 'made to be grave and imposing', the canzonas, with their melodic ♩ ♩ ♩ opening, being more brisk and gay. Gabrieli never specifies recorders or flutes in his instrumental music, and his smallest sonata group is three violins and continuo bass. He set a high standard of craftsmanship in his music, and, through his fame and his teaching, his influence and example spread beyond Italy to Germany, for example through Schütz. Although he wrote no solo sonatas, Gabrieli set the stage for the characterization of the sonata as grave, imposing, exciting in its sonority, dramatically varied by speed and dynamics, highly organized, and carefully crafted. Eighty years later this characterization of the Italian Baroque sonata was powerfully reaffirmed, again in Italy, and with enormous influence throughout Europe, by Arcangelo Corelli.

Three years before Gabrieli's death the first two surviving sonatas for solo with continuo were published by Gian Paolo Cima in Milan in 1610 (Newman, 118). One is for violin, the other for cornett or violin. Most accompanied solo sonatas of this early Baroque period specify violin or cornett, though composers (or publishers) not uncommonly add that their sonatas may be accommodated to any sort of instrument. With this encouragement, and as the recorder ('flautino') is specified in at least three solo/continuo canzonas (Riccio 1612 and 1620/1), recorder-players need have no compunction about playing sonatas and sonata-like canzonas from the early seventeenth century, provided the music is within their instrument's range and sounds good. The experience of playing this music considerably broadens one's approach to later Baroque sonatas as it helps

PL. 3.   Music-making Italian style—but in Germany. This detail from a
fresco depicting Europe by Tiepolo, in the Residenz at Würzburg
(1753), shows recorder, viola, violone, and two singers performing
music identified as by Vivaldi—music by a great Italian composer in a
splendid German setting (in fact the architect of the Residenz, Balthasar
Neumann, is portrayed sitting next to the musicians, just below this
picture). In comparison with French style of the period—see the
Watteau, PL. 4—note the players' energy and fire, in almost shameless
enjoyment in the communication of their music. Note, too, the
splendour of light and shade, the strong contrasts, e.g. between the
opulent folds of the first singer's dress and the plain wood of the side of
the violone, and the deliberate dramatic disorder (equivalent to a
discord) created by the angles of the bows. It is art and music full of
swagger.

to develop the fire, passion, freedom, and sense of adventure associated
with sonata-playing, Italian style (see Pl. 3). With a firm-toned Renaissance
recorder, played at high breath-pressure, the recorder-player can make
some attempt to emulate the exciting tone and virtuosity of the cornett, and
the rich transparency, crisp attack, and versatility of the violin, without
unduly compromising the special qualities of his own instrument. As the
seventeenth century progressed, and the sonata became increasingly
identified with the violin, the vogue for the multicoloured tonalities of the

wide-ranging instrumentation of Renaissance music and the noble sonority of Gabrieli's cornetts and sackbuts was overtaken by the overwhelming demand for opera, with its extremes of expression, which the violins were able to support so well.[1] Display of dexterity and bravura extravagance occasionally threatened the musical substance of some seventeenth-century sonatas. Corelli's sonatas, however, somewhat redress this balance. Nevertheless, contemporary recorder arrangements of Corelli sonatas should be played in a bravura spirit with rich sonority, great drive, and excitement, and intensity and variety of expression that overflows into considerable free ornamentation, especially in slow movements. Do not let us lose sight of the image of the mild and cultivated Corelli looking distorted, wild-eyed, 'agitated like one possessed' as he played an adagio (see Donington, *Interp.* 104).

Wide dynamic range and the surprises of sudden louds and softs contribute to the considerable emotional impact of Italian-style sonatas. It is significant that the first sonata to be published was called 'Sonata pian' e forte', though Gabrieli achieved this simply by having his two four-part instrumental choirs play together for the forte passages. Riccio's canzona 'A un Flautin overo Corneto' (see also the commentary in Ch. 8) contains passages such as the one in Ex. 3.1:

The 'forte' and 'piano' marks appear in the continuo part as well. One of Riccio's 1612 Canzonas for 'Flautino e Basso' ends spectacularly (see Ex. 3.2):

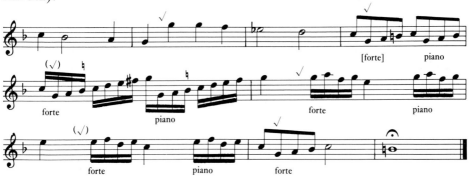

A century later, Vivaldi asks for at least a dozen different dynamic levels in his music.[2] The Bohemian composer Jan Dismas Zelenka, in his oboe trio sonatas (1715-16), marks 'piano forte ffort' during a single held note, and calls for many other dynamic contrasts. Some Italian-style recorder sonatas contain various dynamic markings. For example, the Walsh arrangement for recorder of Corelli's Op. 5 No. 9 sonata contains nine 'piano' and 'forte' instructions in a 56-bar Gavotta; Veracini's sonatas for violin or 'flute' (= recorder, 1716) call for repeats of slow movements to be played *p*, and both he and Corelli liked to end allegro movements quietly; Mancini in his 1724 Sonata 10 in B minor, Allegro, bar 61, marks an expressive 'sigh' passage *p*. However, dynamic variations between loud and soft were generally left to the taste of the performer, so were not often marked by the composer. It is inconceivable that Italian-style recorder sonatas with no such markings were played without boldly expressive and dramatic dynamic variety. This manner of performance also applies to the German and English composers who learnt their art directly (like Handel in Rome) or indirectly from 'the most fam'd Italian masters' (Purcell), though their manner of playing may have been a little more reticent than Italian demonstrativeness.[3]

While a Renaissance descant recorder (Riccio's 'flautino') can produce commanding power, the more elegant and refined Baroque treble recorder rather lacks the decibels needed for solo performances in modern concert-halls. Other Baroque instruments, however, also produce a markedly lower volume than their modern counterparts, but one that was well suited to the performances, often quite informal, that took place at assemblies in private houses or in concert-rooms or theatres that were smaller than those of today. Consider the difference in volume of sound between a Baroque and a modern violin, between the modern metal flute and the one-keyed boxwood Baroque flute with its gentle tone and soft articulation, or between a fortepiano and a modern concert grand. Even in company with other Baroque instruments, however, recorders have the problem that they produce their best tone for performing sonatas and other chamber music at a fairly high level of breath-pressure. This general level of sound leaves a rather narrow margin above it for louder passages without the risk of intolerable coarsening of tone-quality. While the capability for playing softer is therefore all the greater, the soft tones of the recorder can be so quiet that they are overwhelmed by the less dynamically variable sound of the continuo harpsichord. The harpsichord's limitations to some extent narrow the range of dynamics the recorder-player can employ in playing sonatas, so that the recorder's dynamic variety becomes all the more concentrated upon the shaping of phrases. The harpsichord-player may of course change to a quieter registration, but the tonal contrast is usually too great for this to be feasible except, for example, for a complete slow movement, or for repeats. Achieving balanced dynamics is therefore one of the main concerns of a recorder-player when rehearsing for a sonata performance.

The players of a sonata need to find how best to position themselves to achieve good balance, especially in *p* passages. It is essential for a recorder-player to try out the acoustic response of the room he is going to play in before any performance, and, with a critical listener, to judge the effect of playing towards different parts of the room. A recorder, possibly because of its pure tone, is extraordinarily sensitive in its response to room resonance.[4] Conversely, any attempt to play a virile Italian-style sonata in a non-resonant hall is likely to be dispiriting to the player and dull for the audience, the most skilful performance sounding like monotonous piping, and soft tones becoming unacceptably thin, if audible at all. One needs to be cautious, however, about very echoey environments, where fast movements should be played more slowly to avoid blurring, with notes generally shortened and more distinctly articulated.

The recorder-player should, within reasonable limits, adopt the approach of an orator or an actor in putting across an Italian-style sonata with its range of dynamics, such is his need to use every device to overcome the limitations of his instrument. At one moment he will look as though he is playing soft, soulful music; at another his playing attitude will be more aggressive, his recorder held a little higher, his stance conveying the action of playing loud music.

In a large hall, or if playing with a particularly clangy harpsichord, it will probably be necessary to use one's loudest recorder, whether it is 'modern' or 'Baroque', in order to convey the exciting sonorities of Italian-style music. There are, of course, other ways of increasing volume, such as using microphones or various mechanical devices (*RT* 98); or a recorder can be pulled out and blown harder for loud movements, and pushed back in for soft movements; or different recorders can be used for soft and loud movements in the same sonata. As there is little or no pause between the movements of Baroque sonatas,[5] many players would not regard such expedients as practicable, even if they felt they were desirable (however, see Quantz, 59 and 197).

There is no problem in playing a recorder, within its limits, loudly or very softly. One simply puts in more air, or less air. Even on a Baroque-voiced instrument, however, the pitch-difference between a loud and tonally acceptable F′ and a soft and tonally acceptable F′ is likely to be at least a semitone. It will probably be more on a Renaissance recorder or a 'modern Baroque' recorder with a less shallow windway exit. Notes other than F′ vary more or less in this respect.[6] Unlike the violinist or flautist, the recorder-player is faced with considerable difficulties in maintaining accurate intonation at different dynamic levels,[7] especially in a crescendo or decrescendo, all the more so if the latter fades to nothing, *a niente*. Impressions of volume change can be conveyed by tonguing nuances, and by note-length variations (exploiting the silences between notes), but expressive and other considerations limit the extent to which these important dynamic control devices can be used. Ultimately the control must be exercised by fingering. This technique is mentioned by Ganassi,[8] and it is explained in detail in *RT*, chs. IV–VII, and elsewhere.[9]

To illustrate the Italian-style recorder sonata at its best and to demonstrate the dynamic demands it makes on the instrument, one needs to look outside Italy itself. Although there are many fine sonatas by composers working in Italy, relatively few were written specifically for the recorder,[10] the recorder or flute being more usually referred to only as a second designation to the violin. The dynamic effects of many Italian sonatas are conceived in terms of the violin. The Italian-style sonata exerted its powerful influence in northern Europe, where recorders were more in vogue. One thinks especially of Telemann in Hamburg, and the Italian, German, Dutch, Flemish, and even French composers who were attracted to the rich musical life of London.[11] In Germany, princely courts modelled themselves and their music on Versailles (for example, at Augsburg, Johann Fischer wrote French Suites for 'fleute douce'), and Telemann rightly prided himself on his mastery of both the French and Italian styles. His *Essercizii musici* (1739–40),[12] which contain some of his most carefully thought-out music, include two uncompromisingly Italian-style sonatas written specifically for the recorder. One, in C major, is a beautifully balanced mixture of toccata-like exuberance, melodic melancholy, and sprightly abandon in its three movements. The other, in D minor, is a noble four-movement *sonata da chiesa*, demanding the full range of rhetoric and dynamics that characterize Italian style.

Though separated by time and country, both Charpentier and Mattheson associate D minor with religious introspection and gravity (it is also the key of Mozart's Requiem). Frans Brüggen's recording of Telemannn's D minor sonata refers in its sleeve-notes to the 'darker regions of emotion'; Michael Schneider, on his record-sleeve, notes that it is 'permeated by passionate affections', its 'virtuoso passages serving expressive purposes'. David

Coomber says that it is 'full of affect and rhetoric'.[13] He quotes the opening of the 'affettuoso' first movement in his detailed analysis of a Baroque composer's use of rhetorical figures. Coomber especially identifies the initial descending figure in the melody line, which is reaffirmed at lower pitches in the movement's sequential repetitions, as illustrative of uncertainty and of devotion, like bowing the head.

By Telemann's time, as *galant* music came into fashion, the concept of an overriding affect throughout a sonata was giving way to more rapid changes of mood, as in C. P. E. Bach's music. The faster movements of the D minor sonata have been interpreted as lively contrasts with the serious slow movements. Gustav Scheck saw the opening of the Affettuoso as 'the anguished operatic outburst of a deceived lover', but heard Polish dance rhythms (so beloved of Telemann) in the second movement.[14] Certainly in this sonata's C major companion affective contrast between movements is confirmed by the slow movement being in F minor. The D minor sonata seems, however, to gain in power if a dominating serious affect is maintained through all four movements, which in this sonata stay close to D minor in tonality. Telemann seems to suggest this by the 9/8 drive and relative lack of joyful leaps in the last movement (marked 'allegro', not 'giga'). Moreover, the sonata is firmly in Baroque Italian style and has no *galant* sentiment—the third movement does not even have a melody.[15] Having decided upon one's own interpretative approach, one must then be consistent and deliberate in conveying it.

At the outset Telemann uses the Italian device of great dynamic contrast. A double echo appears three times in this movement; to create its full effect, the general level of the movement must be *mf* rather than *mp*. The ardent second movement and the driving gigue also need a generally high dynamic level. The moment of hush is therefore the third movement, which the Schott edition of this sonata marks 'sotto voce', a devotional whisper. The whole movement is given in Ex. 3.3.[16] It will be noticed that the continuo bass part has very little to do—only twenty-two notes, all within an octave's range. The bass note never changes during a bar. The movement is almost a monody, the last half of which is a long-drawn-out but decorated descent from G' to A. There is a slight feel of melodic movement in bar 11, the only point where the merest suggestion of a crescendo out of the prevailing stillness is justified.

Playing the recorder at *pp* levels sacrifices tonal richness, but the thinner timbre perhaps suits the lower dynamic. It needs—very appropriately in this movement—intense concentration to maintain a steady flow of breath at such low breath-pressures. The recorder, even the Baroque type, offers so

EX. 3.3. Telemann, Sonata in D minor

little resistance to the flow of breath that fluctuations which have a dire effect on intonation are all too easily perpetrated. Practising long *pp* notes with an electronic pitch-meter is very salutary. Some players find that placing the tongue high in the mouth (at the highest 'ee' position) offers a slight resistance, so providing a little more control of breath-flow. Others find the visual analogy of a slow-moving river helpful, the current of breath-flow deeply and slowly impelled from the diaphragm and uninterruptedly onwards through the channel between the arched tongue and the upper palate, and outwards through the recorder's windway.

It was noted earlier that an impression of playing softly can be conveyed by shortening notes. This works well in repeats of dance movements or of sections of passage-work where already detached notes can be further shortened. To avoid the impression of a series of pecks, these shortened notes must be all the more carefully phrased. This device cannot, however, be used in a Grave with long legato notes and slurs. Relaxed tonguing can also give an impression of quietness, and this Grave has to be played throughout with slow-speaking, almost dragged, tonguings to enhance the affect. But it is only by refingering, with its attendant tone and articulation problems, that a true 'sotto voce' effect can be achieved.

Different recorders react differently to non-standard fingerings, but here is a fingering schedule for this Grave movement to try out as a starting-point:

Bar 1   A′   Ø 123 4-67; use 7 for fine tuning, or shade a little with 5 if this fingering is very sharp.

Bar 2   F♯′   – 1–3 –––––
         G′   – ––3 –––––

Bar 3   C′   normal C′ but leak 1 to tune. Leaking 3 is an alternative but even more critical to control.

Bar 4   A′   as bar 1; B♭′ use ½6

Bar 5   C♯′   leak 1 and 4 (great care in tonguing): or half-hole 3. Or finger Ø 12– –5–– with circumspect tonguing.

Bar 6   D′   leak 1, a little more than for the C♯′. 1 has to roll back slightly in changing its leaking position.

           An attractive alternative approach to bars 5–6 is to play the C♯′ Ø 123 –567 and the D′ Ø 12– 4567, as the demisemiquavers can then be taken by alternating the movement of fingers 3 and 4. Double-thumbing may help in this fingering (*RT* 85). The music should almost come to a weary stand-still here, before the articulation, *ppp*, of the held up-beat D crotchet that, with a tiny crescendo, impels the music into its next section. This D may be fingered 0 1–3 45––(flattening of E) or 0 –23 45–– (flattening of F′) or, probably best because of its recurrence in bar 8, – 123 456– (a flattening of F♯′).

Bar 7   G′   – ––3 –––––, F♯′ – 1-3 –––––, B♭′ with ½6, and E 0 –23 ––––– or 0 ––3 456–. 3 is down throughout this bar as the 'pivot' finger (*RT* 69).

Bar 8   F♮′   – 123 –––––, A′ as bar 1, E – 123 4–––, D – 123 456–. This fingering leaves 123 in place for the whole bar. This useful alternative F′ is with some recorders in tune with normal F′ at the same breath-pressure, sometimes even flatter. This means that, except with leaking, it cannot then be used as a *p* fingering, and another fingering needs to be sought, perhaps based on F′ as – 12– 45––.

Bar 9   If E 0 –23 –––– is slightly sharper than normal E 0 1–– –––– with the same breath-pressure, which is often the case, this bar can be played with E 0 –23 ––––, adding 45 for the D.

Bar 10   This 0 –23 45–– D fingering can then start bar 10, adding ½6 for C♯. G′, then F♯′, are played with 3, then adding 1, as in bar 2. Still ½6 for B♭′.

Bar 11   A slight crescendo is probably needed in this one bar, bringing fingerings back to normal, but decrescendo to . . .

Bar 12 C♯ 0 12– 34––; this is too sharp on most recorders for normal *mf* sonata-playing, but will then work for the *p* dynamic level here; otherwise 4 can always be slide-fingered (*RT* 60).

The last four notes of the movement are very critical. If they are well played, *ppp*, with plenty of rallentando and a long-held last note and rest, they can produce a hushed effect upon one's audience. Try the following approach. Anchor the thumb so that the thumb-nail is upon the rim of the thumb-hole (*RT* 61) causing only a hairline leaking from the thumb. Slide-finger 5 to produce a very soft A′. This is probably best done by arching 5 to the far side of its hole,[17] which opens up the inner (right-hand) side of hole 5. Then, arching 6 across as well, play the G♯′ with the further, not the nearer, half-hole. Now go back to the slide-fingered A′ by lifting 6, and then, for the bottom A, simply drop the breath-pressure to *ppp* (Beaufort scale 1), articulating the note with an almost imperceptible 'dh' tonguing. A slight pinching of the thumb-nail leak, or pressing down of 5, may be needed if the A threatens to be sharp. If it threatens to be flat, or to go flat during decrescendo, correct this with 5; do not move the anchored thumb-nail to give a fractionally larger aperture as this will create a breathy and nasal tone-quality associated with 'recorder harmonics', an avant-garde effect (*RT* 60). If all is well (steadiness of breath is essential), this A should sound pure and ethereal, and so barely audible that the audience have to strain to hear it while the continuo chord dies away. It must be exactly in tune, dominant to tonic, with the forte D at the beginning of the next movement, and with the As in the harpsichord chords. Technically, one is taking an exciting risk, but such drama is of the essence in Italian-style sonatas.

A considerable amount of practice is needed to be able to remember so many special fingerings in order to interpret the Grave in this manner. A less experienced, or less confident, player might prefer to play this movement with mostly normal fingerings at a *p* rather than a *pp–ppp* dynamic level. It will still be quite effective, though probably not as moving as it can be. Baroque music, like Baroque sculpture and architecture (see Pls. 7 and 6) is, within its structural confines, an extreme and emotional art, and that is how this music should sound, played, as if in religious hush, at the extremes of the recorder's dynamic and tonal potentialities.

Some carefully graded light vibrato on the long notes in bars 1, 3, and 5 of the Grave may add to the effect, but there should be no corresponding dynamic rise. Any other ornamentation is unnecessary. The player also needs to take into account the resonance of the room he is playing in—if he plays too softly in a spongy acoustic, some of his audience may not be able to hear him at all, even if the harpsichord uses its quieter registration. Nevertheless, the audience should feel they need to lean forward to follow the prayer-like sound of this Grave. All expression belongs to the recorder. The continuo parts should be just a neutral harmonic background, as in the 'affetti' sections of earlier Italian sonatas (see Ch. 6).

EX. 3.4. Telemann, Sonata in D minor

The first movement of Telemann's D minor sonata, of which the recorder part from the Schott edition is shown in Ex. 3.4 (the bass is mainly in steady quavers), displays with its concentration of rhetorical figures something akin to a Counter-Reformation fervour (see Bernini's St Theresa, Pl. 7) alongside its Baroque grandiloquence (see the Seville reredos, Pl. 6). No other recorder sonata starts quite so unexpectedly and so searingly as at the recorder's first entry on the fifth chord of the piece (a diminished seventh), after the opening four chords have built up a powerful D minor tonality. All the phrases, mainly downward, call for considerable dynamic undulation, even when the music gets calmer towards the end of the movement before its final sudden outcry at the high G'' in bar 15. The movement as a whole, however, needs to stay loud enough to give the maximum room for dynamic contrast at the three occasions of double echoes.

Playing these echoes presents an interesting problem. The obvious solution is to refinger the third of the three notes on to a 'soft fingering'. This may, however, result in too marked a tonal change to convey the effect of one and the same note being echoed at increasing distances. Take the three D's in bar 2, for example. The 'soft fingering' for D' is Ø 123̶ 4567. On some recorders this may be suitable in tone as the third element, thin and distant, of the double echo. On others, however, this fingering for D' has an acid tone-quality which is in too great a contrast to the open-toned normal D' that forms the second element of the double echo for it to sound like the same note more spacially distanced. It is probably best, therefore, to play all three D's with the same basic normal fingering, thereby keeping them within the same tonal range. The first D', played f, needs plenty of right-hand shading, especially with 4, but leaving 7 and 6 clear enough of their holes not to cause the note to break upwards to the next register, disastrously producing $E\flat'$ or even $A\flat''$. The second D', $(m)p$, is played with normal fingering, using thumb aperture to keep it in tune. For the third D', leak either 1 or 2 (not too much). Clear articulation of this pp note can be achieved by double-thumbing, a high tongue position, and a light, precise 'tee' tonguing (RT 84–6).[18] The length of each of the three notes has to be much the same for a proper echo reiteration, but a little latitude may be exercised in lengthening the first quaver and shortening the third to enhance the effect. Room resonance has to be taken into account. Each note should convey the impression of solitude, the last of inadequacy.

The dramatically delayed demisemiquaver f re-entry in bar 3 will again require some shading. This slur is better balanced if the register change is placed at F'' not at E', but the Ø 1— ———— fingering for E' (with tight thumbing) needed to achieve this does not work on all recorders, or, if it does, may be too uncertain for use at such a crucial situation in the music.[19] Do not allow the descending sequence in bars 3–6 to drop too much in dynamic, otherwise the *f* C′ at the start of the second double echo may sound blurted. The second double echo should be treated in the same way as the first; many players will prefer to slide-finger 3 rather than 1 or 2 for the *pp* C′. The double echo on G′ at bar 11 presents no problem, but choose fingerings that stay in the same tonal range.[20]

Except for cadential trills, no ornamentation, other than the figures Telemann has already included, and a varied vibrato at the tops of phrases to bring out the intensity of the affect,[21] is needed in this movement.[22] Its internal elaboration is as complete in itself as the folds of the drapery in Bernini's St Theresa sculpture (Pl. 7).

Complex refingerings to achieve wide dynamic variety become less practicable in fast movements. On the other hand, the less legato the style of the music, the more can dynamic variation be achieved by changes in note-length. Music in dance styles is particularly susceptible to dynamic change by note-shortening, partly because the unstressed up-beats which contribute in great measure to the 'lift' of a dance can be made to vary so much in their length and in their placing; consider how varied the length and placing of the third beat of a waltz can be. Furthermore, where there are many quavers or semiquavers (or other short notes) in a movement, variety of tonguing becomes feasible as a dynamic device, as the articulation period, or 'transient', of a short note forms a greater proportion of that note than it does of a long note. For example, a very short note played staccato with a strong slowish-speaking tonguing can become almost stifled within its own articulation, a useful technique for passage-work echoes (*RT* 40 and *PB*, Ex. 55). Less extreme, a passage played with a strong tonguing and then repeated at the same breath-pressure and with the same note-lengths but with a medium, less plosive tonguing, sounds softer simply because the attack is weaker.

In playing Italian-style allegros, fire and drive are the qualities most called for, but some bars or sections should be played in a calmer, less emphatic manner in order to contrast with and highlight the power and impetuosity of the main statements. The dynamic ups and downs of the fast movements of Italian-style sonatas need careful thinking out. It is especially important for dynamic as well as expressive purposes to comprehend the pattern and significance of the statements and sentences that comprise the musical paragraphs of a fast movement. The use of sequences within the paragraph structure should also be noted. The first section of the second movement, Presto, of Telemann's D minor sonata (up to the double bar) contains as many as four sequential passages. Not only should the beginning and end of each complete sequential passage be mentally 'marked off' and communicated to the audience by clear phrasing, but the statements that constitute the sequential series may themselves be demarcated by according to each of them a slightly different dynamic level, like shallow steps in broad terraces.[23] This gives the music the excitement of a graded rise or fall in addition to the dynamic shaping of each phrase within the sequence to and from its climax. Sectional and subsectional volume changes, including their variation at repeats, may be referred to as 'structural dynamics', the shaping of phrases as 'expressive dynamics'.

The opening of this Presto movement (Ex. 3.5) places a powerful accent on to the down-beat crotchets preceding minims, creating a punch-and-rebound effect.

Ex. 3.5.

This produces a firm and insistent rhythm that dominates the whole movement, which should be played with great confidence and drive. Perhaps this movement represents the certainties of 'faith', between the 'worship and ecstasy' affect of the first movement and the prayer-like Grave.

The repeats of the second movement demand some ornamentation, but it is probably best to confine such ornamentation to the function of emphasizing notes and figures which already carry stress, a reaffirmation of faith. Ornaments can very easily weaken music, for example by smoothing out leaps intended to sound abrupt or spiky, or, as is the case of the *coulé* slurred on to a beat, detracting from the down-beat definition of a note. In this sonata, ornamentation needs to be restrained, deriving from and underlining the affect of each movement and of the sonata as a whole. Here are two suggestions for ornamentation in the Presto repeats. The first (Ex. 3.6) emphasizes a leading-note on a beat already covered by a slur by giving it a strong half-trill.

Ex. 3.6.

It is tempting to ornament similarly in bar 17, especially as an F'–E half-trill falls so readily under the fingers, but this might be thought excessive. The second suggested ornament (Ex. 3.7)—playing the D' crotchet in bar 44 as  (B♮' C' D')—emphasizes the up-beat which begins the last phrase of this section. This strengthens the agogic accent, which might already have been placed upon the D' beginning the previous phrase two bars earlier.

EX. 3.7.

These agogic accents can convey the impression of the music being driven, headstrong, to its end, too impulsively to allow for any *rall*. The very last note of this movement might, however, be given its full stop with a mordent.

The splendid last movement, the recorder part of which is reproduced in Ex. 3.8, should be as hard-driven as the second movement, but it is far more complex in conception, and calls for greater dynamic and emotional variety, with close understanding between the recorder-player and the continuo-players. Whereas the second movement acquires its energy from the close spacing of the two-beat rhythm, the last movement adopts the huge stride of a 9/8 with nine quavers in most bars, often skidding along in conjunct motion. Its speed needs therefore to be fast enough to convey the effect, carefully established right at the start by the bass line, of one slow, rather lumbering pulse to each bar. A study of the bass line in this movement will tell the soloist—as is often the case—a great deal about how to interpret his part. The 9/8 stride does, however, need a periodic renewal of impetus, and with such long paces it is easy to lose balance, which is what actually happens in bars 10–13, and again in bars 32–3 and 36–7. Indulging one's imagination in relation to the religious affect of this sonata, the movement could be thought to represent conflict between doubt and belief, the human reality after ecstasy, faith, and prayer. Although there are moments of dance-like joy with a very firm one-in-a-bar rhythm when all is well with the world (e.g. bars 39–46), the movement as a whole in this interpretation would be made to sound rather inexorable and discomfiting.

EX. 3.8. Telemann, Sonata in D minor

The third movement dies away on a dominant chord, followed by a pregnant pause of a long crotchet's rest. Then, catching the audience just before they relax, the last movement storms in, a perfectly timed Baroque *coup de théâtre*. The first chord must therefore be loud, but the soloist's first two bars as a whole should not be so loud as to leave no dynamic room for the step up to the next terrace needed at bars 3–4, where the soloist plays the same music a third higher. There should be a slight decrescendo at the end of bar 2 (and a breath) to enable the strong first note of the next bar to be so placed as to impart renewed impetus to the striding pulse now being established. The music gains in regularity and drive with each occurrence of the matching two-bar phrases. At bar 11 the driving sequences are broken. The recorder's repeated neutral Cs form a sort of drone background to a rhythm which shifts itself tantalizingly on to the second, fifth, and eighth of the nine quavers in these bars—a symbol of doubt?—until bar 14 triumphantly re-establishes the 'correct' nine-quaver rhythm with joyful participation from the bass, for here the bass has its first quavers in the movement and it celebrates this renewed confidence by playing quavers throughout the next four bars, while the recorder (bars 15–18), now at a less stressful dynamic, skips along with a new figure incorporating a fast trill at the second beat of the bar. On the repeat of this section the skipping passage might be played even more lightly, *p*, with perhaps a little further ornamentation such as filling in some or all of the rising thirds on the first beat of these bars as two semiquavers, i.e. ♩♫♩ instead of ♩♩♩ . The two echo effects towards the end of each section of this movement must not go unheeded, and they challenge the player's inventiveness at the ornamented repeats. The music should then broaden out, to *f*, at the last four bars of the section.

The emotional climax of the movement is in the two sequential four-bar statements at bars 31–8. Each of these two statements generates an internal 'expressive dynamic' (i.e. non-'structural') of its own through the rise and fall of its pattern of notes. The second four-bar statement, a sequence one note higher, needs to be at a louder, more passionate, dynamic, one step up the terrace of structural dynamics, but retaining the same expressive dynamic curve of the first statement. The middle two bars of each four-bar statement disconcertingly lose sight of the regular 9/8 beat as the slurs from the rising pairs of semiquavers throw the stress on to the second, fifth, and eighth of the inherent nine quaver elements of the second bar, and continue climactically on to the second element of the next bar. The rhythmic hiatus, the sense of losing one's way, is much stronger than in the equivalent passage in the first section of this movement, as the notes to which the stress is transferred are held on as crotchets, the last a crotchet tied to the next quaver, which would normally have taken the second beat of its bar. Meanwhile the bass bravely carries on its steady rhythm. The disorientating effect of the recorder part in bars 32–3, and even more so in bars 36–7, which mount to an anguished high F″, may be even more distressful with a touch of rubato, so that the rhythm is on the brink of collapse until it is redeemed by the strong, stern down-beat at the beginning of bar 34 (and again 38), followed by the recorder's angry throw-away figure on the second beat of this bar, almost as if in disgust at its aberrations and sinfulness. Having survived the whirlwinds of bars 31–8, the recorder again breaks into a dance, with the lightest of accompaniments, its exuberant trilling this time coming on the last beat of the bar, not in the middle. Echo effects and other dynamic challenges, in symmetrical apposition to the events of the first section, recur as the second section progresses. One final challenge is at the very conclusion of the sonata. Should that arpeggiated D minor chord be a last burst of fervour and confidence, or should it die away softly as if the players were by now emotionally exhausted? Is there a *rall.* in bar 69? or should the brakes be applied suddenly at the last possible moment?

Quantz writes (p. 274) 'The alternation of Piano and Forte' (and he refers to the many degrees between—'more than can be expressed by words') 'is one of the most convenient means both to represent the passions distinctly, and to maintain light and shadow in the execution of music.' He might well have referred to Telemann's D minor sonata to illustrate the importance of this dictum.

For further commentary on Telemann's Sonata in D minor, consult the Index.

PL.3–detail (p.42) Recorder Player in Tiepolo's *Europa*

French Style, and Inequality: Lavigne's Sonatas

As J. R. Anthony says in his book on *French Baroque Music* (p. 320), the French sonata was an 'ultramontane importation' from Italy. According to François Couperin, the first French sonatas (called 'sonades' by Couperin) were composed by him in about 1692,[1] and were an outcome of his admiration for Corelli. Baroque 'French style' had been powerfully established by Lully and his contemporaries, and French composers cultivated the kinds of music associated with the glories of Louis XIV's reign and with the rich musical life of the salons of Paris and their 'concerts spirituels'. French involvement with Italian musical taste as it developed in the early eighteenth century at different levels of music, most especially through the Opéra Comique (see Anthony, 152 ff.), was for some time rather ambivalent, particularly with regard to the sonata.

The suite was established in France during the seventeenth century as the dominant form in French lute, harpsichord, and gamba music. As a structure, the suite was both formal and flexible. It could draw upon dances and airs from opera-ballets by Lully and others and include descriptive pieces, thereby sustaining its appeal without compromising its seriousness. It was not until the end of the seventeenth century that the violin, oboe, flute, and recorder came to be used as serious solo instruments (with continuo) in France. This coincided with a renewal of French fascination with Italian music, especially with that of Corelli. The Corelli *sonata da camera* has considerable structural affinities with the French suite, and though French composers imitated aspects of Italian style, these were easily assimilated into existing French forms. The *mélange des genres* during the eighteenth century was an evolutionary process. Lavigne's *Sonates* of 1739 are among the least Italianate of French compositions bearing that title, and they employ what was almost a standard instrumentation for suites—'pour la Musette, Viele, Flute-a-bec,[2] Traversiere, Haubois, etc.'[3] An example of an earlier but much more Italianate French recorder sonata is given in Ch. 8—a sonata which, significantly, appears among a collection of violin sonatas.[4] As the eighteenth century progressed and French violinists of distinction emerged, such as Senaillé and Leclair, both of whom trained in

Italy, French sonatas gradually became structurally closer to the old Italian *sonata da chiesa*. By Leclair's time, however, the recorder was going out of fashion, which happened earlier in France than in Germany or England.[5]

For recorder-players, therefore, the most important eighteenth-century French Baroque solo/continuo form is the suite for *dessus*,[6] with its dance-forms and descriptive pieces.[7] Despite its similarity to the *sonata da camera*, its style and idiom was predominantly French, drawing upon firmly established seventeenth-century antecedents. 'Sonates' were usually conceived with violins in mind (but nomenclature was confused), and increasingly became more violinistic and Italianate in idiom, although sonatas for flute, for example by Michel Blavet, are more common in France than in Italy. In his approach to French Baroque music, a recorder-player needs therefore to be very aware when his manner of playing should be (as usually with suites) totally French in style, and when he needs to take account of Italian influences.

The recorder-player may draw upon a considerable repertoire of French Baroque suites, sonatas, trio sonatas, and duets, mostly written within the range of descant or treble recorders. Although this music is designed to entertain and rarely to evoke strong passions, its perfection within its conventional confines (on paper it sometimes looks very stereotyped and dull)[8] can evoke feelings as profound as those aroused by a fine aria from a Bach cantata.[9] The effect is enhanced because it is so elusive. No recorder-player should ignore such a wealth of music, in an idiom so well suited to his instrument. The considerable pleasure it can give has to be worked for, as much of this music does not come alive unless played in the performance style within which it was conceived.

Dance-forms, upon which so much French Baroque instrumental music is based, impose an internal structure derived from the requirements of the original dance that considerably limits the use of the methods of thematic development associated with Italian-style sonatas. Aggregations of sequences, extended passage-work, and drawn-out cadences cannot be used as flexibly within the confines of dance patterns. Harmonic waywardness is also constrained by the need for key unity, and rhythmic adventurousness cannot go so far as to destroy the dance pulse—though some dances, such as the slow French courantes, are themselves rhythmically complex. Variety needs to be achieved in the larger dimension by sectional contrast, such as the contrasts of the couplets of a rondeau with its repeated main section (refrain or 'reprise'), or mood changes between paired dances. In the smaller dimension, much of the interest of the music is concentrated upon subtle points of detail. Careful delineation and apposition of musical sections and subsections, delicacy and sensitivity of melodic phrasing especially in note-placing, fastidious articulation, rhythmic freedom and variety within the pulse (including the freedom to push and hold back the pulse for interpretational effect), and finesse of ornamentation in creating both melodic emphasis and flow—all these are of the essence in playing French music.[10]

Such emphasis on minutiae makes free ornamentation, which can all too easily become over-ambitious, inappropriate in French-style suites and sonatas. French composers usually say exactly what ornamentation they want, and often provide their own tables of signs and ornaments, though some composers are content with a simple cross over notes to be ornamented. The performer's skill lies not in his improvising new material but in the taste he displays in the exact phrasing of the marked ornaments and in discreet additions at repeats and *doubles*.

The French wrote at length about the difference between their music and that of the Italians, as also did German writers and composers. Although both Couperin and Campra had earlier striven for a *mélange des genres*, it was left to later German composers to arrive at a fully integrated mixture of French 'delicacy' and Italian 'vitality'[11] in the *galant* idiom propounded by Quantz. In terms of playing recorder sonatas (and suites) from the first quarter of the eighteenth century, the differences between the French and Italian styles might be characterized, with the help of these writers, as follows:[12]

French style	*Italian style*
delicacy, 'soft, easy, flowing'	vivacity, briskness, fire
moderation and constraint	extremes of expression, unrestrained
'caress the ear', 'perpetual sweetness'	energy, violence, strangeness
taste, 'goût'	passion, gusto
formality and propriety (with risk of dullness)	novelty and display (with risk of emptiness)
'natural melody, easy smooth tone'	'superfluous artifices, extravagant ornamentation, frequent and harsh leaps'
poise and refinement (see Pl. 4)	urgency, drive, and swagger (see Pl.3)

clarity and elegance	chiaroscuro, dramatic light and shade
'serious, tender, and sustained passions'	'excess of imagination'
mainly dance-based, and character or descriptive ('genre') pieces	more academic pieces, e.g. fugues, and movements indicating strong affects
restrained harmony and prepared dissonances, except for special effects (e.g. discords in Rebel's 'chaos')	dramatic and sometimes surprising discords; frequent dissonant suspensions
rhythmic variety more within the pulse (e.g. by inequality of pairs of notes)	rhythmic variety on a broader scale
accents marked by ornamentation (called 'accens')	accents marked by stress (bow- or breath-pressure)
specified ornamentation integrated into the composition as a form of expression	free extemporization left to the performer, especially in slow movements (Adagios)
French tempo indications and other directions	Italian tempo indication and affect words
less wide-ranging dynamics and tempi	louder/softer, quicker/slower
flute-sound	violin-sound
objective and dispassionate first approach during which the player becomes enticed, charmed, and moved by the music, though his playing attitude never oversteps 'delicatesse' (see Pl. 4)	immediate identification with and total immersion by the player in the affect of the piece. Demonstrative playing attitude (see Pl. 3). Italian music, said Aubert, 'is not to the taste of the ladies'.

These generalizations are valuable as a guide to approach and interpretation, but they should not be applied too literally. Some Vivaldi slow movements 'caress the ear' most deliciously,[13] and some Rameau Tambourins invite unrestrained zest,[14] as do the Tambourins in Lavigne's Sonate I and the Contredanse in Sonate IV. Couperin could be quite academic, though the first fugue in the second *Concert Royal* is on an allemande subject and the second on an 'Air Contre' (= country tune).

PL. 4. The elegant spirit of French music pervades *La Gamme
d'Amour* ('Love's Gamut') by Antoine Watteau (1684–1721). In his
book on the National Gallery (London: Orbis, 1977), Michael Wilson
talks of 'the nervous lyricism of these finely poised, over-refined
characters' in their silken fancy dress 'inhabiting an undefined region
somewhere between reality and fantasy'. Compare these French players
with Tiepolo's Italian performers in Pl. 3.

Campra comments that the French language will not suffer certain things
which get by in Italian music, and eighteenth-century French opera
developed a restrained recitative style of its own designed to make the
words clear. Unlike Italian and most other European languages, French
words have little or no tonic emphasis, and the rhythms of French poetry
and the flow of its delivery derive in part from the varying length of
syllables, not their stress. It is as essential to imagine and feel speech-
rhythms in playing French sonatas (even though they may be dance-based)

as it is in playing Italian sonatas, but more by responding to the recurrence of long and short notes than to stresses on or across a pulse which characterize Italian-style music. French music should be played in a smoother and less accented manner than Italian music,[15] and patterns of note-lengths therefore become all the more significant. It is interesting that the French, particularly after hearing Blavet play, felt that the flute imitated the voice more effectively than the violin, where natural stresses arise from bow movements, the down-stroke being stronger, the up-stroke weaker.

Stresses in recorder-playing are normally created by variations in tonguing *strength*. In French-style music, however, this kind of stress is much less important than it is in Italian-style music, and variety of articulation is achieved more by differentiation of tonguing *duration*, for example by contrasting a quick-speaking 't' (tongued lightly as in speaking French) with a slow-speaking 'r'. Tongued equally gently, the slower-speaking 'r' carries the greater weight by virtue of its length or quantity, and therefore normally corresponds to the long syllable in metre. Moreover, the articulation of 't' takes a tiny silence of time, whereas 'r' rolls off the 't' as if in a single movement of the tongue. This sets up an iambic short-to-long pairing which forms the basis for playing conjunct quavers in French music, with 'r's on the down-beats. (For more on tonguing, see Ch. 5.)

This iambic 't—R' metre is the norm of French music. The more exceptional trochaic metre was shown by placing slurs[16] over the opening pairs of quavers in a piece, and was articulated 'T—r'. This meant prolonging the articulation of the short-speaking 'T' and tonguing the 'r' as briefly as possible to reduce its quantity; the effect must have been very close to a real slur.[17]

The final complexity is inequality.[18] As Hotteterre says, 'you must not always play quavers equally, but you must, in certain time signatures, make one of them long and one short'.[19] This sets up a lilt to the music, cultivated in the current century by jazz and swing players. The following is a brief guide to inequality, derived largely from Donington (esp. *Baroque Music: Style and Performance*, 45–8) and Lasocki.

(i) Inequality is *required* if the composer:
  (*a*) states 'louré', 'pointé', or 'piqué' = 'sharply dotted' (see below).
(ii) Inequality is *likely* if:
  (*a*) the music goes mainly by *conjunct motion* (i.e. stepwise), with notes susceptible to grouping by pairs;
  (*b*) the music is at a *steady speed*, neither decidedly fast nor decidedly slow. If the inclusion of a substantial number of semiquavers within a

medium-pace beat causes the music to sound fast, inequality becomes unlikely. A word such as 'gracieusement' suggests a steady speed where inequality is likely;

    (*c*) the time signature is 2, 3, 3/4 or **C**   (and semiquavers in 2/4).

(iii) Inequality is *unlikely* if:

    (*a*) the music goes mainly by *disjunct motion* (i.e. by leaps, often triadic) BUT disjunct bars within mainly conjunct sections are often taken unequally;

    (*b*) the speed is so fast that inequality would sound restless or lack grace, or so slow that inequality would sound sluggish or lumbering;

    (*c*) the time signature is 3/8, 6/8, or **¢** (and quavers in 2/4);

    (*d*) the same note is repeated several times in succession.

(iv) Inequality is *precluded* if the composer:

    (*a*) states 'notes égales', 'marqué', 'décidé', or 'détaché';

    (*b*) puts *dots* over notes (this does not mean staccato, which is usually indicated by *vertical strokes* over notes; but staccato prevents pairing and therefore also precludes inequality);

    (*c*) puts *slur-marks* over groups of three or more notes.

GUIDE-LINES FOR APPLYING INEQUALITY

1. Inequality is usually applied only to the notes of shortest value which appear in substantial numbers in a movement. In some pieces, however, pairs of quavers and pairs of semiquavers may both be unequal—this depends on speed, etc. Inequality is always contained across or within each beat of the music—the beat itself is never made unequal.

2. The norm of inequality is triplet-like and iambic in metre ♪♩♪♩♪♩ etc., the 'r' being the strong beat by virtue of its much greater length of articulation.

3. If pairs of notes have slur-marks over them, this usually indicates trochaic inequality ('T—r'); such pairs of notes are played more evenly, but still slightly lilting. Confusingly, slurs were sometimes also used to indicate reverse inequality.

4. Reverse inequality '|T–r— |T–r— |T–r—' etc., also known as 'Lombardic rhythm' (or 'Scotch snap'), may be used for contrast. Over-use becomes tiresome.

5. Inequality should sound spontaneous and not mechanical. Other ratios than 2:1 (triplets) should be used, e.g. 3:2. 'It should be proportioned expressively at discretion' (Donington). Above all, it should *lilt*.

6. Odd pairs of semiquavers within a phrase moving in quavers and crotchets are generally unequal, even in Italian-style music (see Ex. 2.2 above).

7. Certain dance-rhythms favour inequality, e.g. sarabande, chaconne, march, minuet, gavotte, and even, if they are not too fast, bourrée and rigaudon; others do not, e.g. passepied (being in 3/8 time), tambourin (too fast), and allemande, if it moves briskly in a mixture of quavers and semiquavers, although in slower, more complex allemandes the semiquavers may be unequal. Italian tempo indications (e.g. 'allegro', 'largo') are rather less likely to suggest inequality than French words. A dance-form repeat may be played more, or less, unequally.

8. Bass parts usually stay steady, even with inequality in the upper part(s), except in passages of melodic or rhythmic imitation.

9. Generally inequality is a performer's option. Its application to enhance expression is at the good taste of the performer.

10. These guide-lines should not therefore be regarded as rules.

Inequality is a subject upon which scholars continue to disagree; for example, some of Donington's statements are challenged by David Fuller in his article on 'Notes inégales' in *New Grove*.

The sonatas of Philbert de Lavigne illustrate many of the aspects of French style referred to in this chapter. They are dance-based, with occasional amusing descriptive pieces, they are full of 'easy, smooth, tunes', and they need variety of inequality to avoid repetitiousness. They are idiomatic for the recorder, and range only over an octave and a half (G to D'), with hardly an accidental in sight. They are lightweight and charming works by a composer who fails to earn a mention even in Anthony's book.[20] Played out-of-style they can sound uninteresting, but the more one applies to them all the nuances of French *bon goût*, the more delightful they become.

The titles of Lavigne's sonatas are as enigmatic as some of those in Couperin's and Rameau's suites. As its first movement shows (see Ex. 4.1), there is nothing oriental about 'La Persan'—but perhaps one of its melodies came from an opera with a Persian setting? A suggested interpretational approach is added to the music (only the recorder part is shown). The A section (played four times) holds this rondeau-form movement together, as is the case with many other Lavigne movements. This section should be played smoothly each time, though on each occasion there should be slight but noticeable differences. There is a great deal of imitation in the bass part. This calls for careful rehearsing and marking of parts, and, above all,

EX. 4.1. Lavigne, 'La Persan'

Frequency of semiquavers in conjunct (stepwise) motion suggests unequal semiquavers

$\frac{3}{8}$ is here a swaying one pulse in a bar rhythm. It does not preclude inequality.

The + trills are original. All other markings are editorial.

careful listening and awareness during performance. The idea of the hemiola at bar 5 and elsewhere is debateable. Hemiolas are common in 3/8 time, but there is no bass support for a hemiola here. It provides, however, a way of varying the four presentations of the A section, other than the more obvious one of dynamic change.

The sections ('couplets') should be well separated and contrasted, as they provide the chief means of variety and liveliness in this movement. The B section (bars 16–24) is shorter than the C couplet (bars 40–52); its change of style from the A section should not be as marked as the later change from the A section to the less symmetrical C couplet. By the C couplet stage of the movement, there is an expectation of a passage which displays greater freedom and originality. Note the phrasing at the end of the B couplet, where inequality has to be tailed away. A rather similar example from the second movement of Lavigne's Sonate I, which is also in 3/8 time and has a falling-third feminine ending to its main subject, is shown in Ex. 4.2.

EX. 4.2.

Rondeau

Pas trop vite [therefore unequal semiquavers]

Here again the inequality has to be smoothed out to prevent jerkiness at the phrase-endings (marked (√)), and to give a fraction more time to take breath if it is needed.

Subtle variations may be made not only in inequality, and in articulation levels, but in the length of appoggiaturas at cadences, even if the following short trill slightly crosses the beat. Italian instrumentalists, it seems, leaned on appoggiaturas, while French players let them speak for themselves as mild, not stressed, discords, and probably held them less, moving sooner into the trill, or even virtually going straight into the trill.

Notes at the top of a phrase, e.g. Ex. 4.1 B′ in bar 2, should not be stressed by articulation but accorded their prominence by a slight swelling of sound after the note has been tongued ('son enflé'), and perhaps sweetened with a reticent finger-vibrato ('flattement'[21]), for B′ using ½7. This means of expression and tone-colouring comes more into its own in slower movements. It is important not to bulge the note into sharpness, so careful shading techniques are needed (*RT* 56–8).

The movements of Lavigne's six sonatas offer interesting challenges in arriving at the best speeds so that there is both contrast and cohesion, but without extremism. A direction against inequality such as 'marqué' in the last movement of 'La Persan' suggests a brisk speed in which inequality would in any case sound fussy or uncomfortable. The second movement is marked 'gaiement'. It is in 2/4 and semiquaver passages proliferate. This precludes quaver inequality; whether the semiquavers are unequal or not depends on how fast the movement is taken. Perhaps, in order to differentiate it from the brisk last movement, this second movement should be at a moderate 'allegro' with at least the conjunct semiquaver passages having a slight lilt (3:2). Then follow a pair of Musettes marked 'gracieusement', suggesting inequality in the conjunct quavers, and a swinging one-in-a-bar waltz-like tempo, faster than the first movement. The section shown in Ex. 4.3, however, with its repeated fanfare-like quavers, might be played, for contrast, strongly and without inequality. The prevailing inequality is resumed at the four descending conjunct quavers before the cadence (i.e. in bar 28).

EX. 4.3.

There are other opportunities in this pair of movements for imaginative dynamic and rhythmic nuances, so that the whole sonata becomes full of personality.

Despite their apparent simplicity, one has to be vigilant in interpreting Lavigne's sonatas. The composer is sparing in marking (+) ornamentation, but discreet additional ornamentation to accentuate his rhythms and melodies is sometimes called for, for example in the repeat of the Sarabande in Sonate VI. Here the slowish unequal quavers have the effect of turning the movement from 3/4 to 9/8 time, while still maintaining the typical sarabande rhythmic emphasis on the second beat of the bar. Sonate IV has a contredanse that even with its 2̸ time signature goes too fast for inequality, a Musette II with three quavers slurred, contra-indicating inequality, and an opening 'Ariete' with slurred pairs of quavers indicating a trochaic rhythm with 'T—r' tonguing and only slight, 3:2, inequality.

The clangorous 'Forgerons' in Lavigne's Sonate VI is marked 'piqué', although it is full of disjunct semiquavers. This cautions against any first conceptions one might have had about frenetic activity in the smithy, and suggests a hammering overdotting with a muscular 'tD' (or even, unauthentically, 'kT') tonguing, possibly at a 4:1 ratio of inequality, which only works effectively at a more moderate speed.

Overdotting of a more serious character was one of the principal eighteenth-century devices to create an effect of grandeur and pomposity in the slow opening and closing sections of a French overture derived from Lully.[22] Lavigne's sonatas provide no examples, but Dieupart's Suite IV opens with the expected 'Ouverture', a 'lentement' section enclosing the usual faster three-time fugato section. The first four bars of the instrumental melody part (in a treble recorder transcription) are given in Ex. 4.4.

EX. 4.4.

By the time Dieupart's sonatas were published (1701) it is likely that the opening section of a French overture, when played at a slowish four crotchets in a bar, would have been double-dotted. Using this piece as an example, such double-dotting might be thought of as a flexible 8:1 ratio, with marked silences of articulation, so that the music might then be played as in Ex. 4.5.

EX. 4.5.

The tonguing 'k' or 'g' might be used, unauthentically, in place of 't' if this helps the player to achieve a crisper, sharper attack. Moreover, the amount of ornamentation in the harpsichord version of these suites suggests that some incisive French ornamentation should be added, not exactly copying the harpsichord elaboration, but in a manner that suits the recorder. A suggestion is given in Ex. 4.6.

EX. 4.6.

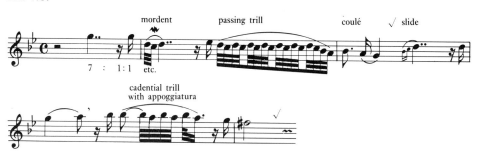

The ornamented French overture was widely copied in Germany, monumentally by J. S. Bach. This should serve as a reminder that other characteristics thought of as aspects of French style permeated Baroque music generally, especially inequality. Freda Dinn, in her *Early Music for Recorders* (p. 41), suggests that the first movement of Handel's G minor sonata (see Ex. 2.1) should be played with inequality, although it must again be emphasized that inequality is a performer's option and that the extent to which a Baroque player might have used inequality, to greater or lesser degree, in his performance of an Italian-style sonata must remain a matter of conjecture (see le Huray, 53). Dotted and undotted versions exist of the opening bar of the Larghetto of Handel's E minor flute sonata, and its prevailing rhythm is dotted over a quaver bass; this may lend support to Dinn's interpretation of the Larghetto of the G minor recorder sonata. Her version of the whole movement is shown in Ex. 4.7. She also proposed inequality for the third movement of this sonata; see below, Ex. 6.7.

Donington[23] puts the question, 'How widely ought inequality to be applied?', and answers, 'This is one of the most difficult questions in Baroque interpretation.' In an Appendix, however, he quotes examples of inequality from Italian composers, including Domenico Scarlatti. Perhaps Couperin's vision of a *mélange des genres* was never far away.

For further commentary on Lavigne's Sonata 'La Persan', consult the Index.

EX. 4.7. Handel, Sonata in G minor

Articulation and Slurs: Herbert Murrill's Sonata and Handel's 'Furioso' (D Minor Sonata)

QUANTZ says of tonguing that it 'is the means by which we give animation to the execution of the notes upon the flute . . . it must animate the expression of the passions in pieces of every sort, whatever they may be: sublime or melancholy, gay or pleasing' (p. 71). How much truer is this of the recorder with its unusually sensitive response to the articulations of normal speech arising from its low breath-pressure and its relaxed and natural lip position. Quantz adds that tonguing 'so distinguishes one flute player from another that if a single piece is played in turn by several persons, the differences in their execution frequently make the work almost unrecognizable.' Tonguing, like one's way of speaking, is a very personal matter, as there is variation from one person to another in the shape of his upper jaw and palate, teeth positions (which dentistry may exacerbate), and the muscularity of the tongue, as well as differences arising from personality, native language, or accent. Moreover, different instruments—different by voicing and bore as well as by size—respond differently to ways of tonguing, though in itself each recorder is responsive to a wide variety of tonguing nuances.

Tonguing has several functions. One is in register selection, although different registers can also be selected simply by blowing harder. In practice, register selection is usually the result of a combination of breath-pressure control and of tonguing. Sharper tonguing excites higher harmonics. On one fingering, for example 0 –23 45––, it is possible by using stronger or lighter tonguing to produce two different notes, in this case D and A′, with no change in breath-pressure (see *RT* 34–5), or even, with breath-pressure change, to play the D louder than the A′. The treble recorder plays from F to D′ in only two registers, however, and the selection of the upper register is so facilitated by the speaker-hole, i.e. by thumbing, that the register-selection function of tonguing in this range is minimal, leaving the tongue free for its prime functions of articulatory expressiveness and of facilitating the playing of rapid passages. The tongue's register-selection function becomes more important for the notes around the more closely spaced register-breaks above D', particularly when one wishes to play high notes softly. In avant-garde music exact tonguing at a register-break can produce so-called 'chords' or multiphonic sounds; for example, the fingering 0 –23 —— can produce with strong tonguing a sound approximating to E, G♯'' and B'', together with a bottom E as a difference-tone (*RT* 64). Notwithstanding the idiosyncratic nature of tonguing, Quantz and other writers[1] concentrate, as this book does, on the function of tonguing as an essential element in expressivity and interpretation.

The expressive power of tonguing will never be realized to the full without complete understanding and putting into practice of two vital principles. The first is that the strength or lightness of any tonguing must be separated in one's mind from the amount of breath used to maintain and continue a note after it has been articulated; generally it is amount of breath that controls the loudness or softness of a note, not tonguing. The second principle is that a tonguing has two qualities which must be distinguished from each other: the power of the tonguing (its strength or lightness), and its speed of articulation (slow-speaking or quick-speaking). These two principles will be considered in turn.

Strong tonguing is brought about by pressing the tongue hard against the teeth-ridge with almost painful muscularity and then suddenly retracting the tongue (without moving the chin) and releasing the weight of air that has built up behind it in the constant flow of breath from the diaphragm. One can, however, isolate this same tongue-movement, miming, as it were, strong tonguing with no breath-flow and therefore no sound. Or one can allow the passage of a tiny trickle of air-flow to create a strangulated strong-tongued staccato *pp*. With constant strong tonguing one can play a series of notes which increase in dynamic from *pp* to *ff*, though in this process a low note may be forced across its register-break into the upper octave. The converse is true, up to a point, with regard to light tonguing, when the tongue rests on the teeth-ridge like a butterfly on a blade of grass. Very light tonguing is not muscular enough to restrain all but the lowest pressure of air-flow welling up behind it; to change the metaphor, the dam will burst. It is possible, however, with careful synchronization, at the moment the tongue retracts to release a high-pressure flood of air, so creating a *ff* note with light articulation.[2] These tonguing-strength variations, with the dynamic of the ongoing note ranging from *pp* to *ff* (or vice versa), will operate with tonguings such as 'r', 'th', and 'y' where there is not a full closure between the tongue and the palate, but only a grazing (fricative) or stricture position. Remember that there are two discrete modes in operation in note-formation—tonguing strength in the strong to light continuum, and air-flow (related to breath-pressure) in the *pp* to *ff* continuum, and that these two modes operate independently of each other.

In loud passages in recorder sonatas, particularly when accompanied by a piano, the recorder-player will want to use a high breath-pressure close to the register-break—9 on the 'Beaufort scale' (see p. 23). This will maximize the excitement of those upper harmonics which make recorder tone more penetrating and strident, giving it a cutting edge. If this amount of breath-pressure is put behind the articulation of a note, however, tonguing will become more like a spit, causing an ugly transient sound at the start of each note which is only acceptable as a special, almost percussive, effect. Moreover, a combination of such high breath-pressure with strong tonguing may result in the selection of a higher register, so the player also runs the risk of playing the wrong note, an octave too high, or worse. In recorder-sonata playing, most notes—and this includes softer notes—are not articulated suddenly at full pressure like a bullet from a gun, but are brought into being by a kind of very rapid extrusion (more like a water-pistol, perhaps). Following the example of Roger North, the diagram shown in Pl. 5 may help to illustrate this.

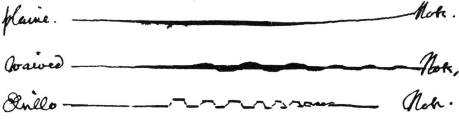

PL. 5. The first three note-formation diagrams were made by Roger North in his 'Notes of Me' (*c*.1695)—Plate II of *Roger North on Music*. North was a viol-player, and his concept of the 'plaine note' derives from the sound produced by the outcurved Baroque bow, held underhand. The 'waived' note is equivalent to recorder breath-vibrato; the trilled note represents the 'close-shake' (Hotteterre's *flattement*), equivalent to recorder finger-vibrato. Beneath is a suggested shape of a Baroque recorder plain long note, showing the faster articulation and formulation of recorder sound as compared with a note drawn out by a viol bow. Like the viol note, the recorder note is developed or nurtured after its short articulation period.

The second principle, the differentiation between tonguing-strength and articulation speed, has already been alluded to in the previous chapter with regard to French tonguing consonants. Articulation speed can be exemplified by repeating the phrase 'One day, two days' in a strictly regular four-crotchet tempo. It takes longer to enunciate the 'w' sound of 'one' than the 't' sound of 'two', so that in effect the time left within the crotchet beat for the vowel sound of the 'u' in 'one' is shorter than the time left for the 'oo' in 'two'. There is a continuum of articulation speeds through the consonant sounds commonly used in recorder tonguing from quick-speaking 't' to slow-speaking 'r' and 'l'. Veilhan's commentary on Quantz (*Baroque Recorder*, 4) aptly refers to these extremes as 'precise' (quick-speaking) and 'unctuous' (slow-speaking). Quantz remarks that 'd', which is slower-speaking than 't', is more suitable for notes which must be 'nourrissantes'.[3] A recorder-player thus has expressive control over the tautness or slackness of the beat (see p. 40). Slow-speaking tonguings can produce bigger-sounding notes, or a more relaxed phrasing, without any change in breath-pressure, but with corresponding loss of definition and sprightliness.

Let us now examine the expressive capabilities of the various tonguing consonants, listed in order from quick-speaking to slow-speaking.

't' Tongue arched with curved tip so that only a small area of tongue touches the teeth-ridge, or below the teeth-ridge towards (or even touching) the upper part of the front incisor teeth. As its formation is different from the normal relaxed position of the tongue, a small lapse of time is required to put the tongue forward into the 't' position, causing a momentary silence of articulation before the note starts, slightly detaching a note from its predecessor. Because 't' is very quick-speaking, it is useful for staccato notes, for separated notes in passage-work (see Ex. 5.3, Handel, 'Furioso', bars 8–10), and for up-beats to new phrases, especially in dance-style music. It has a wide range of tonguing-strengths from strong (English 'tea') to medium (as French or Italian 't') to light (as in 'Scottish' pronounced by a Scot). Strong plosive 't' is very harsh and 'chiffy' (percussive effect in Renaissance dance-music). Much more important as light precise tonguing, especially as 'tee' (with high tongue position to create a high-pressure low-volume air-stream) for the clear production of the recorder's high notes (see *RT* ch. VI).

'k' Palatal reverse-tonguing to 't'. Very quick-speaking. Useful for extremely rapid up-beat notes (see Ex. 4.5) before 't' or 'd'. 'gD' gives a weightier version of this same type of phrasing. 'Ticky-ticky' is the fastest possible double-tonguing for showy demisemiquavers, etc., but is too mechanical for expressiveness. Palatal tonguing is referred to by Ganassi (1535) and Bismantova (1677), but does not seem to have been used in the later Baroque period.

'd'   Tongue slightly down-curved on or just below the teeth-ridge, or more forward. Perhaps because 'd' is voiced from the larynx in normal speech and because a greater breadth of the tongue makes contact with the teeth-ridge area, it carries more weight than 't'. 'd' is nearer the position at which the tongue is normally at rest, so it requires a shorter and more relaxed stroke, and gives a more legato effect than 't' (see Quantz, 71–5: 'd' is used for 'slow and sustained notes').

A useful variant is 'dh', especially for English players who tend to enunciate 'd' too strongly. This is slightly aspirated, and the tongue is flat, extending along the whole teeth-ridge and touching the molars at its sides. 'd', or better 'dh', is standard recorder single tonguing, with a wide range of tonguing-strengths, though 'dh' has less capability than 'd' for strong tonguing (see start of Handel's 'Furioso'). 'dh' corresponds more to the initial articulation of a Baroque bow in string-playing.[4] A light 'dh' is the level of tonguing most suited to cadences, where the articulation should be more relaxed. 'd' ('dh') is also normally used in articulating an appoggiatura or trill.[5]

A lightly articulated 'd' may be used with a light 't' as a form of double-tonguing in the pairing of strong/weak notes in Baroque music, for example at a feminine ending to a phrase. Examples of such double-tonguings in word-form are 'Ditty' or 'Teddy', or in 'Daddy', where the two 'd's are differentiated by tonguing-strength, strong to light. The second element of these double-tonguings is taken on the rebound with no fresh impulse of breath.

'g'   Palatal reverse tonguing to 'd', considered harsh in the Renaissance. Slower-speaking than 'k', as it is voiced in normal speech. 'Dugger-dugger' is a 'safe' tonguing for fast semiquavers as it is less legato than some other double-tonguings. It gives a moment of time between notes for finger-movement while retaining some element of expressivity. A slightly aspirated 'gh' matches 'dh' for tripping more fluently along semiquaver passages, with 'd' for the down-beat or accented semi-quavers. 't' is then used at up-beat semiquavers which start new phrases within the passage-work.

'dl' 'tl'   Advocated by Quantz (79–85) for fast passage-work as a double-tonguing after 'd' or 't' (as in 'diddle', 'tiddle', or 'tittle'). This articulation is also expressive in slower-moving music as it combines a quicker with a slower tonguing, elegantly delineating pairs of notes or longer groups. Quantz acquired this technique from 'ancient' players, and it is therefore probably 'authentic' to use it in earlier eighteenth-century music. Much practice is needed to achieve distinctness—Quantz's exercises are excellent (a lateral tongue oscillation may help to control fast passages). It can be combined for greater legato with 'l' as 'diddle-liddle'. 'dl' does not respond to strong tonguing, so the stronger 'd' takes the down-beat stress even though 'dl' is slower-speaking (*RT* 42).

'l' Limited to the medium to light tonguing-strength range. The tongue is flat across the upper part of the teeth-ridge abutment, air-flow release being spread along the teeth-ridge. A lolling, loose, flabby tonguing, very slow-speaking and blurring rhythmic accents. It is useful for low instruments, and for languid expression. In faster music it can be used in 'multi-tongued' semiquavers; for example, in the group 'D r l t' the first three semiquavers are legato, and the last detached. For smooth and neat triplets try 'doodle-le loodle-li'. 'l' is also useful for rapid articulated slurs.[6] It was the standard direct tonguing for legato passages in Renaissance music, being Ganassi's 'third form' doubled with 'r' as 'lere', with the two syllables almost 'melting into one'.

'r' Archetypal reverse tonguing of the Renaissance ('Diri liri'), especially for *passaggi*; and, with the same forwards and backwards movement of the tongue, an essential component of French-style double-tonguing because of its intrinsic slow-speaking weight. 'r' is articulated as a single fricative tongue-graze at the upper edge of the teeth-ridge with a slightly curved tongue-tip as in Scottish 'baron' or as a single element of a rolled r. 'r' follows perfectly upon direct tonguing consonants, especially 'd' when no change is needed either in the shape of the tip of the tongue or in the breadth of the tongue's contact with the teeth-ridge, and it needs only a very slight upward lift in its placing on the teeth-ridge. After 't', 'd', or even 'l', the tongue can roll back and up under the same impulse of breath, touching the two consonants as if in one movement. 'r' only operates in the medium to light tonguing-strength range, but should be practised as a clearly-articulated medium-strength tonguing, as well as a light tonguing when it almost melts into a slur as in the Murrill Finale (see Ex. 5.9). 'r' has an important use in semi-articulated slurs involving notes in high registers, in association with 'y' (see p.85).

'th' A sort of strangled 'dh', which can be articulated on the teeth-ridge, not necessarily forward on the teeth. Not referred to by Quantz or earlier writers. It has a fairly wide tonguing-strength range and is a very slow-speaking fricative, ideal for accented or weighted second beats after a 'd' first beat, as in chaconnes and sarabandes (see *RT* 46). Hunt (p. 110) illustrates its use on non-accented notes.

'y' See *RT* 51–2. A non-historic half-tonguing. It is like the 'll' in 'Chantilly': the tongue anchors on the molars but does not quite graze the teeth-ridge, impeding rather than holding back the air-flow. Very useful as a slur articulation, especially across the register-break between G′ and A′ or across wide intervals. By insinuating a slight impulse into the air-stream, 'y' can also delineate an accented note within, or at the end of, a slur, as in Ex. 5.1:

deee ee ee Yer er er er   Yer

'h' A non-tonguing controlled from the throat, which may be used in bass-recorder playing or at the beginning of aspirated 'sung' phrases, for example 'Who is Sylvia?'. Was this Ganassi's 'head-breath', or did he really mean 'p' ('the lips control the breath'; *Fontegara*, 14)?

As Ganassi almost suggests, the quality of a consonant is affected by the vowel sound used in the articulation of a note. For example, the 't' in 'heater' is crisper and more sharply defined than the more deliberate 't' in 'hooter'. This is because of the difference in the angle of attack and withdrawal and in the length of stroke of the tongue from its high position near the teeth-ridge in saying 'ee' and from its position much lower in the mouth in saying 'oo'. Experiment by rapidly repeating sounds such as 'daa', then 'dee', then 'doo', and consider the effect of the vowel upon the articulation of the consonant. It is slight, but significant. This gives a greater refinement to tonguing expressiveness, especially in cantabile movements. The vowel sound imagined after the tonguing consonant also enhances the feeling of singing. As a starting point, tonguing syllables may be thought of as 'tee' 'di' 'rer' 'loo' and 'yuh', one's facial expression changing by degrees from a smile to a frown. It is important to vary these syllables in enunciating the imagined words and phrases of sonata movements.

This tonguing variety can 'balance' a phrase to mould its shapeliness. For example, the last movement of Lavigne's 'La Persan' contains the passage shown in Ex. 5.2 (bars 40–4).

EX. 5.2.

Legèrement et marqué

The 2/4 time signature suggests a moderately fast speed. The word 'marqué' precludes inequality. It will be noted that the first three semiquaver groups contain three conjunct semiquavers, and one disjunct. The latter acts in the first two groups as the up-beat to the following crotchet that ends the mini-phrase. The slight separation, the dance 'lift', and the link to the crotchet can all be brought out by tonguing these up-beat semiquavers as 'ti'. The three preceding semiquavers may flow nicely with 'De re le', with 'Der' on the crotchets. The first group needs a clearly defined 'D r l t' as it is the statement of the idea. The second group, in apposition to the first but balancing it, needs the same tonguing consonants but articulated more lightly, although with no change whatsoever in breath-pressure or note-length. The whole bar of conjunct semiquavers (bar 43) will flow nicely with 'diddle diddle duddle duddle' tonguing, which pairs the semiquavers more strongly than 'd r l t' (a 3 + 1 grouping), and avoids any temptation to place a tiny phrase-point '(ʼ)' after the third semiquaver of this bar. 'D r l r' would be too legato for bar 43, overdoing the contrast with bars 40 and 41. 'D g d g' would be too harsh and abrupt, however lightly it were enunciated, because the 'g' is too quick-speaking. The two-quaver feminine ending in bar 44 needs the strength of 'Der' on the first quaver, and a neutral, soft 'te' on the second with no new impulse of breath, as if saying 'Der te' in one word. The wrong type of 't' would be produced if 'ti' were used in this weak position; for example if the word 'Dirty' is tried here the final quaver does not relax sufficiently to balance the earlier part of the complete quatrain-type phrase.

This last pair of quavers, as a falling third from strong to weak, seems a prime candidate for a *coulé*, as follows: filling in the A between the quavers B and G. This, however, would adversely affect the equilibrium of the whole passage as the full length of the quaver B (i.e. not losing part of its length to the *coulé* note A) is required in order to balance the crotchets D and C that have followed the two earlier semiquaver groups. In the background of this passage there needs to be a feel of a firm descending melodic phrase D C B G, in two crotchets and two quavers. A *coulé* between the B and G in this phrase would sound fussy. Moreover, only a few bars back before the passage quoted (i.e. at bar 36), the composer had used a *coulé* in a very prominent manner to round off a phrase-ending. A further *coulé* in bar 44 would be weak and superfluous.

All this attention to detail may seem over-meticulous, even in French music. It is perfectly possible to play the whole of the passage quoted in carefully nuanced single tonguing. But it would never sound quite so elegant.

The balancing action of good tonguing gives shape and 'chiaroscuro' to rapid semiquaver passages, and it is because of this effect, as much as resolving the physical problems of single-tonguing at very high velocity (it becomes impossible to do controlled single-tonguing above a certain speed), that double-tonguing is essential in all fast movements. Ex. 5.3 shows the recorder part for the fastest movement in Handel's recorder sonatas, the third movement of the D minor sonata, Presto or Furioso, with a complete tonguing schedule marked in. It will be seen that it is not only the semiquavers that are made more significant in expressing fury by the process of double-tonguing. The Schott edition by Thurston Dart ('Fitzwilliam Sonatas') is used here only because of its plethora of added slurs—Handel marked none. They are 'non-authentic' but may nevertheless generate various phrasing and tonguing ideas, as well as remind players not to accept editorial markings uncritically (this edition, moreover, does not identify what the editor had added).

Commentary on Ex. 5.3

For the wildest fury, the speed should be fast enough for a feel of two beats to the bar rather than four. One source marks this movement ₵ .

Bar 1	The spirit of the movement would be better captured if the opening two crotchets, played against an outburst of semiquavers in the bass, were thought of as expletives—'Damn!', a rare case for a strong 'D' tonguing in Baroque music.
Bar 2	Slower-speaking tonguings, 'tl' and 'dl', are suggested on the off-beat semiquavers as this gives greater weight than the easier 'd g' tonguing; one certainly could not express anger with the more mechanical and agile 't k' sounds.
Bars 2–3, 9–10, etc.	Too much tonguing variety is fussy, and difficult to remember, so two basic ways are established of treating the semiquaver groups: 'der l t' for those with the opening pair slurred, and 'd dl d dl' for the non-slurred groups. It is not then necessary to mark every bar in the schedule. Of course tonguing schedules such as this are only intended to enable one to acquire good tonguing practices, so that

EX. 5.3. Handel, Sonata in D minor

in reading ahead one associates certain patterns of notes with appropriate tonguings. Lively and expressive articulation should then come spontaneously. It is far too complicated to memorize a whole schedule of tonguing consonants, let alone complete syllables, for the length of a sonata movement, but it generally helps to think in terms of 'eee' syllables for high notes, and 'er', 'ah', or 'oo' for lower notes and at ends of cadences. Certain formulae may then be found useful such as 'tee tittle Durdle doodle' on the opening group of seven downward semiquavers (bar 2), and 'Ticker tacker De ree digger Doo' as an idea for bar 25.

Bars 4-8, 10-12, etc.
These are bars where the editor seems to be suggesting that fury might be communicated not only by Handel's continuous torrent of semiquavers in the solo and bass lines but also by playing certain pairs of notes with an agogic accent (indicated by the slurs), sometimes offset by staccato spitting quavers. In order to display irascibility these pairs could be articulated with forceful 'r's on the down-beats, getting more and more ratty up to the climax (*ff*) in bar 33. Hunt (p. 111) is right to advise caution about weak-to-strong slurring in Baroque music, but see Keller, *Phrasing and Articulation*, 45.

Bar 13
A *f* scale passage down to the bottom of the recorder's range will sound weak unless powerfully articulated, and the bottom F, which takes the strong beat and slur in this bar, will overblow into the next register on many instruments if a strong 'D' tonguing is used, however appropriate such a tonguing might otherwise be. The slow-speaking 'y' tonguing suggested here will give more weight though less definition to this passage, and will be less likely to result in the bottom notes breaking upwards, even with a heavy input of breath-pressure. To avoid blurring, each 'y' needs to be reiterated with considerable muscular force from the back of the tongue. This tonguing should intensify the anger affect of this passage, and the same articulation could then be used in the parallel passage at bar 15.

Bar 19
(and elsewhere). The crosses over notes suggest the possibility of using alternative fingerings for playing these groups at high speed, e.g. E♭ = 0 –23 4–(6)–, adding 5 for D. Such fingerings, however, may not tolerate the strong tonguings needful in this movement, and normal fingerings will then have to be used.

Bars 25 and 27
The 't k's in this section, where fury subsides somewhat, are for contrast. Thurston Dart marks it *più p* (but this means only slightly softer). The slurs up to the B♭'s are questionable and alternative tonguings are proposed here. The slurring in the repeated four-semiquaver groups in bars 31–2 might also be reconsidered, for example tonguing them as 'Te ti re le' or 'De ti le te'.[7]

It will be noticed that in the suggested articulation in this version of Handel's 'Furioso' most of the editor's slurs are shown tongued in one way or another, whereas others are left as 'real slurs' (e.g. bar 24). Recorder slurring is a matter of considerable controversy. Some eminent recorder-players[8] never play real slurs but articulate slurred groups so smoothly and so skilfully that an impression of slurring is given. Their belief is that real slurs on the recorder, even those with only one finger-movement, sound blurred and indefinite, and that the impulse of a tiny tongue-movement into the air-flow gives each note more identity. Be that as it may, a touch of tonguing, 'y' or, if needs be, 'r', is an indispensable aid to slurring across register-breaks and avoiding ugly clicks that prejudice good phrasing. A touch of tonguing also helps to achieve a smooth slur wherever a complex finger-movement is involved. Consider, for example, certain slurs in the first (treble) recorder part of Bach's 'Sheep may safely graze'. The slur E♭′ F″ G″ (first marked *f*, then repeated *p*) involves crossing the obstinate register-break between F″ and G″, which is virtually impossible to negotiate as a true slur, *p*, without a click. A quick touch of 'r' tonguing or a light 'l', at the exact moment of the finger move and a small increase in breath-pressure will, with practice, produce the effect of a slur. To balance the phrase and help hide the deceit of the intruded 'r', the E♭′–F″ part of the slur (which is straightforward as it does not cross a register-break) should be accorded a touch of 'y' tonguing, or a very soft 'r' for players who do not like 'y's. There is an exposed strong-to-weak rising slur from B♭′ to E♮′ at the end of the middle section of this aria, and five bars earlier two consecutive slurs both crossing register-breaks: G′–C♯′, and C♯′–E♮′. Such slurs have to be lightly articulated, but as unnoticeably as possible. In these circumstances the argument for articulating all slurs is made more cogent.

Real slurs do, however, sound slightly different, especially in downward motion, and not to use them is to abandon one of the expressive capabilities of an instrument which is not over-endowed in this respect. Most slurs can, with careful breath-pressure control, be managed as real slurs, especially if the movement of only one finger is involved or if a straightforward alternative fingering is available which does not threaten the tone-quality or shape of a phrase—or perhaps even enhances it. Moreover, slurs were first introduced in early Baroque music[9] with specific expressive intent; downward slurs may represent sighs, for example.[10] The slurs which Handel wrote over the semiquavers in the recurring 𝄞 figure in the Andante of the G minor sonata (Ex. 2.1) sound best played as real slurs. This involves no difficulty except in bar 21, where each of the three slurs can be reduced to a one-finger movement. A′ after B♭′ can be taken by adding 7, closed G′ may be used before the next A′ (see *RT* 77–8), and for the

E♮ after F′ add 3. The steady speed of the Andante will mask any slight tonal or intonational defects of these common alternatives, and the real slurs will help the music to flow more buoyantly.

Baroque composers of sonatas mark in short slurs as an indication of phrasing and expression. Sometimes the indication is shown in the first bar only but is intended to apply to the whole movement. A study of composer's slurs in reliable editions is a necessary preliminary to achieving authentic phrasing, bearing in mind that instrumentalists were expected in the process of performing a sonata to exercise their own discretion in adding slurs. Like other added ornamentation, this would be in a manner compatible with the performance practice of the time and place, and with the perceived affect of the music. Initially, recorder-players have to be reliant upon the knowledge and taste of editors. Further insight into Baroque phrasing may be gained by listening critically to 'authentic' performances, and by studying books such as Peter le Huray's *Authenticity in Performance*, which adopts a 'case-study' approach—a considerable part of his book is concerned with the shaping of phrases.

If Baroque French composers puzzle us by using slur-signs for a variety of different purposes (see p. 66), composers from Vivaldi onwards, and especially nineteenth- and twentieth-century composers, confuse us still further by using long slurs to indicate phrasing (and there could be real slurs within those phrases)—this in addition to the use from the late Renaissance onwards of the slur-sign to show notes tied across barlines. Are the slurs at the beginning of the opening Largo of Herbert Murrill's Sonata (Ex. 5.4) all

EX. 5.4.

real slurs? Or are they articulated slurs—the slur-marks being intended to indicate the legato of the 'cantando espressivo'? Or a mixture of the two? If they are real slurs, what about the passage shown in Ex. 5.5 from the third

EX. 5.5.

movement, 'Recitativo'? Clearly it cannot be a real slur, as this would make the D in this first bar into a dotted crotchet in value, whereas the linearity of the phrase seems to depend on the identity of the three falling pairs of quavers.

EX. 5.6. Murrill, Sonata

*Herbert Murrill told Walter Bergmann that he quite liked the trills being taken from the upper auxiliary, Baroque fashion.

In this sonata a great deal of the effect (or may one use the word 'affect', as Murrill's composition has structural affinities with the *sonata da chiesa*?) depends on grouping—'mini-phrases'—within the long phrases indicated by the extended slurs. Exx. 5.6 and 5.7 set out the recorder parts of the two slow movements of this sonata, 'edited' with real slurs (marked underneath) and phrase-marks added. Like all editions, they must be seen as one person's ideas. The marking of the mini-phrases and slurs does not imply, as it would in Baroque music, a slight actual separation by silences between groups of notes, or the shortening of the last note of a slur, but only a shaping or moulding of phrases within a continuous smooth legato.

It will be noticed that in the Recitativo, which the composer marked throughout with phrasing slurs indicating the imagined word-groups, no 'editorial' real slurs have been added. For example, in the first two bars, if each of the two opening groups of four quavers (identified by (·) s in the interpretation here suggested) were actually slurred, they would be separated from each other too much. They each need to cohere only as much as would the syllables of two four-syllable words within a sentence. To take the composer's slur-mark literally and slur the entire phrase to the end of bar 3 sounds clumsy. Similarly, the suggested paired notes marked with square brackets would sound too glued together (to borrow Quantz's expression) if they were slurred with no tongue-movement. Each player needs to decide for himself how to group the quavers of the Recitativo into words. Should the opening phrase, for example, be grouped 4 + 4 + 3 as suggested in Ex. 5.7, or should it be grouped 3 + 4 + 4? With assured phrase-balancing, the effect of this movement then derives from the flexibility of its pace, 'a piacere' (this allows for quite substantial pauses at cadences, though no rests are marked), from its dynamic ebb and flow within the overall *p* level, and from tonal variety, especially the sensitive use of carefully graded vibrato. Nevertheless, articulation within a very narrow range is also important in order to mould the long undulating phrases that characterize both slow movements of this sonata. Only 'dh' and 'r' are really feasible tonguing consonants in these movements,[11] but they need to be applied with great variety of light tonguing-strengths and, with the 'r', even little differences in the speed of articulation. As the breath-pressure in the Recitativo is never above *mp*, 'dh' is best taken so lightly that it only just closes the air-flow, while the touches of 'r' (mainly on the off-beat notes) become like even weaker 'dh's, just allowing the airstream to penetrate the tongue/teeth-ridge stricture at the precise moment of articulation. These are very small-scale and indefinite tonguing variations, but they are vital in bringing out the beauty of the movement. The only approach to a feel of double-tonguing is the 'd r' of the square-bracketed notes, to express their pairing within the broad arc of the phrase as a whole.

The same gossamer lightness of tonguing is needed in rounding off the slightly diminuendo minims at the ends of the phrases in this Recitativo. In

EX. 5.7. Murrill, Sonata

Recitativo

ongoing playing, a note is normally ended by the tongue returning to a position in readiness for articulating the following note. This is how variety in note-length is achieved, for example in the reiterated crotchets described on p. 36. At phrase-ends, where a more deliberate completion of a note is needed, its sound may be stopped by lightly bringing the tongue forward to the teeth-ridge, rather as in the last syllable of 'London' (see *RT* 53), just sufficiently to stop the air-flow. With a tiny increase in tongue-pressure, the tongue is then ready to articulate the 'dh' at the opening of the next phrase. Alternatively, the air-flow can be cut off, just as neatly, by slightly pressing up the back of the tongue close to the throat, a kind of 'ng' with the 'g' element suppressed. For good control, the sides of the tongue need to be firm against the molars. This gives a slightly less definite note-ending than the 'n' method, and more separation from the articulation of the start of the next phrase. It suits the Murrill Recitativo. Remember that the tongue-movement is very slight in both methods. As the note draws to its end, the tongue should be positioned just short of its final closure-point. An even less definite note-ending, but with the risk of an intonational droop at the tail end of the note, can be brought about by using 'y' tonguing with the closure against the upper palate just behind the 'n' position. This could be effective at the cessation of air-flow when the final note of the Recitativo dies away, but a very delicate 'ng' or 'n' note-ending is safer.

The Finale of this sonata, a jig, relies on lively and consistent light tonguing for its rhythmic drive, and upon slower-speaking tonguing for the contrasting smoothness of the *cantando* section. This jig can be effective with real slurs, but 'D r t' for its basic movement makes it even more jolly. The second movement of the Murrill sonata, Presto, depends yet more on imaginative tonguing, for there are no slurs except the roulade near the end.[12] Double-tonguing is imperative if it is to be played at a speed which constantly and very deliberately contrasts the more or less alternating two-beat and three-beat bars. This requires a velocity that communicates a strong pulse firmly and regularly at the beginning of each bar. Even with the most skilled single-tonguing of the semiquavers it would be difficult to establish the swinging two- and three-beat effect, rather like the compound rhythms of Balkan dance-music. Single-tonguing could also threaten to make the semiquavers sound pecked at.

Even more than in the other movements of this sonata, the soloist has to identify so closely with the pianist[13] that he gets the feeling he is playing both parts himself. For example, the semiquavers at the recorder's first entry, and at re-entries after a semiquaver rest on the first beat of the bar, must all sound as if they had been bounced off the piano's down-beat chord at the beginning of those bars. This calls for great clarity of tonguing, but without over-emphasis.

Ex. 5.8 shows a very controversial tonguing-schedule for the second movement of the Murrill sonata, done out as 'nonsense syllables', and Ex. 5.9 some ideas for the last movement. It will be noticed that it is largely the tonguing which establishes the phrasing, such as in the two long phrases (after the second of the trilled bars) before the recapitulation of the Presto.

EX. 5.8. Murrill, Sonata

The tonguing also establishes the mood of the music, for example how playful the opening of the Finale should be. It is the articulation that gives life to the music.

For further commentary on Herbert Murrill's Sonata, see the Index.

EX. 5.9. Murrill Sonata.

Finale

*Use ∅ --- 45 -- fingering for F♯'', which will only speak when taken as a slur up (a real slur, not articulated) from the previous note (see p. 157).

Ornamentation and Improvisation: Fontana's Sonata Terza

IT is difficult to write briefly about the role of ornamentation and improvisation in the interpretation of Baroque sonatas, even though 'improvisation' is here limited in meaning to invented decoration at places where ornaments are not marked in, rather than the extemporization of completely new pieces of music or extended cadenzas. Styles of ornamentation varied from period to period, from country to country, from one composer (and player) to another, and from one kind of instrument to another. Some composers, such as J. S. Bach, wrote ornamental material into their sonatas,[1] others gave very exact instructions,[2] while others such as Corelli or J.-B. Lœillet often only wrote the framework of an adagio, entrusting the performer to embellish it in an appropriate manner. Professional players ornamented more than amateurs, so the obliging Telemann in his 'Methodic Sonatas' and elsewhere[3] wrote out unembellished and embellished versions of slow movements as a form of instruction in the prevailing *galant* style of ornamentation. General statements about Baroque ornamentation can therefore be misleading, but, as no recorder sonata of the period can be adequately performed without some ornamentation, a player has to embark upon learning how to ornament. He must then improve himself by listening critically to good recorded performances of Baroque sonatas and following the music at the same time, by seeking advice from experienced recorder-players, preferably a good teacher, and by studying books on Baroque interpretation (those listed at the end of Ch. 1 and in *RT* 157–61).

Accordingly, this chapter concentrates on the acquisition of a simple, basically 'correct' trill formula as a starting-point,[4] on understanding the purposes of ornamentation in different Baroque contexts, and on approaching decorative improvisation in a bold and positive manner. Although reference is made to ornamentation practice in the high Baroque period when most recorder sonatas were written, the chapter looks more closely at ornamentation in the early Baroque period. This is partly to encourage a historical approach, and partly to draw the attention of recorder-players to a sonata/canzona repertoire that is still rather neglected;

but it is chiefly because the pioneering sonatas of the early Italian Baroque demanded an exuberant freedom of improvisation from which later, more regulated styles of ornamentation evolved.

Readers of this book are advised to study the chapter on ornamentation in *Recorder Technique* (*RT*, 2nd edn., 111–22) if they are newcomers to the art of ornamentation.[5] This should be combined with the practice in different keys of the eight-semiquaver turned trill. Practice material is available elsewhere,[6] but the 'Three Blind Mice' exercise, republished from two articles in *RMM* (March and June 1984) as Appendix I of this book, adopts a more graded approach than some other exercises, and is slightly more tuneful; it is referred to from here on as 'TBM'. Apart from developing controlled fingering in trills, TBM is designed to establish that the down-beat element of Baroque trills is generally upon the upper auxiliary of the trill. This also applies to the final section of most Renaissance trill-like *groppi*, as at the end of Ex. 6.5 below (see *RT* 114). This usual upper-note dominance continued until well into the nineteenth century.[7]

It is important to remember this trill configuration when the trill is preceded by an appoggiatura, as it is in the cadential trill in its simplest form (see Donington, *Interp.* 241–50), exemplified as the culmination of the TBM exercise (bar 6). A Baroque trill is usually a discord in process of resolving (see Appendix I and Donington, *Interp.* 241–7). It is essential to practice this 'model' cadential trill to perfection, if necessary with a metronome. It can then be generally applied to cadences at the ends of movements or sections in Italian-style sonatas, though it is possibly a little less suitable in French-style sonatas.

Staying within TBM's base key of C major, take as an example the conclusion of the Adagio of Corelli's Op. 5 No. 3 sonata,[8] which is written simply as

EX. 6.1.

with no trill-sign, for that was not regarded as necessary, as all sonata 'adagio' final cadences were decorated. This cadence should, at minimum, be played exactly as at the end of TBM, with note-values quartered, so that it becomes:

EX. 6.2.

hold

Examples abound elsewhere, though, as it happens, most of the cadences in the Handel and Telemann sonatas quoted in Chs. 2 and 3 resolve upwards rather than downwards as in the Corelli example shown above. Cadences approached from below are rather more likely to be turned, with little or no rallentando, as in TBM, bars 4 and 5. Nevertheless, the majority of cadences in Baroque sonatas resolve downwards, and are held back with the customary silence of articulation and 'note of anticipation' (Donington, *Interp.* 247–50). It is suggested that the 'model' downwards cadential trill as in the Corelli example is applied with exactitude to the end of the Larghetto first movement of the Handel G minor sonata (Ex. 2.1)—and notice again that neither the appoggiatura nor the trill is marked in. The note of anticipation, written as a semiquaver, is thereby reduced to a quarter of its marked length. Then try the same formula at the end of the Adagio third movement, even though it resolves upwards: the crotchet becomes a semiquaver. There are examples of downward-resolving cadences at section-ends in the Presto and at the end of bar 10 of the Larghetto. In bar 5 of the Larghetto and in bars 39, 42, and 59 of the Andante, Handel has already written in the appoggiatura note, within the 6–4 chord of the figured bass, which should then be tied over to the succeeding note which represents the trill proper—a D appoggiatura before a D–C trill in the first case, and a B♭ appoggiatura tied over to a B♭–A trill at the end of the Andante, both still complying with the TBM bar 6 model. One needs to be vigilant in recognizing written-in appoggiaturas in Baroque music.

There is an upward-resolving unturned cadential trill at the end of the Affettuoso of Telemann's D minor sonata (Ex. 3.4). Again apply the TBM bar 6 configuration, but with flexibility, hanging on to the appoggiatura for rhetorical effect. Contexts may be found in both the Telemann and Handel sonatas where eight-note turned passing trills (TBM bars 1 and 2) are appropriate, for example in bar 15 of the Handel Andante (Ex. 2.1), though a faster twelve-note turned trill is preferable there, or, with the eight notes played extremely quickly, in bars 57, 59, and 61 of the second movement of the Telemann sonata. Less rapid examples of turned passing trills, occurring in other Handel recorder sonatas, are referred to in Appendix I.

Remember that in the cadential trill the short note of anticipation after the silence of articulation must be articulated with a very light quick-speaking tonguing such as 't', 'k', or 'g'. If, as often happens, old bad habits return of starting trills too early, or of emphasizing the lower auxiliary of the trill, or of playing the note of anticipation too slackly, it is always worth taking a revision course with the Three Blind Mice. Furthermore, the second TBM article sets out most trill- and turn-fingerings of any importance within the context of TBM's range of keys. It should be borne in mind that the fingerings for turns may only work with a slight drop in breath-pressure; this also helps to keep the trill as a whole in equilibrium. As explained in *RT* 121, several other ornaments such as the mordent, the shake or half-trill, and the turn, may be thought of as notes extracted from the eight-note turned trill and played with the same fingerings, neatness, and balance as the model trills in the TBM exercise.

Once these model measured trills are mastered, longer trills, trills at various speeds (especially the common fast unmeasured trill such as those in bars 15–18 and 53–6 of the last movement of the Telemann sonata, Ex. 3.8), trills at increasing or sometimes decreasing speeds (decreasing on the F♯′ trill two bars from the end of the Murrill Largo, Ex. 5.6?), and half-trills across beats, should be manageable with no great difficulty. The recorder, with its plangent tone and precise articulation, makes its best effect in ornamentation when the decoration is neat, accurate, and in perfect balance, a characteristic it shares more with the harpsichord than with the Baroque flute, with its more suave articulation and ingratiating tone, or than with the more brilliant violin, where trills are often played with a sharper intonation to make them stand out (see Quantz, 102). To achieve neat and accurate trills in a variety of keys, the recorder-player has especially complex fingering problems to overcome, particularly as the neatest trills are those which can be negotiated with only one finger doing the trilling. Competence and confidence can only be achieved by considerable study and much practice, taking the behaviour of one's own instrument into account.

Apart from flourishes and slides which, like the scale passages from which they are derived, can often be more neatly played with a touch of tonguing, other ornaments present fewer technical problems. Much ornamention depends on the addition of only one note,[9] such as the appoggiatura in its many guises, the mordent, and the *coulé*. The technique of the 'close shake', *flattement*, or finger-vibrato is almost deceptively simple to acquire.[10]

Recorder Technique, 116–19 sets out in brief the purpose of ornamentation. Again this is an enormous subject, dealt with at length by Donington and Neumann, and succinctly in Lasocki, 'Late Baroque Ornamentation: Philosophy and Guidelines', *AR* 29 (1988), 7–10. With acknowledgement to that article, here are ten basic principles of Baroque ornamentation for recorder-sonata players:

1. A performer's extemporization is a response to the musical invention and ideas of the composer. To a lesser or greater degree it is an involvement

and collaboration with his processes of composition, for example, to bring out a gracefully cumulating sequence (Donington, *Interp.* 193), a well-wrought melodic climax, or a dramatic harmony. The Spanish word for ornamentation and divisions is, very appropriately, *glosas*, a gloss or commentary on the music. The performer should respect any indicated wishes of the composer, and he should recognize patterns of ornamentation already subsumed within the music. The process of extemporization may itself create music in a new form, a kind of induced or inspired recomposition.

2. The kind and amount of ornamentation, and the manner in which it is played, should interpret and express the perceived affects of the music,[11] enhancing the rhetorical figures and devices employed by the composer to communicate those affects. For example, some music may be so down-hearted in affect (see the Handel passage in Ex. 1.1) that it lacks the energy to engage in ornamentation, save for dejected cadential trills. Other music might almost be overwhelmed by its own joyfulness or pomposity.

3. Ornamentation, which often has elements of discord, causes emphasis, or suspense or excitement before repose, as at a cadence. It should therefore be accorded to notes within a phrase or melody where some form of emphasis seems to be needed. This is especially the case in French music with its weak tonic stress, where the ornaments themselves constitute the 'accens'. Vibrato, as a form of ornamentation, creates emphasis and intensity.[12]

4. Ornamentation also enhances the flow of music, easing it forward, or holding it back (often the effect of a mordent). It must therefore respond to the pace and significance of imagined words and phrases, or to the lift and steps of dance-style rhythms.

5. Ornaments should improve and vitalize music, in the same way that written poetry becomes more shapely and meaningful when recited aloud. It should produce a fresh understanding of the music, making it even more breath-takingly beautiful or exciting, particularly in repeats. It gives the performer 'an opportunity to demonstrate his judgement, inventiveness and insight' (Quantz, 318).

6. Extemporization should heighten music by pleasurable variety and surprise, even including an element of modest display of the player's technical mastery or of his instrument's capabilities, especially in repeats. It should be spontaneous and exhilarating.

7. Ornamentation should conform to the harmonic progressions and tonality as well as to the melodic shapes of a piece of music. It must not therefore conceal the music's formal harmonic structure (cf. Pl. 6) nor

PL. 6. A Baroque reredos, in the church of the Caridad in Seville, designed by Pineda in 1670. The exuberant decoration, including the fanciful flying angels at the sides, is all contained within a clearly defined structure—the all-enclosing round arch on firm, thick columns. Even within this, the central painting (Descent from the Cross) is placed within its own well-defined, and repeated, framework of symbolic twisted columns and cumulation of arches. The structural sectionalization and balance of a Baroque sonata movement should always be clearly presented by the performer. Even in the midst of the most fanciful and unrestrained decoration he has to ensure that the structural elements of the basic melody and harmony remain intact and evident.

distort its melodic line out of recognition. For example, the lowest and highest notes of a cadential flourish should belong to the chord within which it takes place (e.g. the 'adagio' cadential decoration at the end of Handel's Larghetto, Ex. 2.1). Free ornamentation should not stray from the prevailing chord sequence (e.g. any arpeggiated ornamentation in bar 13 of this Larghetto), and one should be wary of extending it beyond the tessitura of the movement or section as a whole. Expressive ornamentation should be played lightly, never jeopardizing the natural stresses of the music's basic melodies and harmonies (see Donington, *Interp.* 158–9 and 194). It should be played with flexibility, and rhythmic give and take (le Huray, 41–3).

8. Extemporization should be in the spirit and style of the period and country of the music's composition, ideally expressed in the composer's own idiom.[13] Thus divisions in regular semiquavers belong more to the seventeenth century, while compound arpeggiated triplets belong more to the eighteenth. Filling in descending thirds with *coulés* is rather French, while rapid extended flourishes which finally arrive at a stressed high note are rather Italian.

9. One's extemporization should be adjusted to the circumstances of the performance—for example the resonance of the room, or the kind of audience. It should suit one's instrument. And it should, of course, accord with one's own technical ability, confidence, and feeling at the time.

10. 'Be bold, be bold . . . be not too bold.'

Each of these propositions could be—and most have been—enlarged, authenticated, exemplified, qualified by time, place, or other conditions, or disagreed with; the remainder of this chapter, however, will be most concerned with the last of them. This enjoins recorder-players not to feel diffident or apprehensive about ornamentation. It encourages them courageously to embark upon playing early Italian Baroque sonatas where adventurousness, even a certain waywardness and risk-taking, makes the music wonderfully exciting. The composers of such music include Frescobaldi, Riccio, Cima, Fontana, Dario Castello, and Cecchino. The list raises questions of nomenclature and instrumentation, but these and other composers[14] wrote sonatas and canzonas comprising several sections which contrast in speed, time, and form, to be played by a solo melody-instrument with chordal continuo accompaniment, and where the solo part can effectively be played on a recorder.

Throughout the Renaissance period, recorders and other melody-instruments had been closely involved with vocal music either in supporting singers or in substituting for voices in madrigal parts. Compositions written for wind- or string-instruments had not on the whole, with the exception of dance-music, differed markedly in style from vocal music, especially as such compositions were usually based on vocal originals. During the sixteenth century, however, a more independent style of instrumental music developed in the form of divisions of the melodic lines of madrigals or chansons, involving lengthy improvised *passaggi* 'diversifying a series of notes that are by nature brief and simple' (Ganassi, *Fontegara*, 15). This practice derived from a long tradition of instrumental improvisation, especially in repetitious dance-music, for example in the improvised parts to *basses danses*. The teaching of ornamentation almost monopolized sixteenth-century instrumental tutors such as those by Ganassi for recorder (1535), Diego Ortiz for viol (1553), and Dalla Casa for cornett (1584).[15] As the sixteenth century progressed, the 'continuous semiquaver' type of ornamentation became more complex and florid, with even more rapid figurations, and with more dotted rhythms, but with less division-type continuity, so that the ornaments became concentrated upon the most affective phrases of a melody, and especially upon cadences. Ornamentation in this way responded to the 'new music' introduced by the Florentine Camerata in the 1580s, which emphasized highly expressive monody supported by a chordal bass. It was thus a small step for the solo instrumental decorated versions of madrigals with lute or other accompaniment to develop into instrumental sonatas, transcending the constraints of words.

The vocal antecedents, however, maintained a powerful influence upon the performance style of the early seventeenth-century solo canzonas and sonatas, and their slower sections should be played with the often intense inflections of a Monteverdi madrigal or lament. Frescobaldi, in the preface to his keyboard *Toccate* (1615), asks for his music to be played with 'singable affections', which he has taken care to 'provide abundantly'.[16] Intensifying the most emotive notes in singable phrases with breath- or finger-vibrato certainly impassions this music immensely, as it does later Baroque sonata music. Try, for example (descant recorder), the arioso-like passage from Fontana's Sonata Terza shown as Ex. 6.3 first without and then with the increase in vibrato marked in bars 81–2, preferably finger-vibrato held in tune with a slight crescendo. Notice the invitation to indulge in an echo (marked in here as a double echo, though not by the composer[17]), which requires the use of the slide-fingering techniques mentioned by Ganassi.

In the first descending phrase in Ex. 6.3 the emotive stress is on the antepenultimate note, the longest note of the phrase, i.e. the dotted crotchet B in bar 82. This therefore needs unrestrained nourishing with vibrato. It is frequently the longest note within a phrase that carries the stress, and the composer here brings this out by making the bass of the continuo accompaniment leap up to a high E at this point. The next four bars contain three minims; these, however, could sound rather ponderous unornamented, and weigh too heavily against the opening phrase of this passage. They may therefore be diminished into shorter notes, possibly in the way here suggested. With the ornamentation and the echo effects

EX. 6.3. Fontana, Sonata Terza

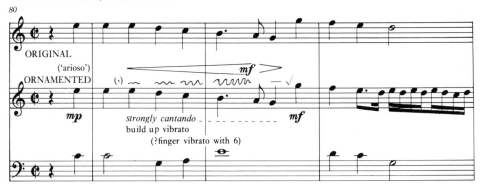

?possibility of bass ornament

While bars 84–5, except for the final note of the phrase (a C crotchet in bar 85 instead of the E crotchet at the beginning of bar 84), contain a note-by-note echo of the previous five-note phrase, the next five-note phrase, here suggested as a 'second echo', is a third lower than the 'first echo'. An alternative interpretation is to play this last five-note phrase contrastingly loud. If the accompanying instrument is a harpsichord, the semiquaver decorations shown in the bass line in bar 86 could enhance the effect of the alternative (i.e. the loud) interpretation, but if the recorder plays bar 86 very softly, such ornamentation in the harpsichord, which necessarily increases its volume of sound, might drown the recorder's 'second echo'. If the accompanying instrument were a lute or other plucked string-instrument, with more dynamic control, then this decoration, played as a mere whisper of sound, could make the 'second echo' interpretation even more dramatically effective.

together, this short passage can be quite striking, provided that leaking fingerings or tonally acceptable alternatives are used to maintain accurate intonation with the continuo—echoes sound appalling if they are flat.

The next sections of Fontana's Sonata Terza are even more dramatic (the

EX. 6.4. Fontana, Sonata Terza

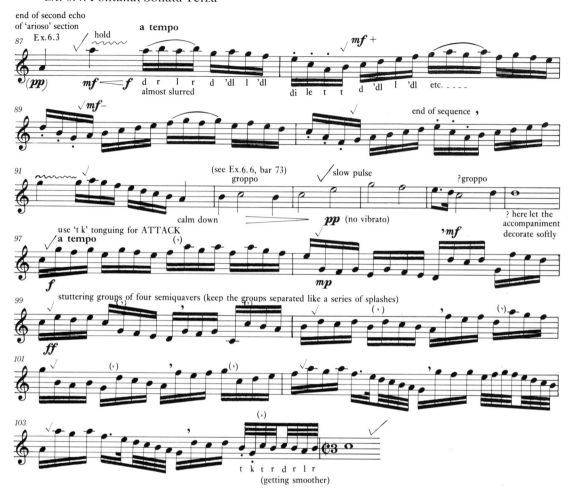

recorder part from bar 87 to bar 104 is shown in Ex. 6.4). After a high A′, which may be drawn out in expectation, like a spring about to snap, the sonata erupts into an ebullient semiquaver passage with only a light chordal accompaniment. This needs to be played at the prevailing pulse of the sonata, *a tempo*. The passage then contrasts with the freer treatment of the two preceding 'affetti' and 'arioso' sections (Exx. 6.6 and 6.3), which call for rhythmic give, though not to the point of losing the sense of an ongoing pulse which binds the whole sonata together. This prevailing pulse, or 'tactus', of the sonata is determined largely by deciding upon a singable speed for the canzona-like start of the sonata ♩ ♩♩. It should sing out, but not so briskly that it becomes difficult to play, or to phrase, the later semiquaver passages. Possibly ♩ = 76 is about right. The semiquavers are therefore decidedly fast; they derive from the florid ornamentation of climactic passages in madrigals. Passage-work in early Baroque music, and often in later Baroque music as well, has a strong melodic element which must be brought out despite the speed. It was partly to accentuate this melodic character of *passaggi* that Ganassi and others advised recorder-players to learn well the use of fast legato double-tonguing. 'Lern wol das diridiride', says Martin Agricola.[18] Moreover, the passage from bars 87–91, like much Baroque passage-work, has its own internal structure; it is a sequence, and this influences articulation patterns, some suggestions for which are given in bars 87–8 at the first statement of the sequence motive. The slur signs added here are not intended to represent 'real slurs' but to indicate very smooth 'd r l r's which 'melt into one' (Ganassi, 14).

After so pell-mell a section, bar 92 should be a reposeful cadence, requiring a *groppo*, i.e. a prepared unslurred turned trill, applying to the C minim and following B crotchet the same formula as is shown for the G minim and following F♯ crotchet in bar 73 of Ex. 6.6. This formula is one of the few decorations of the period accorded a name,[19] among the innumerable varieties of improvised or stereotyped *passaggi*. As Donington picturesquely puts it (Donington, *Interp.* 189), 'an ornament is a short melodic formula which has formed in the tradition of free ornamentation as a crystal forms in a saturated solution.'

The player will by now, if not before, have perceived, perhaps with some trepidation, that there is some even more spectacular passage-work to come. He should therefore savour the respite of bars 93–6, in fact up to the cadential note, the semiquaver at the beginning of bar 97. The music for a few moments almost falls asleep in order to regain energy, while the accompanying lute or theorbo spreads its chords with perhaps some languid decoration in bar 96. The recorder is hardly audible, with alternative fingerings on every note, and even the *groppo* called for by the cadencing in bar 95 goes very wearily—or is it really needed at all? Then the pyrotechnics burst out in a cascade of semiquavers from bars 97 to 103. At bar 102 they explode into demisemiquavers, still played if possible with tongue-movement, but so rapidly that it resembles flutter-tonguing.[20] Most players will have gone over to a crotchet count in this section and perhaps have been forced to slow the tempo down a little, to, say ♩ = 120;[21] a slight drawing up at the end of bar 103 is excusable or even desirable. Ex. 6.4 sets out the top part only of the whole passage from bars 87 to 104 with suggested dynamic and phrasing markings.

EX. 6.5. Notari, Canzona Passaggiata

In this carefully constructed sonata, which is in a cyclical or sandwich form, the sections quoted constitute part of the spicy fillings between the opening and closing canzona-type sections. These, with their dialogue between solo and bass, should not be ornamented except for simple *groppi* at cadences, for decoration could mask the counterpoint[22] and there are abundant opportunities for display elsewhere in the sonata. The two tripla sections dance by too quickly to need decoration. There is a very instructive example of how an entire canzona was embellished in Angelo Notari's 'Canzona Passaggiata' (1613, ed. Peter Holman, Nova 1980). It is interesting to see how some parts are left undecorated, even at a cadence (bar 26), to avoid over-ornamentation and to allow the beauty of tone of the instrument to be displayed. The extract given in Ex. 6.5 might be regarded as a precursor of certain processes of decorative improvisation employed in later Baroque sonatas. Playing such passages, as well as later variation and division music such as van Eyck's *Der Fluyten Lust-hof* (1648), the anonymous *The Division Flute* (1706 and 1708), and Hotteterre's ornamented *Airs et Brunettes* (1723, ed. Lasocki, Nova 1980), should help a recorder-player to arrive at the stage where he cannot resist trying out his own improvisations where opportunities present themselves in sonatas—as they often do.

Display of instrumental timbre and technique was associated from the beginning with sonata-playing, and it must be remembered that many sonatas were written primarily for the composer's own performances as a professional instrumentalist.[23] Recorder-players may have something to learn from noting how flute-type instruments are played in other contexts (for example, the Japanese shakuhachi) in order to display qualities of timbre and technique. Chinese and Irish folk-flautists use considerable finger-vibrato, so that their fingers seem to be constantly a-flutter. Oriental, folk, and jazz musicians use to great effect devices such as *portamento* (gliding from one note to another through the intermediate pitches) and note-bending, i.e. slightly changing the pitch (and often the timbre) of a long note in the course of playing it, either by breath- or finger-control. Singers, whom recorder-players are encouraged to imitate, often use slight pitch modulation for expressive effect. Ganassi shows how *tremoli* (= trills) may be fingered wide—up to a third—to produce a lively affect (*vivace*), or narrow—a semitone or less—to sound sweet and soothing (*suave*).[24] Both Biagio Marini (1617) and Riccio (1620) employ tremolo effects over extended passages, the latter in a recorder and bass (dulcian?) trio sonata with all three instruments 'trembling' together.[25]

There are strong affinities between early music and jazz,[26] for example the use of well-established chord progressions or grounds such as the twelve-bar blues or the Romanesca as a basis for improvisation, the collective discipline of respecting harmonic and sectional structures, rhythmic inequality within the beat, and the need to imitate by ear from one part to another. In both jazz and Baroque improvisation, a player must allow himself to be carried away by the music and its significance, while retaining total control of his technique. Early music and jazz are alike in depending upon a subtle balance between freedom of imagination and invention on the one hand, and reliance upon accepted but changing conventions and formulae on the other.[27] These accepted conventions provided a framework of forms, and a system of ground-rules, within which players of early music could exercise greater rhythmic freedom, enabling them to make room for improvisation. For example, French and English flautists played free preludes before embarking upon a sonata;[28] Ganassi advises that in ornamenting intervals, passing-notes can be overlooked, so that the player may substitute his own extemporized material for what the composer has written from one main chord to another,[29] and such ornamentation can be in irregular note-groups such as 5s or 7s;[30] Frescobaldi advises his keyboard soloists that cadences must be 'greatly sustained [i.e., played more slowly]; and drawing near to the conclusion of a *passagio* or cadence, the tempo must become more *adagio*',[31] though of course such rhythmic freedom is more limited, or contrived, in ensemble-playing. Certain passages in sonatas seem to invite rhythmic latitude, especially in Italian music. Fontana's Sonata Quarta contains several jazz-like 'breaks',[32] while part of the first tripla passage of Sonata Terza veers unnervingly between 3/2 and 6/4.[33] Facsimiles of some later sonatas where composers have incorporated their own ornamentation in slow movements afford a reminder of Baroque rhythmic freedom when a jumble of semiquavers and demisemiquavers may be found not to add up to the number of beats in the bar (and see le Huray, 43). There are many ways suggested by Baroque writers of all periods for playing four semiquavers other than as four equal semiquavers (Donington, *Interp.* 455–63).

In fast or dance-based movements, freedom of rhythm must usually be contained within the pulse,[34] though some dance movements are themselves rhythmically complex, and triple rhythms are subject to hemiolas, which rein back the pulse at cadences.[35] Slower movements are more permissive, especially in adagios where the bass part is written in a manner which does not constrain the soloist's freedom to improvise. Early Italian sonata composers contrasted the strong rhythm of fast sections in a steady two-pulse or a dance-like tripla time with slower-moving sections in long notes where the bass does not engage in melodic dialogue with the soloist.

These slower-moving sections were marked 'affetti' by some composers, while others assumed they would be recognized as such. This is an open invitation to use expressive effects (Donington, *Interp.* 672) and to declaim the music in a free, emotional style, in a highly-charged vocal idiom, adapting phrasing, tone-colouring, and ornamentation to imagined word-rhythms. Within the limitations of his instrument, the player should feel unrestrained. He may indulge in colouring notes by using various types of vibrato or non-standard fingerings, in strongly affective crescendos and decrescendos, and, especially, in ornamentation. Ornaments appropriate to 'affetti' sections include 'Lombardic' (or 'Scotch snap') rhythms played with strong reverse inequality, *tremoli* (i.e. very rapid short trills, or mordents or extended mordents, usually starting on the written note and lasting about half its value), or even the recorder equivalent of the vocal *trillo*. In this fashionable early seventeenth-century ornament, a note is reiterated as a strongly accented pulsating vibrato without interrupting the flow of its sound, starting slowly but gradually accelerating—this can be done with the throat or the tongue.[36]

During the 'affetti' section, the pulse of the music becomes, as it were, a distant background with the bass accompaniment almost static, as the impetus of the music is carried, with great rhythmic freedom, by the soloist's intensity of tone-colour and improvisation in delivering the music's rhetorical affect.[37] This type of ornamentation does not totally exclude short melodic *passaggi*, especially before *groppi* at cadences, but any *passaggi* should not weave far from the melodic notes, except perhaps at the final cadence. Most early Baroque sonatas have sections of this type, usually after a fast passage, and the pulse of the sonata is then picked up in a more flowing arioso-type section, as in Fontana's Sonata Terza, bars 80–7, quoted in Ex. 6.3. Ex. 6.6 presents the 'affetti'-type passage preceding the arioso section of Sonata Terza. It is accompanied only by rather neutral semibreve and minim chords. The written-out ornamented version is given in order to generate ideas, not as a model to copy, for a musicians's response to a call

EX. 6.6. Fontana, Sonata Terza

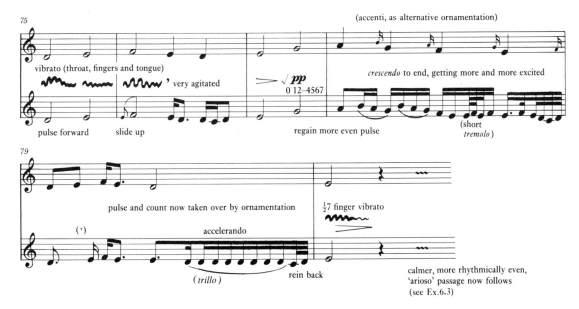

for 'affetti' must be a very personal affair. The illustration in Pl. 7 is to provide inspiration.

Bars 67 and 72: An up-beat to a phrase across a wide interval, especially descending as here, did not seem to attract ornamentation in this period, as it could well have done in later Baroque music.

Bars 68, 69, and 72: The model for the *tremoli* is Diruta (1593; see Howard Mayer Brown, *Embellishing*, 3). After the initial accent needed in the present context, they should be played very fast and lightly (trembling or fluttering), the repercussions being inexact in number but taking about half the value of the minim. Strictly, they should be tongued, but were probably often slurred. Keep breath-vibrato going for the remaining duration of the minim. Attack each one of these three rising minims separately and hard, increasing the intensity and volume. The tremolo in bar 69 can be played by fluttering finger 5 very low over its hole.

Bar 69: Dramatic sudden dynamic contrast after the phrase-mark (a caesura). Note that the whole section is in the form of a quatrain with caesuras. The line-ends are in bars 71, 74 (the half-way point), and 77. Give the music great spaciousness at the line-ends, without quite losing its lumbering pulse.

Bar 70: The sextuplet decoration is used by Notari (see Ex. 6.5) and is marked with a slur—he only uses slurs in 'affetti' contexts. The slurs in bar 78 are also modelled on Notari, who occasionally slurs across beats.

PL. 7. 'Affetti' in sculpture. *The Ecstasy of St Theresa*, by Bernini, in the Cornaro Chapel (1644–7), Santa Maria della Vittoria, Rome. Kenneth Clark, in *Civilisation* (BBC, 1969), quotes (p. 191) from St Theresa's description of how an angel with a flaming golden arrow pierced her heart repeatedly: 'The pain was so great that I screamed aloud, but simultaneously felt such infinite sweetness that I wished the pain to last eternally. It was the sweetest caressing of the soul by God.' He then goes on: 'Perhaps the closest parallel to the combination of deep feeling, sensuous involvement and marvellous technical control is to be found not in visual art, but in music . . .'. In its manifestation of the theatrical power of sculpture and architecture to achieve emotionally affecting communication, the work of Bernini epitomizes the attitude one should adopt not only to early seventeenth-century Italian sonatas but also to later Baroque music.

Bar 73:   The fast notes of the *groppo* should be taken evenly and clearly with 'Doo-ri-loo-ri doo-ri-ler-ri' tonguing. As this is the half-way cadence of the quatrain, the slight rallentando may facilitate the distinct playing of the *groppo*.

Bars 74–6:   The suggestion here, as these low notes are particularly rich in tone-quality on many Renaissance descant recorders, is to generate huge sonority, using breath-, finger-, and possibly also tongue-vibrato all at once. The finger-vibrato with 7 will control intonation. A touch of note-bending[38] by even more breath on the second D would add to the risk and excitement of the passage, as would a portamento glide up to the F at bar 76 (definitely not for purists). Play the F with 5 slide-fingered and vibrato-ing (no 6 or 7).

Bar 76:   The Lombardic ornament here is from an 'affetti'-type section of a Frescobaldi toccata.

Bar 78:   Ornamentation designed to build up in intensity. The ornament on the crotchet F is a common 'affetto', usually marked ♩♪♪♩ (it appears several times in Fontana's Sonata Quarta). The 't' means a very short tremolo, like a catch in the throat (see Neumann, *Ornamentation*, 287–8). The recorder-player can do it with a quick flutter of 'r' tonguing. An alternative approach to this bar, much simpler, is to play a series of *accenti*, common on stepwise descending crotchets (Diruta 1593; Brown, 4), turning each crotchet into ♪♩ —the semiquavers are marked in on the upper stave.

Bar 79:   Here Fontana actually stipulates the Lombardic rhythm. The *trillo* is partly based on the ending of a Caccini aria. Play as many repercussions as you feel moved to, putting the pulse temporarily into abeyance, but picking it up again, recorder and continuo together, after the crotchet rest in bar 80, that is to say at the beginning of the 'arioso' section shown as Ex. 6.3.

It is from 'affetti' passages such as these that the ornamentation of the later Baroque sonata Adagio developed, and by most accounts the emotionalism displayed in Bernini's sculpture of St Theresa pervaded the performance of Adagios, Affettuosos, and other movements, throughout the Baroque period. It is interesting to compare, a century apart, but both within the 'Baroque era', the Adagio of Handel's G minor sonata (Ex. 2.1) with the 'affetti' section of the Fontana sonata. The Handel movement, as one would expect, is more melodic, its impetus (in a loose sarabande rhythm) a little stronger, and the tone-colouring of the minims would probably have been more restrained and polite in Handel's time. Otherwise its approach is similar to that of the Fontana excerpt. Its bass is a simple

EX. 6.7. Handel, Sonata in G minor

chordal accompaniment leaving the soloist room to indulge in his ornamentation; the rhythmic pulse is spread across barlines, flexible and undominating; cadences, which occur frequently, are held back by drawn-out decoration; and the movement is short (31 notes as compared with Fontana's 33), in carefully calculated dramatic contrast with the faster movements before and after it. Even in this calm sonata, Handel's Adagio would probably have been played with intensity and commitment, especially at the climactic high D', rather than dispassionately and coolly. Ex. 6.7 shows Freda Dinn's elaboration, in lilted inequality, of the 31 plain notes of Handel's Adagio.[39] But consider—should the C in bar 4 be tied to the C in bar 5? (it is tied in the autograph manuscript); do the appoggiaturas on the second beats of bars 7 and 8 adversely affect the chromatically rising melodic line (compare with Ex. 2.1)? and should Dinn's downward-slur phrasing at bars 10–11 be retained?

Precept 10 on p. 100, 'Be bold . . .', is drawn from Book III of Spenser's *Faerie Queene*, published in 1589, the year of the Florentine intermedii which contributed so much to the development of musical ideas and forms associated with the Baroque era.[40] It is perhaps all the more appropriate an injunction to encourage adventurous but thoughtful ornamentation and improvisation among players of Baroque recorder sonatas. Ornamentation needs 'practice, and a certain amount of bravado'.[41]

For further commentary on Fontana's Sonata Terza, see the Index.

Further Aspects of Performance

THIS chapter is concerned with certain further points of technique and interpretation in relation to the five sonatas considered in Chs. 2–6. The five sonatas are referred to simply by the names of the composers, so 'the Handel' means the Handel G minor recorder sonata. The points are dealt with under the following headings: speed, repeats, fingering and interpretation, presentation, working in ensemble, and authenticity.

SPEED

Pre-hearing the right speed before the start of a movement, or before a change of speed, is vital to successful interpretation. 'The right speed' does not mean an exact metronome speed, for a movement may be played on the slow side or on the fast side for reasons which involve a considerable exercise of judgement, balancing a variety of factors. Even so, there are limits beyond which a sonata movement becomes too slow or too fast to make musical sense under any circumstances. Getting the right speed is so important that it could have been the subject of a chapter in this book, although for each of the five sonatas suggestions have been given as to how slow or fast particular movements might be played. These suggestions should be considered alongside well-authenticated general advice in books on Baroque performance style such as in Donington, *Baroque*, ch. 3, 'Shaping the Tempo', and in Anthony Newman, *Bach and the Baroque*, on Bach's tempi (especially pp. 24–55), which quotes from Bach's pupil Kirnberger.

It may be helpful to recorder-players, however, to have a general summary of the factors which affect choice of speed in sonata-playing (see le Huray, 36–8). They reach their realization in that well-rehearsed moment of mutual communication between performers just before they start playing, when an agreed pulse becomes firmly established in their minds, is set in motion and impetus, and is then, as it were, joined by the first sounds of the sonata. The impression is as if one were stepping on to an already moving train. This silent understanding between all the players should take place, incidentally, even when one player starts a movement several bars before another's entry.

There are four main factors affecting the speed of a piece in an actual performance. First and foremost is the internal evidence of the music itself, one's judgement as to what the composer might have intended. Secondly, there are considerations relating to the technical ability of the players. Thirdly, there are factors of the resonance of the room in which the music is played. And fourthly there is 'psychological speed'.

Donington gives helpful advice on Baroque tempi as conveyed by time signatures, so-called 'speed words' ('largo', etc.) and by dance-rhythms, bringing out inconsistences in usage and changes from one period or country to another. No soloist should start a sonata without seeing how the bass moves—failure to do this could result, for example, in playing the Presto of the Handel ludicrously fast (see Ex. 2.1). The layout of the chord sequences in the continuo may indicate whether a piece is to be felt one-in-a-bar, or, say, three-in-a-bar. Faster music should go with sufficient lilt to convey the dance-rhythm upon which it might have been based. Allemandes often work well quite slowly as long as they maintain the upright rhythm of the dance—le Huray (p. 37) points out that Corelli in his Op. 2 trio sonatas marks allemandes variously 'presto', 'allegro', 'largo', and 'adagio'. Most minuets should go fast enough for a one-in-a-bar feel; minuets are often played too slowly. Slower music must usually move forward at a singable speed for its imagined words, thus avoiding having to take breaths in mid-phrase. In fact this 'orator test' is valuable in arriving at speeds for most Baroque music. Music with inequality within many of the beats, especially where the interest of the music depends on subtle changes of inequality (as in the Lavigne), should be played a little slower than music with equal quavers; try playing the equal and unequal versions of the Handel Larghetto in Exx. 2.1 and 4.7 and notice how this affects the best singable speed. Similarly, music which is highly decorated needs to go at a pace which gives room for expressive ornamentation. This can often lead to quite difficult decisions about speeds where a section is to be repeated in a more highly decorated form, as the music should not normally have to slow down to accommodate its additional decoration.

Above all, the speed of a Baroque sonata movement must be that at which its perceived affect and its rhetorical forms are best communicated.

Careful reading of Donington, Houle, and others is required to understand the effect of the 'tactus', the late-Renaissance and early Baroque system of keeping time, and of the consequent use of 'time signatures' linked to a system of proportional notation deriving from the tactus concept (see Donington, *Interp.* 650–4). Tactus relates to a speed at which the hand can move comfortably down and up to keep time over the length of a piece of music. The tactus can be held back or pushed forward to suit the most expressive or dramatic speed of the music, but its steady unifying presence in a sonata with many short sections cannot be ignored. Although proportional notation was outmoded by the mid-seventeenth century, the idea of the movements of a sonata being related to a consistent pulse probably affected later Baroque composers.[1]

In early Italian sonatas, such as the Fontana, with their many affectively contrasted short sections, the sense of an underlying pulse is especially important. A compromise between speed of singability of the opening bars and the speed of playability of the very fast passages will usually give a fair idea of what the tactus is. This pulse, or something very near it, should then be maintained in the tripla sections where a minim beat of the previous common time of the opening canzona-type section becomes a whole bar (dotted semibreve, or even dotted breve) in the tripla.[2] This means that the tripla sections, despite the presence of a lot of white notes, go by much more quickly than the player might at first have thought (Donington, *Baroque*, 15). They are lively dance ritornelli. Crotchets in triplas are fast and the quavers extremely rapid, for example at bar 55 of the Fontana, which has eight quavers and two crotchets, against a dotted semibreve in the bass. As the principle of prehearing a change of time must be applied, in the last bar of a common-time section preceding a tripla the players should mentally superimpose triplets into the minim pulse, and each of those triplet groups then becomes a full bar of the next section. Changing back is done by saying 'One and Two and' over the last two bars of the tripla to get back to the original minim and crotchet speed. One must watch out for up-beats which belong to the new speed (e.g. Fontana, bar 42). When this counting method is mastered—though some players have a good enough rhythmic instinct to manage such tempo changes without recourse to expedients of this kind—one can then skilfully introduce the slight rallentandos often needed at the end of sections with no risk of violating the ongoing pulse. All this requires careful understanding with one's accompanist.

The length of any pause between movements of a sonata is an interesting test of musicianship.[3] No recorder sonata is so long that the audience has to be given a rest for coughing, shuffling (or even talking) between movements. Sometimes the follow-on is almost without pause; for example, Murrill marks 'segue' to take his first movement straight into the Presto. A Baroque slow movement ending on a dominant chord has the same feeling as a recitative in opera preceding an aria, with almost immediate follow-on, as between the third and fourth movements of the Telemann, where the change of dynamic should come as a sudden shock. In four-movement sonatas, such as the Handel, there needs to be just enough of a pause between the second and third movements to allow the faster pulse of the second movement to fade away from one's consciousness before starting the third. Substantial pauses between the seven movements of Handel's D minor recorder sonata, from which the Furioso movement is quoted in Ex. 5.3, would be tedious, and would destroy the span of the sonata as a whole. Tempo relationships and the grouping of movements need especially careful consideration when the composer himself appears to have abrogated such matters to the performer. Generally no two movements in a sonata should be played at exactly the same speed, unless this seems to be the intention of the composer, as in the cyclical structure of the Fontana.

The above considerations will help a recorder-player towards arriving at a more or less 'right' speed for the movements of a sonata. How fast he actually plays these movements depends on some more practical matters. Of the five sonatas in Chs. 2–6 one has some decidedly difficult semiquaver passages (the Fontana) and another (the Murrill) includes a tricky Presto; an advanced technique is required to achieve the full dynamic demands of the Telemann, and parts of its second movement do not fall under the fingers. If these sonatas are to be performed, once the right fingering and tonguing for the difficult bits have been established, they will need practising by repetition (see *RT*, ch. X). Should accuracy and confidence even then not be the outcome, the sonata may, regrettably, have to be put aside for the time being until a later occasion when one's general technique has improved through regular practice.

None the less, there is some room for compromise. Most pieces of music have a narrow range of 'right speeds' within which they say best what they mean, and sound good. Within these bounds, however, whole movements (not of course just the difficult passages) may be slowed down, provided the spirit and affect of the movement are preserved. A more deliberate anger may sound almost as effective as all-out rage in Handel's Furioso movement, for example, as so much can be communicated by exploiting the tonguing variety suggested in Ex. 5.3. The same is true of the Murrill Presto (Ex. 5.8); it can be taken more slowly so long as the tonguing brings out the 3/4 and 6/8 swing of the piece. Even the very fast passages of the Fontana (Ex. 6.4) will bear a little slowing down, provided that this does not cause the pulse of the whole sonata to fall below a speed at which the opening canzona phrase can be made to sing. To play the Fontana semiquavers with consummate ease could prejudice the affect of frenzy; they were probably intended to sound difficult, and if the composer's intention is subverted by making difficult music sound easy (as some virtuoso players do) then the purpose of the music is lost. Conversely, the music would be spoilt by incompetent playing. The ultimate test is the reaction of the audience—is this exciting? or is it too slovenly to be tolerated?

Within the limits of the needs of the music, another factor influencing speed where there is room for compromise is the technique or the opinions of the accompanist(s). If the harpsichord-player feels that a recorder-player's proposed speed is too slow or too fast, agreement must be reached or the performance will not be satisfactory, especially if continuo-players are worried about achieving accurate ensemble.

Reference has already been made to the question of room acoustic. Remember that the presence of an audience makes a room less resonant. One must also consider the speaking qualities of one's instrument, particularly in a resonant acoustic which might amplify the harmonics of a tonguing transient and make a recorder—especially a sluggishly speaking tenor recorder—sound fluffy when playing fast detached semiquavers. Speed needs to be adapted to how the instrument sounds best in a particular environment at its optimum tonguing and breath-pressure.

Sometimes a well-rehearsed piece may go stale through over-familiarity. The soloist can rescue a performance so threatened by making a 'psychological' change in the agreed speed of a movement—taking the risk, for example, of playing an allegro a little faster to restore its freshness, or an andante a little slower to inspire the cellist to phrase the bass line more beautifully.

REPEATS

Obviously the continuo-players must know the recorder soloist's intentions with regard to repeats. If a composer marks repeats he presumably does so for a purpose, not just out of habit, and his wishes should then be respected unless there are strong reasons to the contrary.[4] Not repeating can upset the balance of a movement or a whole sonata. In Baroque music, repeats are usually an invitation to play the music again differently. The original pulse and phrasing should be adhered to, but the music should sound different— even more interesting—by touching up the expression, using different dynamics, modifying the inequality, or, especially in slow movements, adding elegant and appropriate ornamentation which enhances the affect of the music. A Gigue section at its repeat may be made even more sprightly by turning a few quavers into semiquavers, or by using new dotted rhythms: ♩♪♪ for ♩♪♪ for example. A few well-chosen changes are often more effective than spectacular ego-trips. Discretion and moderation, but eschewing dullness, were more highly regarded in the 'Age of Reason' than 'enthusiasm'.

During the first playing of a passage to be repeated, the recorder-player should consider how he would like to alter and embellish it when he comes to the repeat. He should listen very carefully for the bass notes which will be his signposts, mainly at the beginning of bars, against losing his way during any free ornamentation, and for the chord progressions that both constrain and inspire his choice of decoration. Without this preparatory discipline he can all too easily become so carried away in an ornamented repeat that he adds an extra beat or finds himself at odds with the harmony. Eighteenth-century solo sonata players were less likely to do this as the music they played from included the figured bass (see Ex. 2.1). An occasional mistake of this kind—during rehearsal—should not, however, undermine a player's confidence or adventurousness.

In the same way that a player observes repeats to respect the composer's intentions, he should as a general rule avoid playing isolated movements from sonatas. Sonatas were usually conceived as entities.

FINGERING AND INTERPRETATION

Fingering as such is not the subject of a chapter in this book, for it is so central to recorder-playing that it dominates discussion of interpretation. It is the chief subject of most tutors and of *RT*. The three main variants of a musical note, other than its length and articulation, are its pitch, dynamic, and timbre. With recorders, fingering is involved in all three. The fingers carry out some of the functions of the lips in other wind-instruments.

As a person learns the recorder he develops new insights into the role of fingering. At the 'mewling and puking' stage he learns (probably, alas, on the difficult descant recorder) that certain fingerings make certain notes; next he discovers that some notes have a second fingering which makes trills and slurs easier to play, (e.g. treble E 0 –23 ----); then his aural musicianship matures to the point where he gradually realizes that the fingerings he has learnt are not always in tune on his recorder so that he adds ½6 to C♯, ½7 to E′, and so on, and that none of these fingerings is in tune when he plays loudly or softly—here begins his mastery of techniques of shading, slide-fingering, and leaking; he grows aware of the different tone-qualities of such differently fingered notes and how they can be used to make music more beautiful and interesting, and his first foray into avant-garde techniques opens up a brave new world of fingering languages, multiphonics, harmonics, and so on; and finally he achieves the ultimate wisdom of recognizing how the fingering of particular notes, and finger-movement patterns for groups of notes, perform a vital role in playing even simple music well.

The Baroque recorder is skilfully designed to produce clear-toned sharps and flats with cross-fingerings. Recorder fingering is therefore complex in terms of the number of individual finger-movements required to play, say, a chromatic scale. It is important to develop flexible and nimble finger-movements in order to play sonatas with accuracy and confidence, prerequisites to good interpretation, but this can lead some extraordinarily adept recorder-players down a primrose path to virtuosity where admiration is gained more by skill than musicianship. Good fingering can only come with much practice (see *RT*, ch. X), especially of difficult scales with many cross-fingerings, such as F sharp major. Work at problem passages (see *PB*), and use books of recorder fingering-exercises; those by Linde, Brüggen, and Alan Davis are also enjoyable as music.

Always use the easiest fingering so long as it is in tune and not tonally inappropriate to its context. This involves reading ahead to plan one's fingering, or sorting things out in a run-through of a sonata. For example, alternation of treble D♯ and F♯′ is common in sonata passage-work; it is clumsy played with normal fingerings with three fingers and the thumb moving in different directions, but simple if one just lifts off the thumb from normal D♯ to get an F♯′ which is perfectly acceptable on most instruments. This F♯′ may in fact be better in tune than 'normal' F♯′, which tends to be flat. This fingering is ideal for the G♭′ to E♭ slur in Malcolm Arnold's Sonatina quoted in *PB*, Ex. 38. A one-finger movement is always the best if tonally acceptable, but complex finger-movements often cannot be avoided. It is then necessary, where there is a choice of tonally acceptable alternative fingerings, for the most complex finger-movement to be placed, if possible, before a note in a phrase which needs a slight accent (see Ex. 2.3).

Although recorders are generally designed to give a fairly even tone-quality over their cross-fingerings, most recorders have notes which are naturally strong and notes which are naturally weak. Plain-fingered notes are tonally stronger than notes with several fingers below an open hole. Half-fingered notes tend to be weak. Examples of strong notes on most treble recorders are bottom G, C, closed G′ (– 123 4567), and A♭′ (– –23 456–), and of weak notes, bottom A♭, C♯, and B♮ (because these two so often have to be flattened to bring them into tune) and C♯′. Baroque music, and much other music, is based on word-rhythms, so, as Quantz points out (p. 123), 'you must know how to make a distinction in execution between *principal* [accented] *notes*, and those that *pass*' (for 'good' and 'bad' notes see le Huray, 14–16). This distinction can be made by note-length, including inequality, by dynamic (slight breath-pressure changes), and by articulation (usually slower-speaking tonguing on weak notes—but not always). However, even all these differentiations together may be upset if a weak note in the music falls on a commanding strong-toned note on the recorder, or if a strong, principal, or accented note in the music falls on one of the recorder's weak-toned notes. One example of refingering to overcome this inherent problem in recorder-playing is given in Ex. 2.2, involving G♯' to A' in a weak-to-strong phrasing context.

Recorder-players need to know each of their instruments well enough to modify their fingerings to respond to expressive needs, in particular when to avoid strong-toned notes. For example, the leading-note E♯' to a tonic F♯' is often more effectively fingered with the tonally weaker – 123 –––– rather than 0 –2– ––––; it is also easier to play that way as only one finger is involved in moving from one note to the other (see *PB*, Ex. 27). Equally, a strong-toned note can be used to reinforce an accent, for example in the first four bars of the last movement of the Lavigne (Ex. 7.1).

EX. 7.1.

Here the strong reiteration of the G' at the beginning of the second bar balances the strong down-beat of the G' which opens the first bar. This second G', however, is only a semiquaver, while the first is a crotchet. So, to give the second (semiquaver) G' something of the same weight as its crotchet predecessor, it could be accorded the extra tonal strength of closed G' (– 123 4567). This also nicely puts the fingers into a better position for the fast semiquaver run up to the D' at the end of the phrase. The two G's at the beginnings of bars 3 and 4 are slightly less strong, being the second line of the quatrain mirroring the opening statement, so they can be played with normal (open) G' fingering, which also better suits the fingering of the downward semiquaver run in bar 4.

Another example occurs in bar 18 of the Murrill Recitativo movement (Ex. 5.7, second bar of the fourth line). The recorder, unaccompanied here, plays four legato quavers F' E♭ D C. If this phrase is to be played in trochaic metre as marked, the E♭ needs to be weaker than the F'. On most recorders normal-fingered F' and E♭ are tonally similar, both being slightly cross-fingered, but the heavier cross-fingering 0 –23 4–6– produces a good but more veiled E♭. Moreover it keeps 2 down as a 'pivot' (*RT* 69) in the phrase as a whole, which makes the fingering of this bar more balanced. As it needs stress in the trochaic pattern, normal-fingered D should be used here. In fast semiquaver passages where its resultant tonal thinness is less apparent, D after E♭ can be fingered 0 –23 45—, giving an admirable fingering economy and fluency to rapid F'–E♭–D–E♭ slurs (and see note on bar 19 of Handel's Furioso, Ex. 5.3).

Another problem in recorder technique which can threaten ideal phrasing is in the production of high notes. Did Murrill really want to slur from E' to F♯'' at the asterisked note four bars from the end of his Finale (Ex. 5.9)? Or did he phrase these last bars with slurs up to the F♯''s only because he had been told about the recorder's limitations in playing these notes? It is in fact not impossible, with care, to play a detached F♯'' on some recorders (see *RT* 89–90 and below, pp. 156–8). Problems with slurring other high notes (in 'Sheep may safely graze') are discussed in Ch. 5.

Detached high notes react best to a precise 'tee' articulation. As stated earlier in the discussion of tonguing (Ch. 5), this articulation takes a moment of time to formulate, which has the effect of slightly separating a note tongued with 't', assisting phrasing in passage-work and elsewhere. Suppose, however, that this phrasing gap is not needed before an isolated high note? There is an excellent example in the last movement of the Telemann:

EX. 7.2.

The phrase-points in this passage probably best come after each of the long tied notes, so that the two final quavers of each bar then move smoothly straight into the next bar with no feeling of break, almost with the closeness of a slur across the bar. However, the articulation of the high F''s in bars 19 and 21 following middle F's is often difficult to accomplish without a momentary silence for their 't' tonguing, although it is less difficult on a narrow-bore recorder with a more fluently-articulating high F''. The clarity of the prominent high F''s at these phrase climaxes is critical, and the first one needs to be played loudly, so they must be articulated with the security and precision of 't' tonguing. By preferring the up-beat phrasing one could thereby be prejudicing the fluidity of the whole passage.

Alternatively, should the whole passage be rephrased so that the phrasing commas come at the end of each bar? This alternative is not without some musical sense, both melodically and in relation to the bass. It gives a moment of time for the articulation of clear high F''s. Then, however, one ought to use this alternative phrasing in the corresponding passage in the second section of the movement (Ex. 3.8, bar 52 onwards), where the technical problem is not as critical, as the climactic high notes are D's, not F''s. A truly brilliant recorder-player would not have to face this intriguing dilemma between interpretation and the exigencies of technique as he would have practised fingering and tonguing so much that middle F' would lead to the high F'' in bar 19 with the same perfect smoothness and ease as the A' at the end of bar 17 leads to the Bb' at the beginning of bar 18.

Of course high notes should be played without anxiety (unless that is part of the composer's intended affect), despite the technical difficulties of playing them. Up to Ab'' (based on either ∅ 1–3 –––(7) or ∅ –23 –56–) these notes, excepting the elusive F♯'', can, with careful tonguing and thumbing, and restrained breath-pressures, be played with as much expressive flexibility as lower notes (see *RT*, ch. VI). A'' appears in a Telemann concerto and in a few modern sonatas (e.g. sonatinas by Peggy Glanville-Hicks and Stanley Bate) but there is little choice of fingering beyond ∅ –2– ––––– with the thumbing as wide as practicable and 2 leaking in an attempt to bring it up to pitch, and it usually needs to be played loud. Sometimes, in the manner of fingering reed-cap instruments and Renaissance recorders, the production of high notes is eased with negligible flattening by adding one or more fingers low down the recorder, such as 5 or 6 for A''. Slight shading, such as 3 or 1 for A'' (with some flattening), can help the articulation and clarity of high notes. Telemann joyously uses C'' in his F major sonata, *ff* ∅ 1–– 4–––.

Renaissance recorders often present problems above C'. Treble D', or descant A', is on some instruments reluctant to articulate reliably with normal fingering, or is weak against the (descant) G' below it, and it is often flat. It is usually better to finger it in the third register, for example ∅ 12– 4567 or sometimes simply ∅ 12– –––7, but this may not work at the *mf* dynamic needed for the very important held A' in bar 87 of the Fontana

(Ex. 6.4). Leaking 4 will usually be found to cure this problem and provide excellent intonational control across the changing dynamic of this particular A′ in the Fontana. Normal Baroque descant G♯′ is often flat on Renaissance (and other) recorders, and Ø 123 –567 is a more reliable and accurate (and flexible) fingering, with 7 being in charge of its intonational control. It also affords a neat A′ to G♯′ trill with fingers 3 and 4 alternating (see Fontana Sonata Quarta, bar 102).

Considerable experimentation is necessary to find the best fingerings, thumbing, tonguing, and breath-pressure to produce each high note on each recorder, and considerable practice to be able unerringly to return to that exact position in the heat of playing a sonata. Only thus can one discover how to achieve the clear quality of high notes that composers doubtless had in mind in writing them, often (as in the Telemann sonata) in dramatically important points in sonatas. This entails finding a way of producing each note so that it articulates cleanly and securely, and so that its inevitable undertones are minimized. In fast music it entails finding fingerings that avoid clumsiness of finger-movement and facilitate neat phrasing; for example, F″ in semiquaver passages with E♭′ and G″ might be fingered Ø 1–– 4–6–, which reduces by two the finger-movements across the F″ to G″ register-break.

Recorder Technique (pp. 124–6) emphasizes economy and lightness in finger-movement, with 'unused' fingers poised low to minimize their downward movement to cover a hole. In sonata-playing the positioning of the 'unused' fingers is crucial, for they need to be held low enough almost to sense the air-stream emerging from the open holes immediately under them, so in effect very slightly shading the pitch without influencing good tone. This enables the recorder to be played at the *mf* level frequently needed to achieve balance and projection in sonata-playing (i.e. 'Beaufort scale' 7) without sharpening the intonation above what it would be at normal consort level ('Beaufort scale' 5) with the fingers held a little less low. This brings three advantages. It gives room for 'structural dynamic' change from *mf* to *p* ('Beaufort scale 4') with the fingers more lifted, without perpetrating intonational indiscretions; it puts the fingers into a position where very small movements will enable expressive dynamics to be brought fully into play with good intonational control; and it has the 'unused' fingers well placed to move down into heavier shading for *f* or louder passages in a sonata. The little finger has to be constantly active in sonata-playing in controlling intonation, hovering around 7, and perhaps never quite leaving the surface of the instrument (though beware! coverage of 7 can cause some notes such as treble D′ to break upwards into the next

register). Even the left-hand little finger has a role to play, not only in
helping to support the instrument but in being a lateral point of reference
and stability in the fine control of the minute movements of the 'unused'
fingers in shading and leaking. A thumb-rest also helps in this respect.

PRESENTATION

Just three points not covered elsewhere.

Reviews of concerts by some fine instrumentalists have referred to the
total engagement of the player in the music, so rapt that 'we felt privileged
to be overhearing a profound private communication between the player
and the composer.' However good the player was, this is a negation of the
attitude and purpose of Baroque performance. Recollection of the image of
the orator (Quantz, 119) should help recorder-players to resist the
temptation to be introspective in public.

At the other extreme, should the player, or someone else, talk to the
audience about the music? Such behaviour is not tolerated in formal
concerts—at least until the encore—but in an informal concert there is
much to be said for spoken programme notes, provided they are short,
clear, interesting, and well delivered. Perhaps a few words about the affect
of the music are allowable, as modern audiences, unlike Baroque
audiences, cannot be expected to recognize the symbolism of affective
rhetorical figures, or even to know that they exist.

Is it advantageous to play from memory? Playing from memory enables a
player to have more eye-contact both with the audience and with the other
players. He is then, without the barrier of a music-stand, better placed to
project the affect of the music upon his audience like an orator or a singer.
Memorizing a sonata involves close listening to chord progressions; this
improves ensemble and encourages ornamentation, and the soloist is more
deeply involved in the music as a whole, not just in the solo part perched on
the stand before him. And he has no awkward turn-overs to cope with.
However, he deprives himself not only of being reminded of the notes he
should play, marked slurs, repeats, etc., but also of those self-instructions,
his interpretative gloss of dynamics, ornaments, and so on, and other
reminders he might have found valuable to pencil in during preparation and
rehearsals. Moreover, if only one player plays without music, the chamber-
music aspect of a Baroque sonata is less apparent. While in theory the
balance of the argument may be in favour of playing from memory, what
really decides the matter is how good one's memory is—it should be good
enough for the player to feel as confident without music as with it. If he feels

anxious and apprehensive of forgetting his part, this will stand in the way of his involvement with the music, and might even convey an unwanted 'affect' to the audience. No performer should look nervous, however he feels. It is futile to try to make a good impression by playing from memory if this compounds the anxieties inevitably associated with performance, which for many players is a stressful experience, though one that is exhilarating and deeply rewarding.

WORKING IN ENSEMBLE

A recorder sonata is chamber music, but with a certain emphasis on the recorder-player, shown from the outset by his standing up while the other players sit.[5] The word 'accompanist' is used in this book; it is convenient, but misleading. The 'accompaniment' is often two people, and could be more. The commonest later Baroque 'solo sonata' group is recorder, harpsichord, and cello. The music is complete, though emaciated, without the cello. Conversely, some sonatas work quite well as recorder and bass without harpsichord.[6] The 'cello' may be a modern cello with a Baroque bow (preferably not a modern bow), a Baroque cello (and bow), or a bass viol. The Baroque bow gives a cellist more sense of the lightness, lift, and detachment of Baroque phrasing. The bass line may be played by a Baroque bassoon, or a modern bassoon if the player can manage to play softly enough and still achieve good tone and enjoy his contribution. A bass recorder is too soft, but the much deeper contra-bass recorder (in F) works quite well in place of the cello if the range of the part is suitable. The harpsichord part may be played on a piano with a small, light tone, or by a chamber organ, or even a larger organ with quiet registration. The early Italian sonatas sound best with chamber organ, or theorbo or archlute accompaniment, or with both. A melodic bass part is only to be used in these sonatas if the composer has so stipulated, as Cima did in his 1610 sonatas (trombone with cornett, violone with violin). Lute, guitar, and various harps make attractive continuo instruments and are soft enough to go with tenor or even bass recorder—two pleasant sonatas by De Moivre have been arranged by David Lasocki for bass recorder and continuo (Hargail). Some recordings religiously use organ continuo for a *sonata da chiesa* and harpsichord for a *sonata da camera*, but the ideal accompaniment, when there is choice, depends more on the affect of the sonata than its denomination.

Reverting to the recorder–harpsichord–cello group, each player, and especially the recorder-player, must appreciate the special role of the cello and the harpsichord in the sonata ensemble. The cello has a very positive, not simply a supporting role. It often engages in dialogue, fugal or other, with the recorder, and sometimes takes the melodic lead so that the recorder may then be accompanying the cello. The security of the pulse is in the hands of the cello and harpsichord together, yet at the same time the cello should be almost as expressive in its phrasing as the recorder. The Handel G minor sonata is a superb example of a bass line that is as interesting as the treble, often more so. It has a foreground part in the second and fourth movements, and only in the short third movement should it gently give way to the recorder, while still expressing the sarabande-like pulse. The steadiness of the cello line should give the player of the melody line freedom to soar and improvise without any anxiety about jeopardizing the rhythmic impetus of the music, or, worse, getting lost. In timbre, the cello contrasts with the soloist. Blending of timbre in chamber-music playing may be desirable in nineteenth-century music, but not in Baroque sonatas. If the recorder, for example, heightens a passage with vibrato, the cellist should underpin this with firm, plain notes. Vibrato, slurs, and other forms of decoration belong only to imitative, conversational, or other passages in the bass line which are of a soloistic character.

The harpsichord part, the realization of the figures, is the greatest test of musicianship—how much to contribute, when to imitate and decorate, when merely to fill in chords, how many notes to put in each chord, and where to spread chords. All this has to be done either from one line of bass notes plus a few figures (see Ex. 2.1), or from an editor's realization, which may be incompetent, inadequate, or just not quite right for the occasion. The harpsichord-player should remember that his main function is to play the bass, whether or not he is supported by a bass instrument, and all his thinking should be from the bass upwards. The left hand leads. The right-hand elaboration should derive from the musical shaping of the bass and solo lines; while not being plodding or unimaginative, it should not be allowed to become the main object of his attention. (For further precepts, see C. P. E. Bach's *Essay*, and le Huray, 98–101 and his note 13 to ch. 6). With modern editions, the keyboard-player is usually the only person who has the whole score before him, and therefore needs to be the most constructive—and diplomatic—person during critical rehearsals.

Nevertheless, a solo sonata 'belongs' most to the recorder-player, who must lead the ensemble. It is his opening gestures, which must be clear and unambiguous, that will be responded to by the other members of the ensemble in pre-establishing the speed, pulse, and spirit of the music, and it is his attitude and appearance as 'the orator' which will determine the mood and affect of the music in the minds and hearts of the other players, producing a cumulative effect upon the audience.

The recorder-player is also responsible for tuning, which should be done in the concert room before the audience arrives, with the room heated ready, if necessary. Tuning on stage during a concert is best avoided, but if it is a matter of necessity, possibly for the cello, it should be carried out unobtrusively. Tuning between movements impairs the flow and tonality of a sonata. The recorder-player's instruments should always be warm before any tuning is carried out. If treble C (descant G) and other notes such as treble C', A, and F are *all* sharp to the keyboard, the recorder-player may wish to pull out slightly, for reducing breath-pressure could spoil the ensemble's balance. He then needs to remember that pulling out causes greater flattening of the middle notes than of the low and high notes,[7] and to be prepared to make the necessary breath-pressure and fingering compensations. If the recorder is flat overall at sonata-playing level to the keyboard, the problem is greater. Some players have tuning-holes in the head-joint of their instrument to meet such an emergency,[8] but otherwise the recorder-player will either have to abandon most of his *p* passages and play the whole sonata loud, or exercise considerable skill and judgement in slide-fingering in places where he had not planned to do this in order to retain dynamic variety, but probably losing tone-quality in the process. The sharp keyboard situation can be so calamitous that the recorder-player must do everything in his power to see that it does not happen.

AUTHENTICITY

As shown in the next chapter, there is no shortage of sonatas specifying recorder. Many of them, however, are the work of minor composers, and recorder-players may therefore envy the greener grass in the neighbouring field of Baroque flute sonatas not only by Handel and Telemann but also by J. S. Bach and Leclair, or even by post-Baroque composers such as C. P. E. Bach. The question of authenticity in instrumentation is thus of concern to recorder-players who want to expand their sonata repertoire.

What one plays to enjoy on one's own or with like-minded friends is not at issue. But what is proper to play to an audience? Here again it depends on the audience, their enjoyment being one's chief object. As the Cambridge Buskers have shown, it is possible to play music on bizarrely wrong instruments and still to convey something of its quality and excitement.[9] Beautiful arrangements from Debussy and Delius exist for recorder groups which enrich the players' experience, and sound good to a tolerant audience—but less good than their originals. Baroque composers adapted their music to the forces available;[10] what mattered was the circumstances of the occasion and the overriding requirement that the audience should be entertained and moved. Some of the most deeply moving accounts of J. S. Bach's keyboard music are played on a modern concert grand piano. It is the insights and musicianship of the player that are paramount. If, however, one had to choose between two players of equal quality and ability, one playing Domenico Scarlatti sonatas on the harpsichord and another on the modern piano, would not the choice usually be the harpsichord performance?

For recorder-players, the music of J. S. Bach is the sounding-board of instrumental authenticity in these terms. Opinions about how Bach might have imagined the sound of his own music, and of what today 'sounds right' or 'sounds wrong' must be very subjective. For the author, a sort of horror descends at the thought of the recorder parts in Cantatas 106, 161, and 175 being played on other instruments, and considerable perturbation at the idea of the great B minor flute sonata being performed on the recorder, although some of the other Bach flute sonatas (despite their having been written in virtuoso terms for a particular flautist) can, even transposed, sound convincing on a recorder if played with respect and understanding. The so-called 'organ' trio sonatas,[11] however, are fair game for arrangement. Some sound better on flute, others, such as the last two, sound better on recorder. As Telemann and other composers suggested that some of their flute or violin music could be played, transposed up a minor third,[12] by recorders, recorder-players need not hesitate to play Baroque flute sonatas on the recorder, transposed if necessary, provided that they seem to 'sound right'. Recordings exist where Couperin's sonatas are played on the recorder,[13] and they do not sound 'unauthentic'.

As already pointed out in Ch. 2, each of the five main sonatas considered in this book should preferably be performed on five different recorders of different designs and pitches. Nevertheless, they can be played adequately on good plastic recorders, so much does musical understanding and attitude of mind transcend instrumentation.[14] A piano accompaniment is obviously less authentic than continuo with harpsichord, but it must also be remembered that the tone-quality of harpsichords varied considerably by country and period, by maker, and by the size of the instrument. Moreover, some harpsichords are designed to make such solo impact that no soft-toned recorder goes well with them. Playing the 'correct' instrument for the music can, however, give the performer a better feel of the style of the time.[15] The possession of sets of recorders of different designs and pitches produces an interesting new problem, for no recorder gives of its best unless it is played frequently. Unused for long periods, especially in a warm dry room, the wood may dry out, and tone will deteriorate.

Another way of getting closer to the mind of the composer is to play from facsimile copies, and some early-music courses now require this.[16] Facsimile copies are not always as easy to read as the Handel–Walsh facsimile in Ex. 2.1, and, as can be seen both from that music and from the critical apparatus in the Faber edition of the Handel recorder sonatas, early printed music is often inaccurate and inconsistent. Considerable experience of Baroque performance practice is needed to know how to phrase the music with slurs, crescendos, trills, and so on, which the composer assumed to be the stock-in-trade of competent contemporary performers of good taste and so did not bother to mark in. Signs for ornaments, accents, staccato, etc. often need editorial interpretation.[17] Figured basses need realization. A rather expensive ideal may be for a recorder-player to get to know a sonata from a good Urtext edition (e.g. the Faber Handel), then, exercising discrimination, to derive ideas from more fully edited versions (e.g. the Schott Handel sonata editions), and finally to study the sonata from a facsimile, perhaps even to play from it.[18] Having the facsimile before him, like seeing a Handel opera in a Georgian theatre, may help the player to imagine the circumstances in which the music was written. While not attempting to recreate a Baroque performance,[19] he should study 'to come closer to the inner vitality of the composer's mind'[20] in the process of achieving his object of entertaining and moving a present-day audience whose backgrounds and attitudes have been formed in an ever-changing musical environment.

Other Sonatas

THE purpose of considering ten further recorder sonatas, inevitably superficially, is twofold. First, these sonatas are drawn from different periods, countries, and styles, thereby providing an opportunity to refer more generally to the range of accompanied solo sonatas and some other related music for the recorder in each period. Secondly, some of the ten sonatas chosen raise interesting points of interpretation and technique that are not fully exemplified by the sonatas considered in Chs. 2–7. The sonatas in this chapter are presented in roughly chronological order.

RICCIO CANZONA (1620/1: VENICE)

Of the five sonatas dealt with earlier in this book, the Fontana Sonata Terza is the most difficult, and the other five in Fontana's set of six are no easier. The difficulties in these sonatas relate to changes of time and to keeping with the accompanist at these points, to the rapid semiquaver and demisemiquaver passages, to the ornamentation of slow sections ('affetti'), to echo effects which need special fingerings, to unexpected rhythms, and to the uncertainty how much to decorate canzona-type sections with *passaggi*. At least Frescobaldi asks that in his five solo canzonas—strong and elegant music which sounds well on the recorder—*passaggi* should not be used; the music is to be played 'come sta', as it is written, in order to keep the fugato between treble and bass clear. Composers such as Dario Castello, whose flights of fancy are very virtuosic, and Bertoli (who wrote the first bassoon sonatas) realized the difficulties of their music even to players brought up on the complexities of mannerist *passaggi*, and expressed the hope (herewith passed on) 'that players will not give up on the first try' (Newman, 107).

Riccio's Canzona is a godsend to recorder-players. It specifies 'un Flautin' (or a cornett) as the solo instrument; it is not long—88 bars; and, though it has its difficulties, it is much easier to play than the Fontana, Castello, or Marini sonatas. The ability of the recorder to play echoes is amply demonstrated in this piece, which makes a feature of them—they are quoted (from the London Pro Musica Edition, ed. Eleanor Selfridge-Field) in Ex. 3.1. They need to be worked out either with alternative fingerings or with thumb-leaking. The echo passage quoted could be played at a weakened, more leisurely pulse-rate as speed can be picked up again at bar 44 in the continuo (and bar 48 in the recorder part), where there are three crotchets on the same note—in this kind of music such a figure usually implies 'a tempo'. There are two short uncomplicated tripla sections which go by trippingly in the basic pulse of the canzona, probably a sort of flexible ♩ = 84 or thereabouts. Bars 62–8, which are also followed by a 'pulse pick-up' figure of three crotchets on the same note in bar 69, suggest by the nature of the melody and the sustained chordal bass part that this section is to be garbed with 'affetti', though it is not so marked. The two sequential phrases in these bars are just long enough to challenge decorative imagination, but they are also short enough for the performer to be able to get by with nothing more than cadential *groppi*. In fact, Riccio's canzona is effective played as it is written, with good rich tone-quality, yet it benefits from ornamentation, which can be added gradually as the player becomes more familiar with the style of this music.

Riccio's music suits a C recorder—a descant, or, with a light accompaniment, a tenor. David Lasocki, in his edition (Zen-On), suggests a tenor recorder, while the London Pro Musica editions suggest a descant, or, following Riccio's proposal in a 1612 canzona to transpose up a fourth, a sopranino recorder. The 1612 canzona with recorder also asks for a bass instrument, ideally a dulcian (a soft early bassoon), but the bass part is reduplicated in the continuo, and, except for three bars, this is also the case with another 1620/1 canzona, 'La Grimaneta', with its tremolo effect. Three Riccio pieces that are not too technically demanding can therefore be played as solo sonatas with continuo, though the presence of the bass instrument is desirable in two of them.

There are solo/continuo sonatas from this period by Tomaso Cecchino (1628; Schott OFB 159) which are easier still as they only have one tripla, and no 'affetti' section. They make an admirable starting-point for a newcomer to this repertoire but are less musically interesting than the two Cima sonatas (1610) or the five Frescobaldi solo canzonas (1628) for 'any sort of instrument'. Several of Frescobaldi's adagios are long-drawn-out cadences to sections, not sections in their own right, and the players have to be alert to manage frequent tempo and speed modifications within a unifying pulse.

The early Italian solo-sonata repertoire suitable for recorder is a small one, as composers favoured groups of two or more instruments and continuo, and the trio sonata developed into a more important Baroque musical form than the solo sonata. The first extant complete publication of a set of twelve solo/continuo sonatas, by Uccellini, did not appear until 1649. These sonatas are entitled 'a Violino Solo, & Basso Continuo', with no suggested alternative instrumentation (Newman, 123), although a few of them, for example Nos. 5 and 12 (published by London Pro Musica), are still playable on a recorder in C.

CORELLI SONATA OP. 5 NO. 12 'FOLLIA' (1700: ROME)

It seems that no recorder sonatas appeared in Italy between 1620 and 1699.[1] Apart from Benedetto Marcello's twelve Op. 2 sonatas (Venice, 1712) which specified 'Flauto' (= treble recorder),[2] few such sonatas were published in Italy during the Baroque period, although the outstanding violinist Veracini dedicated twelve sonatas in 1716 to Friedrich August of Saxony as 'for Violin or Flute',[3] his later sonatas being for violin only. Two exceptions are Venetian publications of twelve sonatas Op. 3 (1720) by Bellinzani, a Corelli admirer, and six 'Flauto' sonatas, resembling Marcello's, by Santini. Far more Italian recorder sonatas were published in London or Amsterdam, not only by expatriate Italians such as Bononcini, Fiocco, and Barsanti,[4] but by Italians who found enthusiastic northern publishers of recorder sonatas, such as the Venetian monk Diogenio Bigaglia, six of whose recorder sonatas were published by Le Cène in Amsterdam in 1725,[5] Martino Bitti from Florence (Walsh and Hare, London 1712), and Francesco Mancini, who published in London (1724) twelve solos for violin or flute appropriately dedicated to the English consul in Naples, his home town.[6] The only return commerce was Robert Valentine ('Inglese') who published several sets of 'fluent and facile' recorder sonatas in his adopted Rome (Newman, 316). In addition there are sonatas that publishers did not discover or wish to publish (either with or without the composer's consent), such as the twenty-nine recorder sonatas of Giuseppe Sammartini that, like some other interesting sonatas, remained in manuscript until recent times.[7]

The resourceful and mercenary Walsh, like his rival Roger in Amsterdam, took less than a year to pirate Corelli's Op. 5 violin sonatas. These long-awaited works, which were to have so great an effect upon sonata-writing throughout Europe, were published in Rome in 1700, and the second part, the six *sonate da camera*, appeared in 1702 in London 'made fitt for A FLUTE and A BASS'. Sonatas 3 and 4 (*da chiesa*) appeared in 1707 in a recorder version 'with the proper Graces, by an eminent Master'.[8]

With this and other precedents, twentieth-century recorder-players may look among the Baroque violin repertoire from Vitali onwards for additional sonatas. Vivaldi wrote some fifty solo sonatas (Newman p. 169); six sonatas all purporting to be by Vivaldi were published in Paris in 1737 as his Op. 13, 'Il Pastor Fido', with the usual French list of fashionable instrumentation (bagpipes, hurdy-gurdy, flute, etc.).[9] They include the splendid No. 6 in G minor. Several of these attractive sonatas sound idiomatic on the recorder, but the Corelli Op. 5 sonatas are so well suited to the superb Cremona violins then being made that their transposition to the recorder creates problems that cannot always be resolved.

On the whole, Corelli's dance-based *sonate da camera* survive the transposition better, and it is a tribute to Walsh's acumen that he first seized on sonatas 7–12, although it is a pity that a better job was not made of their arrangement. There is less violinistic double-stopping in these sonatas, whereas the Allegro of No. 1, for example, has a fugal second entry within the solo violin's double-stopping, with triple-stopping a few bars later. Long 'allegro' arpeggiated movements are exciting on the violin with its stringy attack, dynamic range, and strength of tone; on the recorder such passages can sound 'pecked at' in single or quick-speaking double-tonguing. In slower-speaking, more legato tonguings, which give the required feeling of bigness, the high notes are at risk, and negotiating the rapid cross-fingerings in near-slurs verges on the impossible. The violinistic 'adagio' decorations are instructive, but even if conquered technically can sound mannered on the recorder. In sonatas 7–11 there is only one Adagio movement, and it is one which possesses some melodic flow, not relying for its effect mainly on 'ye graces'. Flutes and recorders thrive on expressive melody.

The showpiece of Corelli's Op. 5 is the so-called 'Sonata 12', the 'Follia' variations, of which there are several editions and recordings. This is underpinned throughout by one hypnotic bass progression. Its melody has inspired composers over four centuries.[10] Even without the original double-stoppings, it remains in its recorder version a tremendously exciting piece to play and listen to, given a cellist who is as carried away by it as much as the recorder-player should be. Of the theme and twenty-three variations, nos. 10 (bar 161) and 18 (bar 266) call for a level of fingering dexterity that can usually only be achieved after hours of practice—and preferably by learning the recorder from the formative years of childhood with the same seriousness of purpose and discipline as is usually expected by teachers of the piano, violin, or flute in mastering scales, arpeggios, and other exercises. Space is here inadequate for a proper commentary on this piece, but two points must be made.

The first is that the spirit of the violin original should not be lost. Every ounce of sonority must be extracted from the recorder at the most powerful breath-pressures it will stand without tonal degradation. Conversely, in the *pp* passages, such as parts of variation 14 (bar 202), which belongs to the keyboard continuo instrument, the recorder should be a mere background whisper. The violin bowing might also inform one's interpretation: variation 1 calls for detached full bow, variation 2 a detached half bow, and variation 5 (bar 81) is possibly 'sautillé', a bouncing bow.

The second point is that Corelli, fine craftsman as he was, had surely, in making the 'Follia' the culmination of a set of sonatas, kept in mind the association of the word 'sonata' with logic and organization. His grouping of the piece into three 'movements' is often overlooked. After the full-blooded announcement of the theme[11] and the first broad-shouldered variation (both 'adagio'), the piece develops its impetus where Corelli marks 'allegro', implying that variations 2 to 7 should be taken almost continuously under one broad span, with a single powerful ongoing surge of pulse until a cadential pause is reached at the end of variation 7 (bar 128). The middle 'movement', starting 'adagio', consists of eight variations of contrasting affects, each requiring its own pulse, so that a slight gap is needed at each change of speed; variations 12 and 13, however, though different in time, are paired under the same continuous 'allegro' pulse, and 14 and 15 are paired under 'adagio'. There is a big hemiola cadence at the end of variation 15 (bars 231-3). At bar 234 Corelli marks 'allegro', signalling the beginning of the 'last movement'; there are no further speed-marks. This should probably be a notch up in pulse from the opening 'allegro'. It starts with the hard-driven variation 16 and strides inexorably on to the very end—the cello only reins back after the third beat of the penultimate bar, so the recorder has to get all its flourishing in at that bar without respite in its onward drive, a final frenzied effect to leave the audience, and probably the players as well, gasping. This, after all is what *la folía* is about.

PAISIBLE SONATA IN F (*C*.1700: LONDON)

Even before Corelli's sonatas were published in London, that most musically cosmopolitan of cities had begun to favour Italian style in preference to the French music which the court of Charles II had sought to emulate at the Restoration in 1660. Even French musicians who settled in London, such as Paisible and Dieupart, wrote sonatas in the Italian manner, following the example of Henry Purcell.[12] As Roger North put it, 'wee found most satisfaction in the Italian, for their measures were just and quick, set off with wonderfull solemne *Grave's*, and full of variety . . .' 'But still the English singularity will come in and have a share.'[13] The return to fashion of the recorder (Hunt, ch. 4) coincided with the growing interest in 'the most fam'd Italian masters',[14] and it is not surprising that in the recorder sonatas of Godfrey Finger, a Moravian who pursued a successful career in London from 1687 until 1701, 'the Humour . . . is principally Italian'.[15] Peter Holman writes: 'The result was something new: a style of instrumental music based on the abstract patterns of Italian *da chiesa* sonatas, but filled with an Austrian virtuosity and an English tunefulness.'[16]

Despite the overwhelming influence of Corelli in the first decades of the eighteenth century,[17] an Englishness of style, something less sumptuous but with more bounce, which one recognizes first in Purcell's music and later in Handel's, pervades the Italian-style English recorder sonata. This is irrespective of the original nationality of the composer. Although one notes that there are certain French traits in Paisible's sonatas, that the Pepusch sonatas have a controlled ponderousness, and that Barsanti's dotted rhythms seem to have the weight of Veracini's rather than the springiness of Purcell's, all show signs of sharing a common English sense of fancy. Compared with his genius brother, Daniel Purcell was a 'journeyman' (Denis Arnold's word) but Daniel's attractive recorder sonatas do occasionally display something of Henry's harmonic adventurousness. London-based composers such as Purcell's contemporaries Topham (twelve recorder sonatas), Parcham, Courteville (sonatas and duets), and Bingham (four suites), then William Corbett, the oboeist Galliard, Henry Thornowitz,[18] John Lœillet,[19] Handel's 'rival' Bononcini, William Turner, and Louis Mercy,[20] though all writing within well-established conventions, seldom lack some aspects of originality.[21] As with music from all places and times, there is much in this recorder-sonata repertoire that is mediocre and sometimes dull, but it is rarely incompetent or trite, and never ugly or characterless. It is therefore incumbent upon recorder-sonata players not only to express to the full the qualities of conventional Italian forms that appealed to musicians such as Roger North but also to seek out and display characteristics peculiar to individual composers, and indeed to each sonata and movement—and occasionally to express the unexpected. As pointed out in Ch. 1, surprise, or even fancy verging on the rhapsodic, is an important element in Baroque music.

The first movement of James Paisible's F major recorder sonata (Ex. 8.1) is an example.[22] The bouncy theme obviously needs to be taken fast, so the semiquavers of the second subject after the first four bars may come as a first surprise to those who have not looked ahead and made allowances. The

EX. 8.1. Paisible, Sonata in F major

demisemiquavers of bars 23–4, written-out *passaggi*-like decoration, come as even more of a surprise. In bar 25 the bass has downward scalic semiquavers against the recorder's held C′, and then—'Adagio'—the music almost stops (the bass has a crotchet chord at the beginning of bar 26 while the recorder's C′ hangs on expectantly). How should the next seven notes be played before the sudden final perky restatement of the 'Vivace' theme at the end by the recorder in bar 28 and by the bass in bar 29? Magnificent and allargando? Or very softly, stepping cautiously (and using echo-type fingerings)? Decorated? (probably not after the preceding outburst). Double-dotted, or more? Or in a deliberate and measured quaver movement? Should there be a pause between the two quaver F′s at the beginning of bar 28? (or would that be excessive?). Whichever way, the final 'Vivace' should make the audience gasp, or even laugh, with surprise.

A point about the semiquavers, and about the demisemiquavers. It will have been noticed that there is much lively thematic exchange between the soloist and the bass in this movement. The bass states the theme in bars where the recorder rests, and elsewhere. The recorder's semiquaver subject, however, is not discussed with the bass as it already contains within itself an exchange of ideas—the second group of eight semiquavers is a kind of reply to the first group of eight, and should be tongued as if by a different interlocutor, perhaps at a slightly lighter dynamic. The demisemiquaver passage in bars 23–4, however, is in effect a decorated rising scale and probably sounds best played in one great sweep while the bass picks out its rising-scale passage below, holding the decoration in place. Should the demisemiquavers be slurred? It is difficult at so fast a speed not to slur. Perhaps the tongue should go a-flutter with the fingers in the hope of some defining synchronization, using the fastest soft articulation the player can manage. This could be 'r' trembling at the tip of the tongue grazing the teeth-ridge, or 'l' with rapid side-to-side movements, or 'y' trembling from the back of the tongue and felt where the tongue touches the upper molars. Fingering needs to be worked out as well. Some recorder-players will prefer to use familiar normal fingerings, while others may find certain easily remembered alternatives helpful, such as either a thumbed G′ after the A′s in bar 24, or closed G′ and alternative A′ for this G′–A′–B♭′ movement (see *PB*, Ex. 38).

It is tempting to trill the following held C′ in bars 24–6, or to colour it strongly with changing vibrato or dynamics, but to do so could detract from the effect of the semiquaver figures in the bass, for this is the only place in the movement where the bass gets a look-in on the recorder's earlier semiquaver interlocutions. Moreover, how this held C′ is treated depends very much on how one intends to interpret the following 'adagio' passage. This movement, written by a Frenchman, is a fascinating amalgam of, as Roger North puts it, Italian-style 'variety' with 'English singularity'.

SCHICKHARDT SONATA IN E MAJOR FROM OP. 30 (*C*.1735: LONDON)[23]

Many German composers wrote music with recorders,[24] but other than Handel, only two, Telemann and Schickhardt, are associated with solo/ continuo recorder sonatas. Telemann wrote 8,[25] and Schickhardt 44, even excluding the 21 sonatas in Op. 30 designated for violin, flute, or recorder; 3 of Telemann's 8 are alternatively for bassoon or recorder. A few collections of recorder sonatas exist in German libraries,[26] on the whole deservedly anonymous. Telemann and Schickhardt both expected recorder-players to exercise facility in clef transposition, and playing a minor third up[27] gratifyingly widens the recorder sonata's boundaries to encompass some sonatas designated for flute, including those by composers from Sweden (Roman) and Holland (the melodious de Fesch),[28] though there are some genuine recorder sonatas by Dutch composers such as Konink and van Noordt (Newman, 341–2). German Baroque composers drew their inspiration as much from Gabrieli and later from Vivaldi as from Corelli,[29] and generally preferred multi-part textures to Italian solo sonata flamboyance or French *naïveté*. This predilection for weight and substance is worth bearing in mind when playing German recorder music, even in technically demanding fast movements.[30]

Both Telemann and Schickhardt were concerned (as this book is) to raise the standards of amateur instrumentalists closer to the level of technique and commitment expected of professional players, although the ability of amateur recorder-players must already have been high, judging by the recorder parts in Telemann's 'Harmonischer Gottesdienst' cantatas, intended for home use. Some of Schickhardt's publications have non-aristocratic dedications, probably to his pupils.[31] His Op. 30 sonatas 'in all the keys' pose enormous technical problems. Their allegro passage-work, slow movements requiring much ornamentation, jigs, and vivaces in keys with six sharps or flats constitute excellent practice in recorder cross-fingerings and trill-fingerings, though the quality of the music would not always justify the effort and nervous tension that would be expended in performing them in such keys.[32] E major, however, is not a particularly remote key (it is used by Telemann in a trio sonata with recorder), but even just the last two bars of the sixth and final movement of the E major sonata

(Ex. 8.2) will show how, away from 'home keys', an awkward border-line exists in recorder-playing where problems of technique, especially in the maintenance of accurate intonation, can compromise a desired interpretation.

EX. 8.2.

It is first necessary to decide how to phrase the passage. Clearly, a comma comes before the first high D', for this is the half-way point, and such phrasing matches the up-beat from the end of the previous bar. There is probably a 'half-comma' after the high E'. In the first half, are the semiquavers paired as rising thirds (trochaic) or as falling pairs across the beat (iambic)? This will depend on how one has phrased semiquavers earlier in this Allegro; Schickhardt's style is rather four-square and the trochaic solution is a probability.

That decided, and assuming a *mf* ⟨ *f* dynamic, one must consider intonation and fingering. Mattheson asserted that the recorder was the 'only woodwind instrument on which one could play perfectly in tune in all twenty-four keys'.[33] Gratifying though this statement may be, the emphasis has to be on 'could'. Remembering that original Baroque recorders were often less well-behaved intonationally than modern recorders, the statement ought perhaps to read '. . . on which it is just about possible, with a critical ear and considerable application, to play perfectly in tune in all twenty-four keys'.

In trochaic metre the C♯ at the beginning of the first bar in this passage will be stressed, and to be in tune at *mf* will certainly need ½6 or more. F♯' as a weak note after D♯ is probably best taken – 1–3 4–––, i.e. lifting the thumb from D♯. The G♯' at its first appearance is in a weak position, so the thumbed version is there preferable, but at its second appearance, where it is the first of a rising pair, normal fingering, with its greater tonal strength, should be used.

The main problem is the D♯'–C♯'–D♯' at the beginning of the second half of this excerpt. With unchanged thumbing many recorders play an interval of more than a tone between these two notes. A more open thumbing for the C♯' and a tighter one for the D♯' may be sufficient to correct this—provided the C♯' at *f* articulates well with the more open thumbing. Often correction by thumbing is insufficient, in which case the D♯' will have to be flattened a little with shading (i.e. with 3 or ½7)—but then the climactic tonic E′ at the beginning of the next bar will need to be brought into tune after its leading-note; and will that modified E′ be in tune with the E implied in the bass realization? or should that E be taken out of the keyboard chord to avoid the problem? (which is tinkering with desirable interpretation on technical grounds). And even so, will the recorder's flattened E′ still sound in tune with the remaining notes in the continuo chord (i.e. C♯ and A)? If this D♯′–C♯′–D♯′ semiquaver group had been slurred, the C♯′ could have been fingered ∅ 123 4567, i.e. adding 3 and 7 to the D♯′. This C♯′ is passable in intonation and its weakness of timbre can be tolerated at speed, but it is unsafe to tongue, as with this fingering slight articulation changes select other notes in the harmonic series of (approximately) F♯′, C♯′, F♯′ and B♭″. While a case could be made out on interpretational grounds for slurring these three semiquavers, it would be dubious practice to write in a slur for no other reason than to resolve a problem of technique.

Worse difficulties follow at the penultimate beat of this passage. This has a turned cadential trill from G♯′, first held as the appoggiatura, trilling to F♯′ and concluding with an E turn. Ideally this should sound as effortless as a turned cadential trill on other notes, say on E, D, and C, but it happens to be very awkwardly placed across the recorder's main register-break. Such a trill, however, is likely to be encountered frequently in any Baroque piece in E major. No solution starting with the thumbed version of the G♯′ ought to be considered because in all cadential trills the appoggiatura should ideally be strong in tone-quality, and thumbed G♯′ is a weak-note fingering. Both a held appoggiatura and the final held note of a trill need to be good in tone and intonation, with, if possible, a one-finger trill in between. This cadence should therefore start on the strong open G♯′, with or without 1.

With 1 down (provided this does not over-flatten the G♯′), the only way to play the trill in tune is with the pinched thumb and the little finger trilling together, which is clumsy, and gives a squeezed-sounding F♯′ not consistent in tone with the G♯′ or the final E. If it is used, the crossing of the register-break for the E turn after the trill is either with normal fingering or by using 0 ––– –––– (i.e. lifting 1) for the F♯′ of the turn. At the speed of a trill the tonal weakness of the thumbed F♯′ might not be too apparent, and this solution does have the advantage of producing a trill without clicks. Some recorders may trill nearly in tune with ∅ 123 4ˣ567.

The second approach is to start without 1, i.e. G♯′ – –23 456–, and trill across the register-break. Trilling to normal-fingered F♯′ produces an unacceptable mess of clicks, but they are much reduced if the trill is taken with 4, and 3 leaks slightly.[34] If it works (it does not on some recorders), this fingering will sharpen both the G♯′ and the F♯′ a little, but they can be shaded with 1. If the leaking of 3 is *exactly* right, the E turn can then be done with the thumb (a very risky but neat fingering). The tonal quality of this trill-fingering is good, but no trill played across the register-break can be negotiated without some 'clickishness', though even this might be tolerated in this particular context—exploiting the slight clicks to give brightness to the final notes of a long sonata.

The third solution is to reduce the trill to a half-trill on to the F♯′, to use normal fingerings, and to cross the register-break (twice) with quick touches of tonguing as in a fast slur, holding the F♯′ momentarily before the turn (using E – 123 4–6– after the F♯′, perhaps). This is still none too easy, but it could be the safest way of resolving the problem. On the other hand, it allows considerations of technique to pre-empt the ideal interpretation of a full cadential trill. How a player responds to this dilemma depends partly on the way his instrument reacts to various fingering alternatives.[35]

A player who is forced to use, for this and other trills, fingerings which on his instrument are difficult to manage or are tonally or intonationally suspect, may be tempted to minimize many trilling problems by prolonging the appoggiatura (on a good fingering) and reducing the number of repercussions of the trill, possibly, as suggested above, down to the two repercussions of a half-trill. Whether this is acceptable or not depends on each musical context. It could be argued that different musical instruments impose. quite legitimately, a particular manner of performance to suit their technique. Nevertheless, whatever Mattheson and Schickhardt might have implied, the recorder is certainly not a 'well-tempered' instrument in remote keys.

ANNE DANICAN-PHILIDOR SONATA IN D MINOR (1712: PARIS)[36]

The freedom of instrumentation which applies even more to French Baroque music than it does to German sonatas provides the recorder-player with a wealth of solo/continuo music during the period from Couperin to Rameau, especially in the form of French suites, where the recorder is often listed among other fashionable instruments of the time. Once the manner of playing French music has been understood, he can enjoy suites by composers such as Jacques Hotteterre, Marin Marais, Saint-Luc, Dornel, Caix d'Hervelois (one of whose suites is discussed in Dinn, *Early Music for Recorders*), and Nicolas Chédeville.

Generally, French freedom of instrumentation applies less to sonatas

(Lavigne was an exception), which French composers conceived in violinistic terms, emulating Italian models. Nevertheless the transverse flute acquired considerable popularity in early eighteenth-century France (as a little later in England), and composers such as La Barre, Blavet, Boismortier, and Naudot left flute sonatas that are playable on recorders, more particularly on the voice-flute in D. One sonata, in D minor, from a collection published in 1712 by the oboeist Anne Danican-Philidor,[37] is, unusually, marked 'pour la Flute à bec'. Moreover it has Italianisms comparable with those of Couperin in his music inspired by Corelli.

Playing French Baroque music derived from Italian models presents some fascinating interpretational problems. French Corellian music remains French in manner, and later when Vivaldi's music was all the rage in France (it still is), the language of Vivaldi came across with a strong French accent. Even when forms such as fugues are used, the French version could rarely be mistaken for a fugal movement of an Italian or German sonata.[38]

The French solo/continuo suites mentioned above whole-heartedly require the interpretative approach described in Ch. 4, but how far does one exercise French style in the more Italianate Philidor sonata? Do French rules of inequality apply? In playing French suites the *flattement*, or finger-vibrato (Hotteterre gave fingerings for each note), would have been used, though with subtle and elegant variety, to colour many longer notes; does this apply to the Philidor sonata? The answer to these questions is almost certainly in the affirmative, so deeply ingrained were French performance practices. Thus the Courante should be taken at a deliberate, not a fast, speed, with delicate hints of inequality in the few bars where conjunct quavers predominate, adding piquancy to the movement's strongly phrased rhythms. It is significant that the movement after the Courante is marked, by contrast, 'Les notes égales et détachéz'. *Flattements* should certainly be used in the opening 'lentement' (note the use of French rather than Italian tempo indications), but with almost Italian dynamic variety, including echoes.

In this sonata both the second and the last (fifth) movements are marked simply 'Fugue'. The concluding fugue is a fiery affair in 4/8, a fast Italianate time signature in which even conjunct semiquavers are likely to be equal. It seems reasonable to conjecture that the more Italianate the music the less French musicians would have used French mannerisms, so here even some rather French-looking phrase-endings in strong-to-weak falling thirds[39] might not have been accorded the customary *coulé*. Nevertheless, the ornamentation crosses are placed in a manner which seems more French than Italian.

The second-movement fugue is in 6/8 with a complex up-beat 6/8 3/4 alternating rhythm redolent of a courante. An interpretational problem of this very interesting sonata is that this fugue is followed by an actual Courante, before a slower movement. Speeds and styles need to be chosen by the performer for these three middle movements, which provide sufficient, but not too much, contrast. The second-movement Fugue is not typical of Italian fugues, and much more resembles the wonderful Fuguéte in Couperin's 'Quatorzième Concert' of *Les Goûts réunis* (1724)—an incomparably French piece despite certain Italian characteristics.[40] The association of a dance-form with fugue occurs elsewhere in Couperin's music,[41] suggesting that this Philidor fugue should be invested with the lightness and lift of dance-based French music, without however losing its gravity; the player needs to imagine a *ballet de cour* with Baroque staging. Much depends on the gentle lift of up-beats, and refined tonguing. The rhythmic drive should be restrained, and the lines of implied quatrains within the music should be balanced, with delicately placed dynamic ebb and flow both within the lines and contrasting them. The long notes invite the tint of a *flattement*, using for F', for example, a distant vibrato-fingering such as ½6. The effect of poise and refinement, as in the Watteau painting in Pl. 4, should be total, and far removed from Italian passion.

J.-B. LŒILLET SONATA IN D MINOR, OP. 1 NO. 2 (C.1710: AMSTERDAM)

The mixture of Italian and French styles pursued by Couperin and achieved much later by Telemann and Quantz, but through the new *galant* style, is evident in the sonatas of J.-B. Lœillet. He and his cousins, John and Jacques, were brought up in a musical family in Ghent, and were exposed to the popular Italian style. Like his cousins he acquired something of the musical manners of his adopted country—Jean-Baptiste worked in Lyons, John in London, and Jacques in Munich (and later in Paris), but, unlike most Baroque emigré composers, e.g. Dieupart, the Lœillet family retained so strong a loyalty to the style they had first known that an editor of their music, R. P. Block, considers that 'on stylistic grounds the works of the three Lœillets are barely distinguishable'. J.-B. Lœillet's Op. 1 sonatas are more Corellian than the more ingratiatingly tuneful sonatas of his Op. 3, from which a movement is quoted in Ex. 1.2, but one should always consider whether they sound even more attractive with a slight French accent, especially the use of inequality.

J.-B. Lœillet is regarded by many recorder-players as their 'third sonata composer'[42] after Handel and Telemann, and he wrote forty-eight recorder sonatas (twelve in each of Op. 1 to 4), not just six or eight. The first two in Op. 1 are among the best crafted. They could be used to exemplify the art of thematic extension—how themes can be spun out by deferring cadences (see the commentary to the Leigh sonatina, Ex. 8.5, for an example of the use of this device of thematic extension by a modern composer). The reference here to Lœillet's Op. 1 No. 2 sonata, however, is limited to one point, that is to illustrate the principle of thematic unity.

Composers of Baroque sonatas not infrequently achieved a sense of coherence between movements of a sonata by employing subjects that belong within the same family melodically and/or harmonically. Consider, for example,[43] the opening notes of the recorder part of the second and fourth movements of the Handel G minor sonata (Ex. 2.1). The first four notes are the same in each case, with the same dotted relationship between the second and third notes. Indeed, the first two bars of the Larghetto, the first four of the Andante, and the first six of the Presto use only the same six notes D F♯' G' A' B♭' and C'. Use of this device can easily be overlooked by the performer, but its realization is necessary for a full understanding of the music. In performance these related themes should be announced clearly and with a certain deliberation; it would be wrong to ornament them, at least at their first statement. Another example of thematic relationships between the beginnings of movements is in the 'Pastor Fido' Op. 13 No. 6 sonata in G minor ascribed to Vivaldi. Yet another, not quite so apparent, is in the openings of the five movements of Lœillet's Op. 1 No. 2 sonata (taken from the Bärenreiter edition HM 43), which are shown in Ex. 8.3. It will be noticed that, except for a passing quaver A' in the Giga,

EX. 8.3.

Giga

Gavotta

the opening notes of the Adagio and the Giga are the same. The opening of the Gavotta rises from D to A′, as do the first two notes of the fugal theme of the Allegro. This fugal theme closes on F, the major key of the Largo; the openings of both the Allegro and the Largo rise to a held A′, and then follow a similar melodic path (A′ G′ F′). Playing these openings one after the other at roughly the same speed will show their relationships more convincingly. Try playing the opening phrases of the first and last movements of Lœillet's Op. 1 No. 3 sonata (Ex. 8.4) at the same speed, and their thematic relationship is immediately apparent, binding the sonata together in Baroque symmetry.

EX. 8.4.

Largo

Gavotta

PUGNANI SONATA NO. 3 IN F (*C*.1767: LONDON)[44]

The career of the Baroque recorder sonata ends splendidly in about 1740 with the publication of Telemann's two recorder sonatas from *Essercizii musici*, for after then sonatas designated for the recorder become a rarity, though the instrument was played until into the nineteenth century.[45] Walsh and other publishers had long provided fare for players of the 'common flute' by arranging violin sonatas, not only those of Corelli but flute or violin sonatas by composers such as Castrucci, Geminiani, and Dall'Abaco (an eminent Italian violinist working in Munich; Newman, 261–3), and there are also some modern arrangements of violin sonatas by French composers, such as Francœur and Senaillé. Rameau had given instructions as to how the violin part of his *Pièces de Clavecin en Concerts* could be suited to the transverse or 'German' flute, and Leclair, like Senaillé, had indicated flute as an alternative to violin for certain of his sonatas, and it is thus a small step to playing these sonatas and the Rameau *Pièces*, some of the finest instrumental music of mid-eighteenth-century France, on the recorder. Because of the range of this music it may need to be played on a tenor recorder in flat keys and a voice-flute in sharp keys. Certain flute sonatas published in London (or Edinburgh) during this period are similarly playable on recorders, such as those by John Stanley, Roseingrave, McLean, and Giovanni Boni, and this treatment may be accorded to flute sonatas by Quantz, Frederick the Great, his young sister Anna Amalia, and (dedicated to her) the Duettos of Christoph Schaffrath. Insatiable recorder-players may look at the flute sonatas of the three Lœillets (despite their tally of fifty-four recorder sonatas), and at the flute and oboe sonatas of Handel, and may extend their legitimate piracy of Telemann to his many sonatas for other instruments, including the six Partitas of *Die kleine Cammermusic*, for oboe (or violin, or flute) yet very attractive on descant recorder. Descant players may also explore the six sonatas by Domenico Scarlatti, written, unusually for him, just as melody line and figured bass.

Looking to the second half of the eighteenth century, there are still some sonatas that seem to 'sound right' on recorders. The flute sonatas of C. P. E. Bach may possibly be across the borderline of suitability both in range and style, but just to attempt to play them opens up new realms of recorder expressiveness. Mozart's flute sonatas[46] do not 'sound right' on the recorder, though this does not prevent a recorder-player with the necessary technique and like-minded friends venturing upon Mozart's music, or Haydn's 'three sonatas with flute and cello accompaniment'—the Piano Trios 15–17—or indeed some other of his trios. Four simple sonatas by James Hook have long been in Schott's catalogue, and there are many more by him—they need to be played with a rollicking lift in the style of dances at the Bath Assembly Rooms in Jane Austen's time. There is music with an attractive Scottish lilt in sonatas by General John Reid, and in the suites by his publisher James Oswald called 'Airs for the Seasons'. Some sonatas by J. C. Bach and Abel, who worked together in London, and by Gaetano Pugnani, a London visitor, are also playable on recorders. The approach to these sonatas has to be totally different from one's approach to Handel or Lœillet, so considerably did musical style change between the eras represented by Telemann and by Haydn, even though the lifetimes of these two composers overlapped by thirty-five years.

The most startling difference is that the keyboard, from being part of Baroque continuo support, has now become the dominating sonata instrument, although it had been treated as 'concertante' by J. S. Bach in

PL. 8. Rococo architecture parallels the *galant* style in music. Both depend more on curves than on straight lines—the church at Wies in Bavaria (Zimmermann, 1746–54) is oval, not rectangular. Flooded with light and whiteness, touched with gold, the building seems without weight or thrust far removed from the power and grandiloquence of earlier Baroque style. Structure is still important, but ornament often conceals formal shapes. The overall affect is one of pleasurable sensibility.

his violin sonatas and three of his flute sonatas, as well as by Telemann in at least six sonatas with flute. A set of six of Pugnani's sonatas are, typically, 'for the Harpsichord with an accompaniment for a Violin or Flute and a Violoncello'.[47] Such sonatas could often be played on the harpsichord alone. So the former 'soloist' must now take more of a background seat.

Galant sonata form is generally in three movements, a slowish flowing first movement, not uncommonly marked 'amoroso', a moderate Allegro, and a triple-time finale, probably a minuet: this is how the structure of a standard solo sonata was described by Quantz in 1752 (pp. 318–19). Harmony has become more subservient to melody, including the new 'singing allegro', and the melodic line is longer-reaching, often impelled onwards by the arpeggiations of an 'Alberti bass'. Cadences are much more spaced out, so that, with the slower harmonic pulse, melodies may insinuate at will, charmingly adorned with curvaceous written-out ornamentation, often in fast triplets or sextuplets. The music has more unexpected twists, both in its melodic phraseology and in its harmonic progressions. Its internal structure is thus far less apparent, although in the more serious movements the introduction of an affectively contrasting second subject assumes greater importance, for example the C minor second subject (bar 22) of the central Allegro of Pugnani's third sonata in the publication of *c.*1767.

The principles of communication of affect through the commitment and oratory of the performer remain as strong as ever,[48] but the object of the music has become to convey pleasurable feelings or sentiments rather than more abstract virtues and states of mind. Baroque symbols became fusty and old-fashioned, and a new lightness and grace animated music. 'Its aims were to achieve an intimate, sensitive and subjective expression; gentle tears of melancholy were one of its desired responses.'[49] A comparison of the interior of Wies church illustrated in Pl. 8 with earlier Baroque architecture, such as the buildings illustrated in Pls. 1 and 6, shows how taste had changed.

The many recorder-players who must have attempted the Pugnani sonata edited by Carl Dolmetsch in 1960 have probably found it superficially attractive, but nevertheless oddly elusive. Possibly the music would reveal its qualities more, and the player feel more confident in his approach and interpretation, if he first studied the sonatas and other instrumental music of C. P. E. Bach (perhaps recorder-players generally do not listen enough to other music) to become more familiar with the idiom of mid-eighteenth-century music. He might also gain insights by visiting rococo buildings and gardens of the period. Nevertheless, it is extraordinarily difficult for a recorder-player to capture the spirit of this 'rococo' music. The slightest coarseness in the flow of a melodic line or the slightest clumsiness in shaping curlicue turns and triplets (register-breaks notwithstanding), or indeed too much pushing of ornaments which should unfold in exquisite naturalness, or too much intensity in the essential dynamic changes, will render ineffective the very effects upon which this music depends. It has to be accepted that the flute has the greater dynamic and expressive flexibility needed to elucidate this kind of music.

LEIGH AND BERKELEY SONATINAS (1939: LONDON)[50]

After two hundred dormant years, the recorder sonata in England had an auspicious revival with the commissioning in the late 1930s of 'a series of Sonatinas for treble recorder and piano by some of the most talented young composers of the time—Stanley Bate, Lennox Berkeley, Christian Darnton, Peggy Glanville-Hicks, Eve Kisch, Walter Leigh, Peter Pope, Alan Rawsthorne and Franz Reizenstein'.[51] They became part of Carl Dolmetsch's repertoire in Wigmore Hall and other concerts, and such encouragement led to compositions by other composers, including Herbert Murrill, Gordon Jacob (three recorder/piano pieces and a splendid Suite for recorder and strings), Edmund Rubbra,[52] Cyril Scott ('Aubade'), Martin Shaw, and Arnold Cooke.[53] Sonatinas and sonatas of quality have been written by Wilfred Mellers (a thoughtful and attractive Sonatina), Malcolm Arnold (1953, as well as a solo and a concerto for the Danish recorder virtuoso Michala Petri in 1988–9), Robin Milford, Colin Hand, Patric Standford, and Michael Short, and Suites by Norman Fulton and John Gardner, both for Carl Dolmetsch Wigmore Hall recitals.

While several twentieth-century composers of recorder music have drawn upon the forms and melodies of earlier music, often to very beautiful effect (e.g. in Rubbra's music—all with harpsichord rather than piano—and in the second movement of Martin Shaw's Sonata), both Leigh and Berkeley represented more recent styles. Parts of Leigh's Sonatina are reminiscent of the elegiac manner of Vaughan Williams and other English composers of his time.[54] The second movement is a dream-like pastoral of an English summer's day, perfectly conceived for the recorder.[55] The accompaniment flows in semiquavers almost throughout the movement (the recorder rhapsodizes on its own in bars 37–42). Ex. 8.5 gives the recorder part to this movement, together with a suggested interpretation/technique 'commentary', and also an English countryside picture (Pl. 9) to inspire the imagination.

EX. 8.5. Leigh, Sonatina

There are some points in the 'commentary' written on this music which are not wholly evident:

1. Note the structure of the movement: Section 1 bars 1–10, a 'quatrain' (bars 1–4) in short 'mini-phrases', followed by three longer phrases; Section 2 bar 13–23 (piano from bar 10) with more spun-out phrases, a process of 'thematic extension'; Section 3 bars 24–34 (piano from bar 23) with phrases gathering in intensity with semiquavers, then declining with languid triplets; Section 4 bars 34–42 immediately following 3 with no gap, its second half unaccompanied (piano chord at 37 dying away), all more rhapsodic and spun out, more intense with the

PL. 9.   A suggested image of an idyllic English countryside to inspire playing of the second movement of Walter Leigh's Sonatina—lush green meadows, a blue sky with light clouds blown by a gentle breeze which, as in the demisemiquaver rufflings in the music, disturbs the surface of the placid river. Interestingly, Rachmaninov said that imagining a picture helped him compose. This picture, in assisting interpretation, has added poignancy, for it is of Grantchester with its Rupert Brooke connections, and both Walter Leigh and Rupert Brooke lost their lives during a war. Walter Leigh would have known these meadows well when he was a student and later Director of Music for the Festival Theatre in Cambridge.

repeated C's at bars 35–6, and demisemiquavers that suggest the ruffling light breeze in the picture; Section 5 bars 42 to end, the piano resuming the theme and the semiquaver accompaniment, while the recorder, taking over at bar 45, eases the movement to a quiet end, dying away with the piano chord. Note also that the recorder plays the theme only at the beginning of the movement, and that most of its part is like a cumulating improvisation, or a descant, above the theme which is played by the piano at each section, except Section 4 , which is a rhapsodic extension of Section 3 . The recorder has a kind of countersubject at bar 13, reiterated in bars 14, 16–17, and 24.

2. Leigh marks *p* at the beginning, but it is one of only two dynamic markings throughout the whole sonatina (the first movement is marked *mp*), so he evidently intended to leave dynamics generally to the performer (or thought the recorder had none). In this movement the dynamics should vary slightly from one section to another, and within sections should follow the contours of the melodic line. Nowhere should the movement get loud.

3. The whole movement should be very legato, with real slurs where marked,[56] and an even movement from one note to another with little stressing of individual notes within phrases. Each note bears the same weight and impulse as its neighbours, with no Baroque strong-weak pairing of notes. Intensity is controlled by differentiated vibrato, and punctuation within the long phrases should be left to the harmonic movement of the accompaniment. The melody should be spun out, almost continuous, with breaths taken frequently and inconspicuously.

4. It is therefore important to avoid allowing register-break clicks to interrupt the smoothness of the slurs. Use closed G' – 123 4567 if, as it usually will with practice, this affords a smoother transition from F' to G' across the register-break than does normal G' to normal A'. If closed G' is tonally or intonationally unacceptable, first try sweetening or tuning it with a leaking fingering, e.g. 1, and, if this does not work, use normal fingerings with a touch of tonguing (hopefully unnoticeable by the audience) to negotiate the slurs at bars 14, 25, and 26.

5. Sensitive note-placing in relation to the more or less regular semiquavers of the accompaniment is of the essence in this movement, for example the shaping of three against two in the falling triplets, and the duration of the crotchets in bars 36 and 47 before they relapse downwards. The feeling of a gentle breeze coming and going can be captured by tiny speedings up and slowings down with the rise and fall of the music, but this must be contrived with infinite subtlety or it could sound mannered. Music of this kind can easily become a travesty of itself.

6. Great care is needed in ending the last note with its decrescendo, and keeping it in tune (see p. 90 and *RT* 53).

The Leigh, Berkeley, and other twentieth-century sonatinas were written with the strong tone-quality of an Arnold Dolmetsch recorder in mind, an instrument designed to balance better with the piano and to be accepted by contemporary composers as equal in status to other modern wind-instruments. The Leigh sonatina could sound adequate on a softer Baroque recorder; the Berkeley sonatina could not. Berkeley makes few concessions to the recorder in his sonatina with its sonorous piano part. Indeed, it is conceived as a flute sonatina and is frequently so performed. Berkeley writes *ossia* alternative notes for the recorder here and there, but they are musically less satisfactory. Recorder-players should play the flute version if they can manage it. Nevertheless this fine sonatina sounds even more exciting on the recorder than it does on the flute. With a recorder there is a sense of struggle which well suits the tempestuous first movement and the spikey last movement. Nor has the composer been insensitive to the recorder's limitations, for in the slow movement where the recorder is in its low register the recorder part is marked *f* and the piano part *p*, and there are similar dynamic differentiations elsewhere. Berkeley marks the recorder *ff* only twice in the whole sonatina, whereas Stanley Bate in his sonatina has in the course of one movement (fortunately the last) marked *ff* seven times, as well as one *fff*, calling for violent hammering tonguings well suited to Bate's music of a machine age. It should, however, be remembered that all dynamics are relative and are as much a matter of attitude as decibels. The surges of piano sound in the Berkeley sonatina come where the recorder is resting or playing penetrating high notes. Even so, the recorder-player should be outgoing and uninhibited in playing this and much other recorder music with piano,[57] aiming at the fullest possible tone, with the diaphragm and associated muscles 'feeling big' to create and support a generous air-flow. This approach should not, however, cause the player to overlook the many places in this sonatina where delicacy of phrasing is needed, for example at the cross-rhythm of the second subject entry in Section '3' of the sonata-form first movement, a subject which is both tender and epigrammatic in contrast with the drama and eeriness of the sonatina's opening theme. There are many subleties of harmony, particularly in the languorous slow movement.[58] This sonatina as a whole has the elegance and urbanity one would expect of a composer schooled in a French tradition.[59]

Technically, the Berkeley sonatina presents many problems (see, for example, *PB*, Exx. 17 and 30), quite apart from its F♯''s (see next section). The opening theme (Ex. 8.6) lies across the recorder's central register-break:

EX. 8.6.   Moderato (♩· = 60)

Should the slur be half-tongued with normal fingerings, or should a fingering be used which holds this slur, usually marked *p*, within one register, thereby affording some interesting tonal changes? Played softly, the opening theme slur could be fingered, as a perfect slur within the upper register, as A′ 0 123 4–67, F♯′ 0 123 4567, and G♯′ 0 123 45–7, but with 5 and 6 staying low over their holes to prevent the A′ and especially the G♯′ from being sharp. As the dynamic builds up, one then needs to work back to normal fingerings for this slur, giving tonal change as the sound becomes less squeezed, certainly by bar 10 and probably sooner. At the beginning of the last movement with its jazzy rhythms,[60] the three trumpet calls can be played louder by not tonguing the A′. In this last movement the slurs from A′ to F″ and back (and then A′ to F♯″) work best with no slurring assistance from the tongue, despite the register-break crossing. The trills in the first movement start firmly on the note marked, definitely not from the upper auxiliary; Berkeley's Sonatina has nothing Baroque about it.

SCHOLLUM SONATINE (1966: VIENNA)[61]

Despite Hindemith's influence in the field of *Gebrauchsmusik*— uncomplicated music to be used at home, in schools, etc.—German composers writing such music, which included several recorder sonatas, did not always avoid dullness. Exceptions are Harald Genzmer, whose sonatas remain in print, and Walter Roehr, who has written some tuneful and easy sonatinas for descant recorder and piano. As in England, sonatas have tended to be written with a well-known recorder-player in mind. Thus a long and extraordinary sonata was written by Koerppen for Ferdinand Conrad in 1957, and Arnold Matz's interesting 'Sonata Contrappuntistica' (1979) was dedicated to his mentor Walter Bergmann. Recorder-players and teachers such as Bergmann in London, Hans-Martin Linde in Basle, and Staeps in Vienna all wrote good recorder sonatas.[62] Other highly regarded sonatas are those by Henk Badings (1957),[63] by the Dane Niels Viggo Bentzon (1973—'bracingly different', commented Paul Clark in his review of it in *RMM* 5 (June 1975), 69), and by Eliodoro Sollima, teacher at the Palermo Conservatorio (Hunt, 157). There is a dashing Sonatine by Heinz Walter among other interesting music (Linde, etc.) in Schott's *Modern Music Book* (OFB 137). Recorder sonatas or sonatinas have also originated from France (Georges Migot), the USA (Colin Sterne and Maurice Whitney), and Argentina (by Eduardo Alemann, 'Sonatina Francesca' for treble recorder and guitar), and a considerable number from Germany, for example by Helmut Bornefeld, Hans Poser, and Wolfgang Stockmeier.

Currently many of the most interesting compositions for recorders are in the field of avant-garde music, for which the structures and tonalities associated with the sonata may seem inappropriate. This music is considered with insight and discrimination in Eve O'Kelly's book. Nevertheless, even in Japan which, like Holland, has produced a notable school of avant-garde composers using the recorder,[64] at least one recorder sonata has been written in recent times.[65] While not using avant-garde techniques, Alan Bush, in his Duo Sonatina, Op. 82 (1981), probably the best recorder sonata of the 1980s, extends the compass and variety of the sound of the instrument by requiring the player to switch during movements between descant, treble and tenor recorders.[66]

Several composers, influenced by Schoenberg and others, have adopted serial techniques, sometimes in a modified form, in writing recorder sonatas. Serial technique involves constructing a tone-row out of all twelve notes of the chromatic scale and restarting this tone-row (which may be used forwards or backwards, turned upside-down in either direction, or transposed) as a means of logical composition without tonality. Tones may be used at different octaves. A tone should not be repeated before the row is completed, as this might emphasize one note, and risk implying the tonic–dominant melodic and harmonic patterns of an outmoded form of music. In playing such music, dynamics and expressivity may be used, but not in a manner that causes one note to take upon itself greater significance in the music than the other notes of the tone-row.

Serial music must therefore use all the twelve notes of the chromatic scale, including F$\sharp$, and it would be unreasonably limiting to a composer to forbid its use, on purely technical grounds, in the uppermost register of the treble recorder. Thus Robert Schollum's Sonatine, although the composer is not absolutely strict in his approach to the serial technique of composition, uses high F$\sharp''$ four times in its first movement, and once each in the second and third movements. Other twentieth-century composers have been unwilling to avoid this note, including Murrill, Berkeley, and Rubbra, and the first movement of Stockmeier's Sonatine has a high F$\sharp''$ as its triumphant conclusion. F$\sharp''$ also appears in Baroque recorder music derived from flute music to be read a minor third up, if the original contains D$\sharp'$ or E$\flat'$. It must therefore be mastered, not avoided.

There are five basic ways of playing F$\sharp''$ on the treble recorder.[67] With many recorders none of these is very satisfactory. Which method is used depends partly on how one's recorder is constructed and how it behaves with these possible fingerings. It also depends on the context in which the F$\sharp''$ appears in the music. These five methods are:

1. $\emptyset$ 1— 4—— needs very careful double-thumbing (*RT* 85), and it is

usually necessary to leak 1 slightly, as far as can be managed without making articulation impossible or causing the note to break downwards, in the hope that this will raise the pitch of this fingering to an accurate F♯″. Sometimes the stability and articulation of the note is improved by adding 3, with or without leaking, which, surprisingly, does not cause flattening, but this can push the note upwards across the register-break to G″. If adding 3 works, however, this facilitates leaking either or both of 1 and 4 to bring the F♯″ into tune, even when played softly. Will only respond to light precise 'tee' tonguings, not to strong or slow-speaking tonguings, but can, like Method 2 below, be slurred up to from notes beneath with considerably fewer problems. This method is much less likely to be available on wider-bore modern recorders than on narrow-bore recorders (if it articulates at all on a wider-bore recorder it will probably be too flat).

2. 0 ł–– 45 –– with careful double-thumbing. Generally available by slurring up to it from a note below, e.g. from E′, as at the end of the Murrill sonata (asterisked in Ex. 5.9) or in bar 24.2 of the Berkeley sonatina. Will work from other thumbed notes, e.g. D′ (end of Murrill) or even A′ (Berkeley bar 20.5). 1 has to open sufficiently to bring the intonation up to pitch, but without the note breaking downwards. Tone liable to be coarse, and tends to degenerate if the note is held on, though adding ½7 may stabilize it. Useful for F♯″ as a short note, provided the interpretative context of the music requires the necessary slur up to it.

3. ∅ 123 4567 Thumb very tight. Tone-quality thin, but improved with 5 leaking very slightly. Much too sharp on many instruments, but at speed, after a sharpish G″ ∅ 1–3 4–6– with wide thumbing, this will do service as the F♯″ of a downward G major scale passage. Could be in tune at low breath-pressure as a very soft F♯″. In the sitting position, it can, with care, be brought into tune by shading (not covering) the recorder's end, or bell, opening. Nevertheless, according to how the surrounding notes are tuned, first by the maker and then by the player, on some recorders (especially basses and Renaissance-design instruments) this fingering, a flattening of G″, can produce a reliable F♯″ which may then become the normal fingering for use in almost all contexts. Equally, on some instruments the fingering ∅ 1–(3) 4––– in Method 1 above, a sharpening of F″, may be found to be reliable enough, having regard to the intonation of its neighbours, to serve as an all-purpose F♯″.

4. ∅ 1–3 4–6(7)X, i.e. G″ with the bell-hole covered. Clear in tone; intonation is sharpish but easily brought down by 5; responds well to different tonguing strengths. But, unless the recorder has a bell-key (*RT* 98), the player has to be sitting down to cover the bell of the recorder with the knee (the bell covered, not closed—no need to be airtight).[68] If 'stabbed

down to' during playing, tense the lips or use the chin to prevent the recorder mouthpiece knocking the front teeth. This is the best F♯'' for the final note of the Stockmeier Sonatine first movement. With a bell-key, this or Method 5, whichever is the better in tune, or a close variant, would become a 'normal' fingering for F♯'' in most contexts (see Waitzman, *Art of Playing the Recorder*, 99–100).

5. Ø 1–– 4**5**––X, i.e. F'' with the bell covered and 5 rolled back as necessary to bring the note up to pitch. An excellent, clear, accurate note, but same problems as Method 4. This, or Method 4, can be used for the sustained F♯'' in Rubbra's 'Meditazioni', provided the player is sitting down or has some other way of covering the bell.

Recorder-players may follow in the footsteps of Ganassi in discovering yet more fingerings for high notes, including the elusive F♯''', or its equivalent on C (or D) instruments. For example, the author's Albert Lockwood low-pitch tenor will not produce C♯''' by any of the Methods 1 to 5 above, but plays it accurately with the fingering Ø ––– 456–.

Exx. 8.7–10 show the six F·''s from the Schollum Sonatine with suggested 'solutions' from Methods 1 to 5 above for players without an 'all-purpose' F·'' fingering. It should be noted that, rather oddly, the music is written in 'Tr⁸', German treble consort-music style, with middle F' on the lowest space of the stave (*PB*, Exx. 63, 66, and 67).

EX. 8.7.

First movement   Fliessend (Flowing)

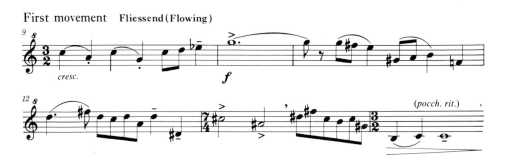

Bar 11 Method 3; after G'' Ø 1–3 4–6– with thumb wide, then squeezed for the F♯''
Bar 12 Method 2
Bar 13 Method 4; hold the recorder with the end just touching the knee for the D♯', so that the thrust to the bell-covered position is as little as possible.

EX. 8.8.

(First movement, continued)

Bar 23   Method 5; with, if available, a bell-covered fingering for the E′, e.g. Ø 1––
––––X and, unavoidably, a touch of tonguing across the resulting
register-break—in fact the slur may, alas, have to be abandoned. As this
bar is marked *f* it may not be necessary to roll back 5 to get the F♯″'s in
tune. Anticipate the bell-covering by getting into position at the G′ at the
end of the bar 22.

EX. 8.9.

Second movement **Langsam (Slow)**

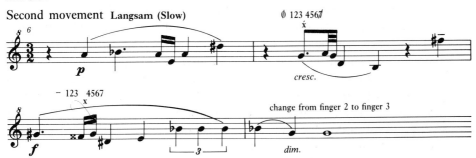

Bar 7   (end) Method 4; plenty of time to get into position during the rest. Note
the four different fingerings for G′ (as F double-sharp in bar 8) in this
passage in order to make the most of the marked dynamics.

EX. 8.10.

Third movement **Sehr rasch (Very quick)**

Bar 20   Method 4, but at this speed a potential tooth-breaker unless the bell is
covered in playing the preceding F′ (this will not adversely affect the F′).

Note that Method 1 has not been used, as it is normally only available as a
tongued F♯″ on Baroque-model recorders, though if it is available it affords
a good solution to the F♯″ in bar 13 of the first movement. Music as
thoroughgoing as this Schollum Sonatine needs the power and bite of the
modern recorder, perhaps even its touch of coarseness, to convey its full
effect.

SOME CONCLUDING CONSIDERATIONS

Throughout this book recorder-players have been encouraged to cultivate expressivity, using dynamic variety with associated intonational control, different modes and gradations of articulation, and the colouring of notes by breath (vibrato) and fingering devices, in order to achieve affective contrast between movements and sections and to shape phrases persuasively. There are limits to this process; it can be overdone.

First, recorder-players should not give their audiences the impression that they are trying to push their instrument beyond its capabilities. It might then be thought that the player would prefer to perform his sonata on a different instrument such as a flute or a violin, with its greater expressive range. There are points before extremes when dynamics and tonal variations will still sound natural on the recorder, though these extremes will vary from one instrument to another. Forced coarse *ff*s and wispy *ppp*s are not likely to give pleasure to an audience, especially if they are out of tune, and should be reserved for occasional special effects.

Secondly, in the same way as an orator does not emphasize every word or even every point, or as a writer deliberately uses insignificant turns of phrase in a sentence in order to draw attention to those words that matter most, a good musician does not lovingly model every phrase in his music. Too much attention to detail may cause the player and the audience to lose sight of the structure and significance of the sonata as a whole. Constant unremitting emphasis is very tiresome. Without sacrificing the balance of the music or losing the interest of his audience, a player may put across particular passages in an almost neutral manner. This applies, for example, to some Baroque passage-work designed only to maintain impetus across a transition or modulation. Some phrases are of secondary importance and without being peremptory should be accorded their proper place in the scheme of things. Then the main subjects may be fully characterized within the environment created for them. It is upon their presentation that the audience should feel that the greatest care has been lavished.

This book has also emphasized the importance of a player understanding the music he plays and its background, even attempting to enter into the mind of the composer who created the music he interprets. However much thought and care a player has put into analysing a sonata, and into taking into account the circumstances, attitudes, aesthetics, and performance practices of its time, his presentation of a sonata will be totally vitiated if two things are missing: accuracy and spontaneity. A minor slip may pass unnoticed by an audience enjoying a performance, and must not be allowed to distract the player; everybody makes mistakes. No amount of enthusiasm or 'authenticity', however, will make up for inaccurate intonation, reading or time errors, poor ensemble, sloppy fingering, and so on. Practice and rehearsal should bring the players to the point where, having chosen music which is not too difficult for them in the first place (and music they all like and want to play), they feel reasonably confident of giving an accurate performance.

Given that starting-point, the substance of this book implies that players with a better understanding of the music they play are likely to produce a more interesting and committed account of a sonata, and that this interest and commitment will, with good presentation, convey itself to the audience and increase their enjoyment of the music. Even if the audience remain unmoved, the players themselves may have enjoyed a more enriching experience. On the other hand, no performance should sound academic, ostentatiously demonstrating 'correct' ornamentation, or displaying (perhaps mistakenly) an absence of vibrato. However profound the players' understanding of a sonata and its background may be, they should imagine they are playing the music for the first time, identifying with an audience many of whom may be hearing it for the first time.[69] There is an art that conceals art. A bit of unpremeditated ornamentation on the part of the recorder-player, a new shade of pathos in an 'adagio', or even a slightly changed tempo, can rekindle latent fire, and the performers and the audience alike will enjoy the spontaneity and freshness of the music.

APPENDIX I

'Three Blind Mice' and Baroque Trills[1]

EX. App. 1.1.

(etc.)

The exercise below has four main purposes:

1. To establish neat, accurate, and reasonably authentic standard patterns of trills suited to many Baroque contexts as a sound basis from which greater flexibility in trill ornamentation may then be developed; and, in particular,

2. to ensure that these standard patterns place the upper auxiliary of the trill on the beat;

3. to familiarize the correct use of long appoggiaturas; and

4. to employ the necessary alternative fingerings, especially on the seventh note of eight-note turned trills.

EX. App. 1.2.

8-note turned passing trill (bars 1, 2, and 3)
Appoggiatura and turned trill (bars 4 and 5)
Cadential trill, unturned (with appoggiatura) on final cadence (bar 6)

	Key:	starting on:
PRACTISE on	C	E (as written)
	B♭	D
	F	A
	G	B
	F (upper octave)	A′
	D	F♯′
	E♭	G′
	A	C♯

Count slowly as shown, with metronome if necessary. Gradually increase speed until the count can become four minims with no loss of accuracy. Finally speed up to two beats in a bar.

Try the effect of starting on C or F′.

This exercise is based on 'Three Blind Mice', a simple and well-known tune that uses only the eight notes of a major octave scale. The advantage of using a familiar and simple tune is that it is quite easy to transpose it aurally into other major keys, and it will also work in minor keys. It is not then necessary to follow written notes—the tune with its three trill patterns can be played blind. You then concentrate entirely upon the sound produced, and in this particular exercise upon achieving a perfectly balanced trill, one with all the semiquavers of equal length and with the correct (but very slight) accentuation on the fifth semiquaver: note how the semiquavers are grouped in the exercise. Tonguing or vocalization is given as an additional aid to achieving control and balance in the trills.

Seventeenth- and eighteenth-century teaching material provides so many different examples of trill patterns that the concept of standard patterns of trills is open to challenge. The three basic patterns in the exercise are starting-points, and they are good and necessary starting-points. They incorporate common factors in Baroque practice, two in particular. The first is that ornamentation should, although it may sound extemporized, always be neat and controlled and relaxed, not messy or obtrusive. The second is that, for the shorter trills at least, the weight is upon the upper rather than the lower auxiliary note of the trill. This in itself implies that Baroque trills start with the upper auxiliary upon a beat. An appoggiatura is a discord, and the listener is held in suspense awaiting the pleasure of resolution upon the concord, a sensation particularly in evidence in a full cadence. The trill is a discord trying to resolve itself, not a concord harking back to a discord of the appoggiatura. The trill acts therefore, with the utmost Baroque *politesse*, as a transition, beguiling the hearer by extending the suspense of the appoggiatura, touching upon but just holding off its full resolution. In the case of the unturned cadential trill (last bar of the exercise), it holds off the final resolution of the chord sequence until the last possible moment, after a brief but vivid anticipatory rest. It is necessary to understand the purpose of trills to play them well (see Ch. 6). Even recorder-players often play trills the modern way ('upside-down'), starting too soon and landing heavily with the lower auxiliary on the beat; Baroque delicacy and pithiness are then lost. Perhaps the three blind mice will help players to remedy this common fault.

The exercise proposes three standard trill patterns. The first one to be learnt to perfection (in all keys) is the eight-note turned passing trill. Unturned passing trills—which in the first bar of the exercise might be represented by eight semiquavers E D E D E D E D—occur, but probably less frequently. In contexts of *rising* minims, passing trills would generally be turned, especially where the trilled minim is a leading-note (e.g. B trill to C). Passing trills are normally short, and eight notes is perhaps the average length. Moreover, the same eight semiquavers, usually unslurred, with the turn, were a standard Renaissance formula at the end of the *groppo* (Ex. 6.6, bar 73), and would have been assimilated into Baroque ornamentation as an inherited pattern. Furthermore, it is easier both visually and aurally to perceive the balance of an eight-note turned trill than a shorter or longer one. A six-note turned trill may, for the purpose of ensuring its accuracy, especially in starting with the upper note on the beat, be taught as two triplets, slurred as six: this gives a neat twist to the accentuation but is misleading, as the balance should be Dee–er–ee–er–or–er.

Bar 3 of the exercise reaches the highest note of the melody and consolidates the turned passing-trill pattern given in bars 1 and 2. Conveniently, the tune now repeats itself, so the feel and balance of a long appoggiatura followed by a turned trill, resolving upwards, can be conveyed by tying the minim C on to the first semiquaver C of the same trill. The only difference, but a most important one, is that the 'tonguing' changes from 'Dee– Dee–er–' etc. to 'Dee– Ee–er–' etc. This pattern is consolidated by its repetition in bar 5.

It is in the unturned cadential trill that the fault of starting the trill too soon, and on the lower auxiliary, is most common. If the first semiquaver D in bar 6 falls on the second beat, the weight of the trill becomes a concord. If one overcompensates by holding back the first finger-stroke on to the D too late, again it will threaten to fall into a concordant position (i.e. that of the third semiquaver of the pattern). It has to be just right. To assist in achieving exactness, the exercise models the final cadential trill as closely as possible upon the previous eight-note turned trills. In effect it is exactly the same as the turned trill until the sixth semiquaver when, like the mice, it has its tail cut off. At the sixth semiquaver the trill movement suddenly stops and that semiquaver is held on, becoming a quaver, unstressed but given importance by being very slightly held, as if the note were being pinned to the paper. This small piece of rubato just leaves time for the tiny articulatory rest and for a crisp, very short, eleventh-hour demisemiquaver, almost stuttering on to the final relaxed tonic minim. Note that the demisemiquaver happens at such speed that it is not possible to use 'd' tonguing. Only 't' or 'k', the fastest-speaking articulations, can be used. If the final demisemiquaver in cadential trills is made too long, the whole piece of music becomes limp; it loses its Baroque tautness and precision.

The type of cadential trill here recommended as a starting-point may be called a 'three-stroke' trill because the second finger strikes D three times, the last time held down. Note that it strikes on the 'er' of the vocalization, off the beats. This can be practised away from the recorder at any time which might otherwise be wasted by making the back-and-forth tongue movements in the mouth silently (for 'ee' the tongue is further forward than 'er') and synchronizing a finger-movement with the three 'er's of the pattern. Thus: for 'Dee—Ee' hold the first finger firmly down (e.g. on a table). Then, exactly as the tongue goes back for 'er' put the second finger down; lift it for 'ee' (on a subsidiary beat), down for 'er', up for 'Ee' (the 'and' beat) and finally down for 'err'. A little press with the held-down first finger on the 'Ee' at the beginning of the trill will help in getting this movement exactly right. This three-stroke cadential trill pattern is the shortest that constitutes a trill, for with only two strokes the ornament would be a shake or half-trill. In fast music, however, a shake may be substituted for a trill after an appoggiatura. Many trills are of course longer than three strokes, where the music allows the time, or the appoggiatura is shorter. As some Baroque tables of ornaments show, such trills, though beginning with the upper auxiliary dominating, may, rather than prolong the implied discord, change their balance so that they end with the lower auxiliary dominating. This happens by insinuating a triplet into the course of the trill. Longer trills may not be even, for several Baroque authorities talk of trills getting faster. But, initially, total mastery must be gained of the three-stroke regular trill before experimenting with the many variations that are called for in different musical contexts. To use this three-stroke pattern in all contexts would be committing the sin of inflexibility, which is almost as venal as the sin of inaccuracy or sloppiness; almost, but not quite.

If the mice become tiresome, there is excellent trill practice to be found in Handel's recorder sonatas. Try the first section of the last movement of the C major sonata. This is in 3/8, which often suggests a one-in-a-bar beat (as in a passepied), but here needs to be counted in a fast three to give the long semiquaver passages in the bass enough time to breathe. It is in effect a lively minuet, fast enough for eight-note turned trills (eight demisemiquavers) to be a valid interpretation, although regular twelve-note turned trills are better—but faster and more difficult to keep under control. The notes of the trills are the same as in the 'Three Blind Mice' exercise, complete with a fast cadential trill after a hemiola (then use three or two strokes for the trill). There is great opportunity for turned passing trills in rising minim contexts in the second movement of the D minor sonata, although at hornpipe-speed there may be time for only six-note, rather than eight-note, turned trills. Some of them involve fingering problems.

The turned passing trill in bar 2 of the 'Three Blind Mice' exercise uses E as the seventh note with an F′ on either side. Trills, and especially turns, are the natural habitat of alternative fingerings. This in fact is the only one in the exercise as written. Most recorder-players will automatically in this context use 0 –23 for E rather than 0 1––. The latter requires the movement of two fingers in opposite directions, which is much less easy to accomplish neatly than moving one finger (3) only; moreover, the alternative leaves the normal F′ fingering in place. When the exercise is played in other keys all sorts of fingering problems arise. The over-riding purpose of the exercise, however, is to achieve accurate basic trill patterns, irrespective of key. It is therefore wise to pause at this point while you master 'Three Blind Mice' trilled in C major, and to leave the fascinating complexities of turned-trill fingerings in more distant keys for later study. So get out your metronome and set it to eight steady beats to the bar (♩ = 92). Be sure the final bar is accurate, and go straight back to the beginning without *rall.*, or pause. Then gradually speed up the count, maintaining absolute accuracy and balance in the trills. You are now taking the first steps to becoming trill-perfect.

SOME TRILL FINGERINGS

'Three Blind Mice' (hereafter TBM) bar 2 contains the most common alternative fingering, E 0 –23 ––––, here used for the F′–E turn. It illustrates three maxims applying to alternative fingerings. The first is that, in using alternatives to simplify fingering and slurring in fast music (all trills are fast, though not uniformly so), aim at a one- or two-finger movement to replace the more complex movement involved in normal fingerings. The second is to use a normal fingering—F′ in this case—as the starting-point before employing alternatives. This is especially true when, as here, the context is from a normal note to an alternative-fingered note and then back to the normal note. The fingering of the normal note should not as a rule have to be disturbed when going on to the alternative. The third is to revert to the normal fingering for a held note, here for the E minim after the trill. This, however, may not be necessary if the alternative is as good in quality and intonation as the normal fingering, which is the case with E on most recorders, or if the quality and intonation of the alternative is better suited to the particular musical context. Many alternatives are too poor for a held note, but they may be perfectly acceptable for the note of a turn or trill, which passes by so quickly that its weakness is not perceived.

The TBM exercise is set out in C major, but should then, as suggested, be played in other keys, starting with B♭ major as this key introduces, at the third trill, the important closed G′ alternative. It starts with a D–C passing trill with a B♭ turn; that poses no problems, but the second trill and turn, F′–E♭–D, does. It occurs frequently and must be mastered. Start with normal F′. Then add fingers until the F′ is flattened a tone to E♭. 0 –23 4–6– may be the solution, but instruments vary. Taking off 3 will bring you almost back to F′, near enough for you to trill F′–E♭ with that one finger. Avoid multi-finger trills if possible, as they are less precise. The turn on D may be achieved with 0 –23 45––, involving a quite simple movement of 5 and 6. This is a poor quality, sharpish D, but it is useful slurred at speed, with a slight drop in breath-pressure, in this type of context. So for the minim D of bar 2 after the trill you must revert to normal fingering. Note that during all this the F′ fingering stays down, providing a firm foundation for the other finger-movements.

TBM bars 3, 4, and 5 played in B♭ major slur B♭′–A′–G′. Start with normal B♭′, and trill to A′ with the little finger, covering both half-holes. Now comes the problem. We are in the upper register and normal G′ is on the other side of the register-break, being the highest note of the lower register. To use it would cause those 'clicks' of crossing register-breaks which are the recorder-player's chief enemy. You must therefore use the closed G' fingering—all fingers down, thumb off. This entails adding 5 and moving the thumb off from its 'pinched' position, and this movement itself can cause a slight click if not perfectly synchronized. But in fact the little-finger alternative A' fingering Ø 123 4–67 works without the thumb. The secret therefore is to remove the thumb during the A' on the way down to G' and to put it back during the A' on the way back up to B♭'. This needs practising slowly at first.

TBM in lower octave F has to be managed with normal fingerings on its first two trills. The third trill needs alternative E, and the D for the turn can usually be found by adding two fingers, i.e. 0 –23 45—, as given above, with a drop in breath-pressure.

TBM in G, beginning on B, again has to be started with normal fingerings. It helps to hold 5 down firmly for the B–A–G turned trill in bar 1. The E turn after the F♯' of the third trill responds to the device of 'adding fingers below', such as – 123 4–6–.

The upper octave F' TBM requires the closed G' for the A'–G' trill in the first bar. Whether one starts on little-finger alternative A' depends on how good that note is on your instrument in intonation (?too sharp), tone, and tonguability. It is certainly an advantage in the appoggiatura situation of bar 6 to get straight on to it, thumbed of course for better quality. Once the trill movement has started, leave the thumb off. Now comes the rub. To get to the F' turn you *must* cross the register-break. This means that the fifth semiquaver, G', must be normal fingering. It may help in this difficult movement to press 2 down and almost throw the other fingers in a bunch off the recorder. The same problem occurs with an F♯' turn after an A'–G' trill, as in D major. The good management of the closed and open G' in trills and slurs is fundamental to recorder technique.

The C'–B♭'–A' turned trill calls for the little-finger alternative A' (thumbed). It is a matter of personal preference whether to trill C'–B♭' with both 4 and 6, or with 4 alone with 6 staying down. The same is true in the lower octave: should one trill with 467 together (all in the right hand), or with 4 only with 67 down?

The turn of the high F''–E'–D' trill involves the crossing of the register-break between E' and D', which with normal fingering is, with careful breath-control, manageable on the way down, but decidedly clickish on the way back up. Some recorders, with careful thumbing, will, however, slur back up from D' to E', without crossing the register-break, by lifting 2. The other, more usual, way is to add fingers on to normal E' in its own register, maybe with 67 in the right hand and shading with half 3 in the left, a little tricky.

The vital fingerings for TBM in D major are closed G' (see above), F♯' as 0 ——— ———— (a Renaissance favourite) in the F♯'–E trill after a normal F♯' start, and Ø 12– 45—— for the B' turn after C♯'. A slight drop in breath-pressure over this turn may help, as it does with many other alternative-fingered turns.

The first trill in the E♭ version, starting on G', calls for a quick move from the

0 –23 4–6– E♭ turn to normal E♭. Next we encounter the problem of trills with A♭′ (*RT* 79). In this context the solution may be to play a slightly sharp B♭′ by half-holing 6 (finger bent position) and then use the thumbed A♭′ trilling with 5. 7 may then account for the G′ turn. The turned trill E♭′–D′–C′ is difficult because of the register-break at E♭′. Start with normal E♭′. For the E♭′–D′ trill you will have to shade with ½3 and trill with 7, but you may want at the sixth semiquaver to go on to normal D′ in readiness for the C′ turn. This method becomes well-nigh impossible if you substitute D♭′ for D′ by trilling with 3 and 7 together (or with 7 only, or even 2) because of the click on the slur down from E♭′ to D♭′ when the normal fingering comes in. So stay on the trill-fingering ∅ 12ˣ3 4567 right up to the C′ at the turn.

The first trill in TBM in A major is a problem. Normal fingering? or trill sharp with 3 on 0 123ˣ –56–? The third trill loses its terrors if you are able to stay in the thumbed register and trill A′–G♯′ with the little finger—a useful alternative on many instruments, though rather sharp. The F♯′ turn may then work (with gratifying simplicity) with 6 (see also Ex. 8.6). For trill problems in E major, see pp. 141–2.

TBM in minor keys will show up the few remaining trill-fingerings of importance. C minor requires at the outset the 'one-and-a-half-below' fingering for D after E♭. This is 0 1–3 45ˣ6– with 5 trilling, but reverting to normal D at the sixth semiquaver before the C turn. E minor requires the thumbed G′ ∅ 123 4567 for the turn in the second trill after B′–A′. This pinched fingering with a pinched sound is of importance in G′ slurs with the upper octave where virtuosity matters more than an open tone. The C♯′ turn after the E′–D♯′ trill in this key is best taken as ∅ 123 4567. In B minor the third trill requires ∅ 123 –56– for A♯′, and the thumbed G♯′ (add 4) for the turn. F minor starts on A♭′ with normal fingering – –23 456–. Add 1 and 7 for the G′ trill (closed G′) and trill with these together, or with 7 alone, or perhaps with 4. Throw all the fingers except 2 off at the sixth semiquaver for open G′ and the F′ turn.

The innocent-looking challenge at the end of the TBM exercise ('Try the effect of starting on C or F″') will take you into A♭ major (four flats) and D♭ major (five flats). These remote keys are the breeding-ground of alternative fingerings to enable you to manage turned trills smoothly. They do not, however, reveal principles not already covered here. Though you may therefore run yet further with the three blind mice, they may take you into blind alleys of recorder technique— better to concentrate on other things until a particular trill problem arises in preparing a piece of music. If you can maintain perfect accuracy and poise at a reasonable speed in the three basic trill patterns in the TBM exercise in the eight major keys listed in the exercise and the four minor keys mentioned above, you will have the technique to face up with confidence and equanimity to the teachings of Baroque writers on ornamentation and their scholarly interpreters such as Mather, Donington, and Neumann. But you still have a long way to go!

APPENDIX II

Suggestions for Starting to Explore the Recorder-Sonata Repertoire

Where, for the convenience of readers, a particular edition of a sonata is mentioned in this list, and elsewhere in this book, this is not intended to imply that it is necessarily the best edition. Where a sonata is available in more than one publication, one's personal choice will depend, among other considerations, on how the music is edited (particularly in the realization of a figured bass), clarity of printing, lay-out for playing, cost, and availability. Some of these sonatas are discussed in the book; see the Index for references.

EARLY SEVENTEENTH-CENTURY ITALIAN SONATAS

Riccio, Canzona 'A un Flautin' (see Ex. 3.1 and Ch. 8) for descant or treble (London Pro Musica, or Zen-On).

Tomaso Cecchino, 3 Sonatas, D, Tr or T (Schott OFB 159). The change to triple time should be to the slower *sesquialtera*, i.e. the bar-length stays at the same pulse.

Easy Music of Monteverdi's Time, vol. 2 (Dolce Edition) contains similar music from this period for descant and continuo.

LATE SEVENTEENTH-CENTURY ENGLISH SONATAS

Get into the feel of the period with George Bingham's easy suites (Schott). Then try . . .

Daniel Purcell, Sonata in F (in Schott OFB 78). Remember that 'largo' is not slow, and 'allegro' is moderate.

Godfrey Finger, two impressive sonatas in Schott OFB 27, and, a little more difficult, the fine Sonata in C minor Op. 3 No. 2 (Nova). Walter Bergmann transposed another of Finger's treble-recorder sonatas for descant (Schott OFB 1022).

HANDEL

The G minor sonata (Ex. 2.1) is probably easiest, at least for the recorder player.

Then try the F major (No. 4 in the Faber edition—see Ex. 1.3) and B flat (Faber No. 5). The only technically difficult Handel sonata movement is the Furioso of the D minor sonata (Ex. 5.3). The problems in these sonatas are interpretational, especially where and how much to ornament.

TELEMANN

The least difficult of the Telemann sonatas is the F major from *Der getreue Musikmeister* (Schott, etc.); the high C''' in the last movement can be avoided. Even without it, this sonata overflows with high spirits.

LŒILLET

Of J.-B. Lœillet's forty-eight sonatas, start at the beginning with Op. 1 No. 1 in A minor, and then try Op. 1 No. 2 in D minor (see Ex. 8.3) and No. 3 in G major (all in Bärenreiter HM 43). Go on to Op. 3 No. 3 in G minor (Ex. 1.2), and then, more difficult, No. 5 in C minor, with its beautiful third-movement Rondo (Op. 3 sonatas available from Musica Rara, ed. Block, or Schott).

OTHER NORTH EUROPEAN LATE BAROQUE SONATAS

Thornowitz, Sonata da Camera in F, and in G (Schott Eds. 10083 and 10814).

Bononcini, *Divertimenti da Camera*: Sonata IV in G minor (with A minor in Schott OFB 10).

Schickhardt, Sonata in C, Op. 23 No. 2 (Schott OFB 91). Sounds harder than it is.

Pepusch, Sonata VI in F, the last of six (?oboe) sonatas in two volumes (Noetzel N3149) for descant recorder. Unusual and easy.

de Fesch, Sonata in B flat (Universal UE 12602, arr. Staeps).

ITALIAN BAROQUE SONATAS

Marcello, Op. 2 Nos. 1 and 12, both in F—but some difficulties in the final 'Ciaccona' (No. 1 Hargail, No. 12 in Schott OFB 1000).

Martino Bitti, Sonata in A minor (with C minor sonata in Bärenreiter HM 191).

Vivaldi, Sonata in F, RV 52 (Schott OFB 115). Unusually easy Vivaldi. Its D minor companion (OFB 116) is not difficult either, despite some rhythmic games in the last movement.

FRENCH BAROQUE SONATAS

The Lavigne sonatas discussed in Ch. 4 make an excellent introduction to French

Baroque style, as does a Sonate by the English emigré Henry Eccles (Schott OFB 132). Chédeville l'Aîné's four 'Sonatilles Galantes' (Noetzel) provide rather similar fare. Then, progressing greatly, let Freda Dinn (*Early Music for Recorders*, 54–8) take you through four movements of De Caix d'Hervelois's Suite in G for descant and keyboard (Schott Ed. 10016).

LATER EIGHTEENTH CENTURY

James Hook, two sonatas for descant, two sonatinas for treble (Schott)—easy and jolly. The original was for keyboard with violin or flute accompaniment.

TWENTIETH CENTURY

Many modern sonatas were written for virtuosi, though there are some in a more *Hausmusik* style, e.g. those by Bender and Zipp, and descant sonatinas by Roehr and Migot (all Schott). Staeps's 'Sonate im alten Stil' (Doblinger) ranges only over (descant) C to E'. Attractive non-sonata pieces include, for treble recorder, Edmund Rubbra's 'First Study Pieces' (Lengnick), Robin Milford's 'Three Airs' (Oxford), Antony Hopkins's 'Four Dances', and John Graves's Divertimento (both Schott), and, for descant recorder, suites by Christopher Steel (Novello), Benjamin Burrows, and Antony Hopkins (both Schott), and the Intrada and Waltz from John Turner's 'Four Diversions' (Forsyth).

NOTES

Notes to Chapter 1

1. Newman, chs. 2 and 3. On p. 8 he defines Baroque era as roughly 1600 to 1750, though 1740 or even 1730 may be regarded as nearer the point where Baroque style was giving way to the new *galant* style. Baroque music is normally characterized by the presence of a figured bass. This implies a mode of thought about the structure of the music in harmonic terms which sets it apart both from earlier Renaissance polyphony and from mid- and late 18th-c. music, with its slower harmonic rhythms (i.e. rate of change of chords) and its greater emphasis on tuneful melody and the expression of pleasurable sentiments.

2. This is generally the case, but some sonatas, easy ones in particular, were played by gentlemen amateurs for their private enjoyment (see Buonamente's letter of 1627 to Duke Cesare Gonzaga, Newman 37—the Duke was excused ornamentation). Another possible exception is guitar music. A guitar tutor published in Paris in 1626 by Luis de Briceño claims that 'two thousand people now entertain themselves and express their thoughts and troubles through the guitar'; but even in this self-communing situation it is ideas and emotions that are expressed, not just the music itself.

3. Georg Muffat, 1701 (see Newman, 33–4). On the status of the musician as an entertainer, see Lorenzo Bianconi, *Music in the Seventeenth Century* (Cambridge: Cambridge University Press 1987): 'the [professional] musician was essentially an artisan-supplier of highly qualified services' (p. 88). Professional recorder-players are rather a modern phenomenon. Most recorder-players who performed and taught professionally in earlier periods did not practise the recorder exclusively. For them, the recorder was a second instrument after the oboe or violin. Some acquired a high level of technique, but not at the level associated with Baroque violin-playing, or with 20th-c. avant-garde recorder technique. It may be 'unauthentic' to use, as is sometimes suggested in this book, elements of modern technique in playing Baroque recorder sonatas, such as certain non-historic tonguings or 'soft' fingerings, but their use is surely justified if a player can thereby more effectively convey the significance and spirit of the music, and achieve the Baroque player's objective of moving and entertaining an audience.

4. One needs to except 'sonatas' used as short introductory or incidental pieces within larger vocal works (by Purcell, for example), and also short keyboard sonatas of the Domenico Scarlatti type.

5. Extent in purely instrumental music is achieved in various ways. For example, in the early 17th c., fancies, such as those of Gibbons, increased in length, with sections of different speeds and moods, becoming more like sonatas. Instrumental dances were grouped into thematically coherent suites (e.g. those of Peuerl, 1611).

6. From Italian 'sonare'; see Newman, 17–18. During the Baroque period the title 'Sonata' gradually evolved from meaning any instrumental composition to one for a small

number of instruments, and then to its general early 18th-c. use as a piece for one instrument with thorough-bass continuo, or for a solo instrument, especially keyboard (see Newman, ch. 5).

7. e.g. J.-B. Lœillet.

8. 'Solos' is the title normally used in England, although the performance of a sonata in the later Baroque period usually called for three players (see Newman, 21, 19, and 65).

9. e.g. Quantz, 90, where he discusses phrasing.

10. A similar view of Quantz's relevance to earlier Baroque music is expressed by Anthony Newman in his *Bach and the Baroque: A Performing Guide to Baroque Music with Special Emphasis on the Music of J. S. Bach* (New York: Pendragon Press, 1985), 7. (There are some later references to this book: its author should not be confused with William S. Newman, the writer of *The Sonata in the Baroque Era*.) Quantz, then almost 30, admired Handel's 'magnificent' music when he heard the opera *Admeto* in London in 1727, and he regarded J. S. Bach's organ-playing as the closest to perfection (Quantz, 339).

11. e.g. J.-P. Freillon-Poncein, *La Véritable Manière d'apprendre à jouer en perfection du Hautbois, de la Flûte et du Flageolet* (1700), and Jacques Hotteterre le Romain, *Principles of the Flute, Recorder & Oboe* (1707), tr. and ed. David Lasocki (London: Barrie and Jenkins, 1968).

12. See ch. 11, para. 10 (p. 122): 'Good execution must be first of all true and distinct . . . You must try to make each sound as beautiful as possible . . . You must avoid slurring notes that ought to be articulated, and articulating those that ought to be slurred. The notes must not seem stuck together. The tonguing on wind instruments . . . must always be used in conformity with the aims of the composer . . . ; this puts life into the notes . . . the tongue [must make] proper movements suitable to the piece to be performed. Musical ideas that belong together must not be separated; on the other hand, you must separate those ideas in which one musical thought ends and a new idea begins, even if there is no rest or caesura.'

13. For example, Donington quotes from Sir Thomas More's *Utopia* (1516), where music is to 'move, stirre, pearce and enflame the hearers myndes' (Donington, *Interp.* 111).

14. Quoted in Donington, *Baroque*, 2. Readers of this book are also urged to read the sections on the affections in *New Grove*, esp. para. 4 of the entry 'Rhetoric and Music', by George Buelow. See also Quantz, Introduction, p. xli.

15. Palpably so in Dryden's poem 'Alexander's Feast or the Power of Music', set by Handel.

16. Charpentier's list from his *Règles de composition* (1692) is given in Anthony, 189. The passage from J. Mattheson, *Das neu-eröffnete Orchestre* (1713), is reprinted in full (in Hamburg German) at the backs of the Noetzel edition (four vols., N3572–5) of Telemann's *Fantaisies pour le Clavessin, 3 Douzaines* arranged for treble and tenor recorders; a summary (in English) appears on pp. 401–2 of George J. Buelow and Hans-Joachim Marx, *New Mattheson Studies* (Cambridge: Cambridge University Press, 1983). Rameau's two paragraphs on the affective suitabilities of different keys are in his *Traité de l'harmonie* (1722). Heinichen (1728) opposed the notion of key/affect relationships. See also Quantz, 164.

17. Telemann, *Sonate metodiche* (1728) in E minor, C minor, and A minor. See *PB* Ex. 12 for advice on how to undulate.

18. Explained more fully, with an example, in Quantz, 254–9.

19. An interesting commentary on the doctrine of affections and figures of Baroque musical

language is in Manfred Bukofzer's *Music in the Baroque Era* (New York: W. W. Norton, 1947), 388–90. This, and a similar passage in Claude Palisca's *Baroque Music* (Englewood Cliffs, NJ: Prentice-Hall, 1968), 3–4, is quoted by David Lasocki in 'Quantz and the Passions: Theory and Practice', *EM* 6 (1978), 556–67. This article is of special interest to recorder-players as it applies in detail Quantz's descriptions of affects to his trio sonata for recorder, flute, and continuo. Gregory Butler, 'The Projection of Affect in Baroque Dance Music', *EM* 12 (1984), 201–7, quotes extensively from Thomas Mace's *Musick's Monument* (1676). Mace's 'humour' is the equivalent of 'passion' or 'affect'.

20. C. P. E. Bach, *Essay on the True Art of Playing Keyboard Instruments* (III, 13), quoted in Donington, *Interp.* 113–14. The series of quotations from More to Mozart (ibid. 111–16) admirably illustrates the development of the 'theory of affects'.

21. *Der vollkommene Capellmeister* (1739), 146, quoted by Buelow in *New Mattheson Studies*, 400. This apparently extreme statement needs to be taken at its face value in Baroque terms. As Cuthbert Girdlestone pointed out in his book on *Jean-Philippe Rameau* (London, 1957; repr. New York: Dover, 1969), 527–33, theorists in the 18th c. universally regarded words, and visual forms and symbols such as dance, as the prime means of artistic and spiritual communication, which music then greatly supported and enhanced. Deprived of this partnership with words, purely instrumental music could only strive, against odds, to depict 'the temper, disposition or frame of mind, passions and mental reactions characteristic of man' (p. 530), i.e. affects. Players of Baroque sonatas who failed to communicate affects, however showy their performance might otherwise be, risked accusation by the cognoscenti of producing 'nothing but vain noise' (D'Alembert, cited by Girdlestone, 533).

22. For the relationship, in terms of affect, between operatic and instrumental music, see le Huray, 33–4.

23. David Lasocki and Eva Legêne, in the first of three articles on 'Learning to Ornament Handel's Sonatas Through the Composer's Ears', *AR* 30 (1989), 9–14, 102–6, and 137–41 at 10–11, have shown that in a cantata aria Handel composed in 1707–8 which is very similar to this sonata movement both in melody and bass, the key affect words include 'weeping' and 'dejection'. They quote the whole aria with its words, which suggest not only the affect of the movement but also nuances of phrasing and style of ornamentation.

24. The rhetorical figure *catabasis*.

25. 'embellishments must never contradict the prevailing sentiments of the principal melody' (Quantz, 125).

26. Jean-Marie Leclair, in his preface to the *Quatrième livre de sonates* (1738), writes: 'Tous ceux qui voudront parvenir à exécuter cet ouvrage dans le goût de l'Auteur doivent s'attacher à trouver le caractère de chaque pièce.' ('All those who wish to succeed in playing this work in the taste of the composer should apply themselves to finding the character of each piece.')

27. For example, the *New Grove* article on 'Rhetoric and Music' says that Mersenne in his *Harmonie universelle* (1636–7) 'emphasized that musicians were orators who must compose melodies as if they were orations, including all of the sections, divisions and periods appropriate to an oration'.

28. Cf. Leon Battista Alberti, *Della pittura* (1436), referred to on pp. 11–12 of Angelica Goodden's *Actio and Persuasion* (Oxford: Oxford University Press, 1986). Girdlestone

quotes Rameau's statements that music must 'conform to the general rules of poetry and painting' in imitating and depicting 'objects which would have roused real passions in us' (*Rameau*, 528).

29. J. Mattheson, *Der vollkommene Capellmeister*, pt. 2, ch. 14. Mattheson tells us most about how the six parts of a speech in rhetoric may apply to a sonata movement. These parts are: (1) *Exordium*, in which the purposes and intentions of the movement, especially its affect, are set out to prepare the listener and arouse his attention; (2) *Narration* (or exposition); (3) and (4) *Proposition* and *Confirmation*, balancing and corroborating the theme, taking us to the end of the first section of the movement (which may be repeated for emphasis); (5) *Argument*, the longest section, in which the most rhetorical figures and devices are likely to be employed, where statements from the first section are developed and subjected to scrutiny by harmonic and melodic rearrangements, perhaps challenged by a modulation or a counter-subject; and (6) *Peroration*, where the nature of the opening statement is reaffirmed, usually in the original key.

30. J. S. Bach was praised by Abraham Birnbaum, instructor for rhetoric at Leipzig University: 'He knows the parts and the advantages which the elaboration of a musical piece has in common with the art of rhetoric' (quoted by August Wenzinger in 'Expression and its Interpretation in Baroque Music', *AR* 11 (1970), 8–15 at 9–10).

31. David Coomber, 'Rhetoric and Affect in Baroque Music', *The Recorder* (Melbourne), No. 3 (Nov. 1985), 23–7, shows the rhetorical forms employed in the first movement of Telemann's D minor recorder sonata. See also le Huray, 22.

32. Rameau, when discussing the grouping of pairs of notes in phrases, makes comparisons both with poetry and with symmetry in architecture; see *Nouvelles réflexions de M. Rameau sur sa demonstration du principe de l'harmonie* (1752), ed. Erwin Jacobi, in *Jean-Philippe Rameau: Complete Theoretical Writings*, v (Rome, 1969), 129.

33. Theron McClure, 'Making the Music Speak: Silences of Articulation', *AR* 29 (1988), 53–5. concludes: 'The principle I used in making these "silences" was to gather the notes into "beats" that produce groups of "mini-phrases", adding rhythmic energy to the musical expression. Practicing such varied groupings in a piece can help us discover new meaning that we might otherwise have missed. By analyzing the printed text of our music in this way, we are taking a rhetorical approach that helps us conceptualize it as words, phrases, and sentences. Then our delivery of a sonata becomes like a delivery of an oration, as we use the *silences d'articulation* along with other enunciative devices such as beautiful tone, dynamics, varied articulation, and ornaments, to move and persuade our audiences.' See also Hermann Keller, *Phrasing and Articulation* (London: Barrie and Rockliff, 1965), especially ch. 6, 'The Construction of Groups through Articulation'.

34. Quantz goes on, rather reassuringly, to say that 'Good natural ability is for many a detriment rather than an advantage.' 'Too great a dependence upon talent is a great obstacle to industry and subsequent reflection' (p. 19).

35. Rhetorically, the two introductory bars form the *exordium* (see n. 29 above)—'A good beginning is half the job' (Mattheson). Though the melody is the same as the first line of the quatrain, it should be played in a different manner, as if stage-curtains were being drawn back to reveal the story-teller who then embarks upon the *narratio*. le Huray (ch. 8) describes how Momigny, a contemporary of Mozart, analyses the first movement of the D minor String Quartet K. 421 by considering it as an operatic aria.

36. Quantz (p. 231) says that Affettuoso movements 'must be played seriously'. It seems that they were not usually as ornamented as Adagios—none of the ornamented slow

movements in Telemann's *Sonate metodiche* are called Affettuoso. The simple poignancy of this movement would be spoilt by much ornamentation—certainly no more than is marked by the composer (crosses) or the editor (crosses in brackets). The 'et Grave' implies a slow 'affettuoso'; but it should be fast enough to lilt in siciliana rhythm (described by one writer as 'a kind of slow pastoral gigue'; see *New Grove*) with the dotted figure almost double-dotted. A delicate touch of tonguing within the slurs sounds attractive.

37. Donington, *Interp.* 392–404, gives a résumé of dance styles and speeds, noting how speeds changed with time (e.g. sarabande) and country (e.g. courante). See also Quantz, 289–92. For a detailed study of this aspect of performance, relating dance to poetry and rhetoric, see Betty Bang Mather, *Dance Rhythms of the French Baroque* (Bloomington: Indiana University Press, 1987).

38. This 'apotheosis of the dance' may be traced in the varied treatment of *basse danse* themes such as 'La Spagna', in keyboard variations on dance melodies or grounds (e.g. 'La Follia'), in complex pavans (e.g. Dowland's 'Lachrimae'), and in the development of the dance suite from dances linked by key and/or melody as entertainment during banquets (e.g. Schein) to the seriousness of a Corelli *sonata da camera* or a Bach partita. Even the grave sarabandes of Bach's cello suites need to be played with the up-beat lift of the original dance.

39. See Newman, 24–5, quoting Sébastien de Brossard's dictionary of *c.*1710.

40. Leclair, in the *Avertissement* to his Fourth Book of Sonatas (1738), says it is 'ridiculous' to change the tempo of two rondos made for each other, playing the major faster then the minor (ed. Ruf, Schott). On the other hand, C. P. E. Bach, in his *Versuch* of 1753, translated and edited by W. J. Mitchell as *Essay on the True Art of Playing Keyboard Instruments* (1753) (London: Cassell, 1949), says that 'Passages in a piece in the major mode which are repeated in the minor may be broadened somewhat on their repetition in order to heighten the affect' (p. 161).

41. Mattheson: 'If the melody of a minuet is only sixteen measures [bars] long (for it cannot be shorter), then it will have at least some commas, a semicolon, a few colons and a few periods [full stops] in its make-up. Many a person would scarcely think that; yet it is true' (*Der vollkommene Capellmeister*, tr. Harriss, 451–2). Mattheson then gives an example, quoted as 'curious' in M. Mathis Lussy's 19th-c. book on *Musical Expression* (London: Novello, n.d.).

42. The common analogy with painting was used by Roger North (1728; North, 116 and 118–19): he saw musical composition as a 'parallel state' with painting, as well as by Quantz (pp. 124 and 172–3), Leopold Mozart (1756), and Alessandro Scarlatti, who used the word 'chiaroscuro' in a letter about his opera *Il gran Tamerlano* (1706); see Wenzinger, 'Expression'. Sylvestro Ganassi (*Fontegara*, 1535) compared the recorder-player to 'a gifted painter'.

43. Angelica Goodden, in *Actio and Persuasion*, 113, quoting from an article on 'Courante' in Pancoucke's *Encyclopédie methodique* (1782–93); he goes on to say that failure to convey some affection of the soul is 'an abuse of the art'.

44. Mattheson, *Der vollkommene Capellmeister*, tr. Harriss, 451–66.

45. 'Learning to Ornament'. The Handel reference is to a cantata aria 'Bella gloria in campo armato', and the ornamentation is upon the word 'guerra' (war). The subject of rhythmic symbolism is dealt with in depth in George Houle's book *Meter in Music 1600– 1800: Performance, Perception and Notation* (Bloomington: Indiana University Press, 1987).

46. Donington, in his *String Playing in Baroque Music* (London: Faber, 1977), says of this music: 'a touch of wildness in our fiddling does not come amiss' (p. 73).
47. e.g. see Donington, *Interp.* 104–5 (Le Cerf de la Viéville), and Quantz, 322–6.
48. Couperin's trio sonata 'Le Parnasse, ou L'Apothéose de Corelli' (1725).
49. For Scheibe's description of a sonata (1745) see Newman, 27–8.
50. See Donington, *Interp.* 386–419, and *Baroque*, 11–19. There is also a full discussion of Baroque tempo indications and their relationship to strong/weak Baroque metre in Anthony Newman, *Bach and the Baroque*.
51. The use of sequences, recurrences, and echoes in Baroque composition is well described by Arthur Hutchings in *The Baroque Concerto* (London: Faber, 1961), 39–44.
52. Edgar Hunt's edition of this sonata phrases the last bar of this passage as follows (my added commas are placed on the assumption of a continuation of the up-beat phrasing of the previous bars):

Hunt's realization of the bass differs considerably from that of the Lasocki–Bergmann edition. He gives activity to the keyboard right hand where Handel's bass— ♪|♩ ₇♪♩ ₇♪|♩ etc. throughout this whole passage—has rests, i.e. on the second and fourth beats of each bar. Bergmann's realization is in simple chords, retaining the series of rests. This helps to bring out each group of four low notes in the soloist's dialogue response figure. In the interpretation suggested in Ex. 1.3 the 'character' that acts as underdog in bars 20–2 decides to assert himself in bar 23 by breaking the sequence and striking a high D'. Yet another approach to bar 23 is to phrase the semiquaver groups on the four beats of this bar (retaining Hunt's slurs), thus:

If this change to a down-beat four-crotchet rhythm is adopted at bar 23—though it is not suggested from the layout of the bass line—it is logical to phrase the parallel passage in the first section of this movement, i.e. the first half of bar 10, in down-beat pairs of semiquavers, rather than in two groups across the beat, that is to say as in example (*a*) rather than in example (*b*):

All possibilities should be tried, slowly and with pauses at potential phrase-points, with the continuo part (for a phrasing dilemma can often be resolved by reference to the underlying harmonic sequence). The preferred interpretation should then be played with resolution, as if none other had existed.

53. For example, an unexpected key change may occur near the end of an 'allegro', as in several sonatas by Veracini. The conclusion of the last movement of Leclair's G major sonata (Bk. 2, No. 3), a 3/8 Allegro Assai, is particularly interesting. Ten bars before the end the soloist plays a four-bar scalic passage in E flat while the keyboard concludes a series of modulations with a cadence in A flat; yet in two short bars Leclair contrives to get back to G major for a jubilant final restatement of the movement's main theme. Such moments should be relished.

54. Quantz was very insistent on the importance of studying other people's performances (Quantz, 18 and 116). Considerable interpretational insights may nowadays be gained from listening to radio programmes which compare a number of recorded performances of the same piece of music.

55. I recommend, in addition to the books by Donington and le Huray, Frederick Neumann, *Ornamentation in Baroque and Post-Baroque Music* (Princeton, NJ: Princeton University Press, 1978), Howard Mayer Brown and Stanley Sadie (eds.), *Performance Practice: Music after 1600* (London: Macmillan, 1990), esp. pp. 3–19, 80–6, and 117–46), the articles in *New Grove* referred to elsewhere in this book, and *Companion to Baroque Music*, ed. Julie Anne Sadie (J. M. Dent: London, 1990). This compendious volume provides an overview, by country or region, of Baroque music and musicians (pp. 3–347), followed by sections on the vocal and instrumental resources, and the forms and genres, of Baroque music (pp. 351–405), and on performing-practice issues—national styles, ornamentation, and the idea of authenticity (pp. 409–46).

Notes to Chapter 2

1. e.g. Handel, 'Heart, the seat of soft delight' from *Acis and Galatea*. See Hunt for recorder associations (pp. 47–9) and for use of the recorder by Handel (pp. 68–73), Purcell (pp. 49–51), and Bach and Telemann (pp. 76–85).

2. Hunt, 73.

3. Quantz (p. 315) suggests that a three-movement concerto should be about fifteen minutes long.

4. e.g. by Baston, Babell, and Woodcock (Hunt, 62). Several of these concertos are available in reductions for descant recorder and keyboard.

5. See Douglas MacMillan, 'The Recorder in the Late Eighteenth and Early Nineteenth Centuries', *The Consort*, 39 (1983), 489–97 at 489.

6. Sylvestro Ganassi, *Fontegara* (Venice, 1535) (the first recorder tutor) ed. Hildemarie Peter, tr. Dorothy Swainson (Berlin: Lienau/Hinrichsen, 1956), p. 12.

7. $a' = 415$ is a rough approximation to the chamber-music pitch used around 1700 in various towns in northern Italy, Germany, and England, though not to the pitch used in France, or in Rome, which seems to have been about a semitone lower. Even today there is no universally agreed standard pitch, and pitches higher than $a' = 440$ are in use in Europe. At one point plastic recorders were being made in Japan at $a' = 442$.

8. Though Hotteterre mentions half-holes, and a few original Baroque instruments have them.

9. The best comparison between the 'Baroque' and the 'modern' recorder is by Bruce Haynes, 'The Baroque Recorder: A Comparison with its Modern Counterpart', *AR* 10 (1969), 3–8. Eve O'Kelly's book includes a history of recorder design (ch. 3).

10. The 20th-c. recorder has been provided with various 'improvements' which further affect volume and tone-quality; see *RT* 98–9. For the bell-keyed recorder, see Daniel Waitzman, *The Art of Playing the Recorder* (New York: AMS Press, 1978).

11. See Ganassi, *Fontegara*, 89: 'Remember that you can sound every note softly by slightly uncovering a finger hole and using less breath . . . You should half-close the holes somewhat more or less as your ear requires and as you feel to be right.'

12. It is possible for an experienced recorder-player whose fingering is quick and well controlled, whose breath-control is good, and who has mastered the art of avoiding clicks at register-breaks, to make a recorder give forth a stream of beautiful sound such as one associates with the most acclaimed clarinet-playing. Beautiful as it is, such a sound is not Baroque. Creamy-smooth cantabiles belong more to the Romantic era (see below, n. 31). Except where slurs are marked or are an adjunct to expressive phrasing, 18th-c. performance style was generally more detached—it is significant that Beethoven thought Mozart's piano-playing sounded 'choppy'. Eighteenth-c. books of instruction for woodwind instruments emphasize variety of articulation and the metrical pairing of notes. Baroque recorder sonatas should therefore be played with clear and varied tonguing consonants, displaying the clarity and balance of the phrase-patterns that constitute the fabric of their music.

13. On many recorders it is difficult to sharpen C without considerable loss of tone-quality or undue gain in volume. So it is best to start on C as one of the recorder's least variable notes. For the same reason C is a better note for tuning up with a harpsichord or other recorders. Treble A, and more especially A', are less good for tuning (except with strings) as they have more intonational flexibility. One should never tune recorders with notes that tend to be sharp, as A' often is. Moreover, a harpsichord in non-equal temperament will probably have been tuned from a C rather than an A tuning-fork.

14. Such as 'closed' and thumbed G's, E, 'one-and-a-half-below' D, F' (– 123 ––––), E♭ (0 –23 4–––) and thumbed A♭' (see *RT*, ch. V).

15. Breathing and breath-delivery techniques for recorder-playing are dealt with more fully in Walter van Hauwe's *The Modern Recorder Player*, 2 vols. (London: Schott, 1984–7) i, pt. 3, ii. 60–72, and also in Waitzman, *Art of Playing the Recorder*, ch. 4. For recorder maintenance, follow advice given by the maker of the recorder as regards oiling, revoicing, etc., but see also Edward L. Kottick, *Tone and Intonation on the Recorder* (New York: McGinnis and Marx, 1974), and Adrian Brown, *The Recorder: A Basic Workshop Manual* (Brighton: Dolce Edition, 1989). It must also be remembered that the tone-quality of some recorders may deteriorate after around two hours' continuous playing; they then need a good rest to dry out.

16. J.-B. Lœillet's Op. 1 No. 1 A minor sonata, first movement, played very slowly, is suggested as the victim for this difficult but fascinating exercise, as it is neatly sectionalized by frequent cadences and rests. Try to stay in tune throughout the exercise by shading, etc. (*RT*, ch. IV). The movement could be subjected to the following tonal changes, several of which involve degraded sound, especially the low-volume variants:

    1. *mf*   medium breath-vibrato (*RT* 33)
    2. *p*   strong tonguing, low breath-pressure staccato (*RT* 108)
    3. *f*   light, soft tonguing and strong breath-pressure

4. *ppp*   'harmonics' (*RT* 60–1)

5. *mp*   tone-change by forked fingerings—use no normal fingerings (*RT* 66–7)

6. *mp*   light flutter-tonguing (*RT* 51)

7. *fff*   breath-pressure 9 on the edge of the register-break, no vibrato

8. *mf*   finger-vibrato (*RT* 107)

9. *mp*   slight leak at lips, a touch of 'white noise' (*RT* 105)

10. *mf*   tongue-vibrato (*RT* 107–8)

11. Playing very slowly, *messa di voce* (see Ch. 5, n. 4) on long notes with finger-vibrato intonation control (Donington, *Baroque*, 33–4 and Quantz, 165–6)

12. *f*   'k' and 'g' tonguing (*RT* 41–2)—Dalla Casa, 1584, thought this horrific ('far terribiltà').

Even without going wholly avant-garde, there are other possibilities.

17. Playing avant-garde music opens the mind enormously to the recorder's capabilities. For an excellent account of avant-garde recorder techniques see O'Kelly, 82–115.

18. Ganassi says 'it is possible with some players to perceive, as it were, words to their music . . . with this instrument only the form of the human body is absent' (*Fontegara*, 9). John Hudgebut in his *Vade Mecum* of 1679 (Hunt, 54) writes 'of Instruments . . . there is none which comes closer in Imitation to the Voice' (he is referring to the 'Flagilet' and 'Rechorder', more especially the latter). Three hundred years later, Luciano Berio called the recorder 'such a human instrument' (O'Kelly, 55 and 116).

19. Tonguing in relation to the steps of various dances is discussed in George Houle's article 'Tongueing and Rhythmic Patterns in Early Music', *AR* 6 (1965), 4–13, and in Mather, *Dance Rhythms*.

20. Nevertheless, O'Kelly (pp. 86–8) is able to expatiate upon the recorder's potentialities in dynamic range and in varieties of timbre and harmonics, with the use of 'non-standard' fingerings. She also points out that it is the only 'early music' instrument to have acquired a substantial repertoire of avant-garde music.

21. For example, Charles Bâton's suites (1733 and later) were, like many others, for 'les Vieles, Musettes, Flûtes Traversières, Flûtes à bec et Hautbois' (viele = hurdy-gurdy, musette = small bagpipe). The 'Pastor Fido' sonatas, published in Paris as Vivaldi's Op. 13 in 1737, offer a similar freedom of instrumentation, including violin. Many Baroque violin sonatas do not use the G string; with D as the lowest note they become more accessible to flautists, and thence, transposed up a minor third as was customary, to treble-recorder players.

22. Published music might be 'apt for voices or viols' or 'for Viols, Violins or other Musicall Winde Instruments' (Holborne 1599; see Hunt, 27).

23. Handel's Op. 1 comprises four 'flauto' sonatas, three 'traversa', three for violin, and two for oboe.

24. The Lasocki–Bergmann edition (2nd edn.) gives the background to the autograph sources and the Roger and Walsh publications of these sonatas, and makes full and instructive comparisons. It seems that the recorder sonatas might have been composed in about 1725, though worked over again shortly afterwards in Handel's process of making a fair copy. They are carefully crafted works of Handel's maturity.

25. Even Corelli, who distinguished the two types of sonata carefully, has some sad minor-key movements in *da camera* sonatas (e.g. the beginning of his Op. 2 No. 4), and an unecclesiastical 'Giga' in his *sonata da chiesa* Op. 5 No. 5 (see Newman, 34–6).

26. A gavotte normally starts with two crotchets on the second beat of a two-minim bar.

Handel originally put the barlines in this position before revising the work (see Lasocki–Bergmann edn., p. 70, fig. 1), and he placed them there in a later reworking of this movement in the G minor organ concerto, Op. 7 No. 5, where it is marked 'gavotta allegro', not 'presto' (see Lasocki and Legêne, 'Learning to Ornament', 12). It is often instructive to compare a composer's different versions of what is essentially the same music, for example Handel's Op. 1 No. 11 'flauto' sonata with his Op. 4 No. 5 organ concerto, both in F major, as well as to note similarities such as that between this recorder sonata and the early F major trio sonata for two recorders and continuo (ed. Hogwood, Faber).

27. Quantz suggested ♩ = 120 for a gavotte, (or, better here, ♩ = 60).

28. The Walsh edition places a slur over all three notes of the reiterated ♫♪ figure except in bar 8, where the slurs are only over the semiquavers, and in several other bars (e.g. 10 and 43), where the careless engraver has left them out altogether. The Lasocki–Bergmann edition, derived from the autograph manuscripts, slurs the semiquavers only, adding a few slurs Handel had overlooked.

29. For the use of 'pulse' and 'beat' see Ch. 6 n. 34.

30. Baroque players did not usually mark parts in this manner, as they were accustomed to the idiom, although they occasionally marked in their ornamentation. Experienced players today may feel they have no need to mark parts. Marking parts can make the music look fussy, may stand in the way of discovering new interpretations and phrasings, and discourages spontaneous improvisation. Written-out ornamentation can hide the underlying melodic line and harmonic progression, and make the music appear more complicated than it is (consider the effect of Exx. 4.5–7, 6.7). Nevertheless, at the learning stage, one's private marking of a part or score serves as a valuable reminder of points agreed in rehearsal, and of other matters. The full marking-up of a piece of music as described in *RT*, ch. XI imposes a discipline and completeness upon the process of preparation for performance. Use a soft pencil, and be prepared to rub out first ideas.

31. In his article 'Making the Music Speak', Theron McClure shows five different ways of phasing a three-bar passage from a Telemann solo fantasia. He goes on to contrast the Baroque process of 'breaking up the flow into small clusters of notes that form musical syllables and words' with 'the long connected lines of nineteenth-century melodies'. Liszt wanted the musical patterns that permeated earlier music to be avoided or smoothed out in playing his compositions (A. Newman, *Bach and the Baroque*, 20). If Liszt and Handel had written identical melodies, their internal emphases and presentation would have been different. A Handel melody should be enjoyed as a consummate balancing of constituent parts within the span of the music as a whole, and not played as an almost seamless stream of sound in the style of Liszt or Wagner.

32. On phrasing, see Ch. 1 n. 52. Couperin was not prepared to leave phrasing to the whims of his performers, and he indicated phrase-points with commas; see Donington, *Interp.* 471 and le Huray, 54–5.

33. le Huray, writing on note-length and on legato and staccato in 17th- and 18th-c. music (pp. 16–18), quotes C. P. E. Bach: 'Notes that are neither detached, connected nor fully held are sounded for *half* their value . . . Crotchets and quavers in moderate and slow speeds are usually performed in this semi-detached manner.' This, taken with other evidence, suggests that in the preceding Baroque period the longest of four crotchets in a bar, at least in a lively 'allegro' rather than an expressive 'adagio', would have been accorded only about a ⁵⁄₁₀ note value. The art of a modern player in communicating the

spirit of a Baroque sonata to a modern audience is to achieve this detached style without allowing the music to sound desiccated, and without undermining the flow and span of the music's balancing phrases.

34. See Ex. 9 in *PB* 6, where phrases are contrasted by tonguing alone. It is vital in that exercise to banish note-length and dynamic differentiation utterly, however strongly the melody tempts one to employ them.

35. It is assumed in all exercises proposed in this book that the player is producing good and well-controlled basic recorder sound (see above, n. 15, for references to breath-control exercises).

36. On 'perceiving' words in instrumental music, see above, n. 18.

37. See musical dictionaries under 'agogic accent'.

38. McClure, 'Making the Music Speak', quotes Couperin: 'the feeling or "soul", the expressive effect . . . is due to the cessation and [delaying] of the notes, made at the right moment' (*L'Art de toucher le clavecin*, 1717).

39. Lasocki and Legêne, 'Learning to Ornament', show from Handel's cantatas how Handel related ornamentation to expressive rubato. Handel used well-chosen decorative motives to hold back words or phrases, or to push them forward, intensifying the emotion behind the notes. There is an excellent example of a rhetorically held-back note in the main subject of the Andante of Telemann's flute Sonatina Quarta (Schott/ Amadeus BP 484).

40. See Lasocki, 'A New Look at Handel's Recorder Sonatas', *RMM* 6 (Sept. 1978), 2–9 and 71–9 at 75.

41. If it is too sharp, 6 can be pushed further across to shade its other half-hole.

42. A device much used by Couperin and occasionally by J. S. Bach (le Huray, 55–8 and 8–12) in their keyboard fingerings. Negotiating awkward finger-movements takes a moment of delay, which imparts a slight stress of separation upon the following note.

43. Closed G′ can be tuned with 7 or 1 to sharpen, and with 0 to flatten, but this is impracticable at speed.

44. The virtuoso violinist Tartini, however, said that 'This ornament produces a very good effect on the final note of a musical phrase, if this note is not too long . . . ' (quoted by Newman, *Bach and the Baroque*, 185).

Notes to Chapter 3

1. On the question of orchestration in mid-17th-c. operas, see Donington, *Interp.* 52–4.

2. le Huray, writing on Baroque dynamics (pp. 38–41), provides a table of the principal dynamic markings used by Corelli, Handel, J. S. Bach, and Vivaldi (the most). He argues that crescendos and diminuendos, rather than 'terraced dynamics', were much used in Italian-style music for the dramatic shaping of phrases, and for 'marvellous effect' (Scipione Maffei, Rome, 1711).

3. Purcell wrote (dedication to *Dioclesian*, 1690) that English music is 'now learning *Italian*, which is its best Master, and a little of the *French* Air to give it somewhat more of Gayety and Fashion'. In following Italian models in his 1683 trio sonatas, his aim was 'principally, to bring the seriousness and gravity of that sort of Musick into vogue', and he refers to 'the power of the Italian Notes and the elegancy of their Compositions' (Newman, 307). See also Quantz on Tartini (p. 324): 'a master at performing difficult feats upon the violin', 'abandoning the singing style'.

4. In a medieval mystery play performance in recent times, one recorder filled the great space of St Albans Cathedral with thrilling effect, resounding from every vault and gallery.

5. See Ch. 7 n. 3.

6. Pitch-variation in relation to breath-pressure is less with all or most finger-holes covered, greater on open notes such as G′ – –2– ––––. It must also be borne in mind that the recorder's natural propensity is for the low notes to be softer than the high notes. To achieve an even level of volume, high notes should therefore be given less breath than low notes. In sonata passages where low notes need to be played loud and high notes soft, it helps to give the low notes added weight by slightly lengthening them and slightly shortening the high notes—see Bernard Thomas's introduction to *The Baroque Solo Book* (Brighton, Dolce Edition, 1989).

7. Examining bodies ought therefore, at least at the higher grades, to require recorder-players to demonstrate their ability to control intonation by playing notes, or even scale passages, at different dynamic levels. Ultimately a recorder-player should be able to play complete downward scales crescendo and upward scales decrescendo.

8. See Ch. 2 n. 11.

9. e.g. in *PB* 26–8, by Alan Davis in *Treble Recorder Technique* (London: Novello, 1983), 41–2, and, especially, in an article by Scott Reiss on 'Pitch Control: Shading and Leaking', *AR* 28 (1987), 136–9.

10. Sonatas specifying recorder were written by Benedetto Marcello, Diogenio Bigaglia, Martino Bitti, Paolo Benedetto Bellinzani, and Alessandro Santini.

11. Examples of composers of recorder and flute sonatas attracted to London from Italy: Francesco Barsanti, Giuseppe Sammartini, Giovanni Bononcini, and Pietro Castrucci; from Germany: Handel, Pepusch, Gottfried Finger, and John Ernst Galliard; from Holland: Willem de Fesch; from Flanders: John Lœillet; and from France: James Paisible, Charles Dieupart, and Louis Merci. To this list should be added Francesco Geminiani; two of his six flute sonatas were published by Walsh for recorder.

12. The scheme of the *Essercizii musici* comprises 10 solo sonatas and 12 trio sonatas, exercising Telemann's own ingenuity and skill in writing idiomatically for groupings of six different instruments, including recorder, and thorough-bass.

13. 'Rhetoric and Affect in Baroque Music', 25.

14. 'The Recorder Sonatas of Telemann', *RMM* 2, No. 8 (Feb. 1968), 236–8.

15. Compare this meandering movement, full of harmonic uncertainty, with the charming *galant* melodies of the third movements of Telemann's *Sonate metodiche* (recorder version ed. Bernard Thomas; Brighton: Dolce Edition, 1990).

16. The choice here of the Schott edition of the Telemann sonata (ed. Ruf) is not intended to imply that it is necessarily the best. Such a judgement depends on many factors, and is to some extent subjective, particularly on the part of the continuo harpsichord-player. Some harpsichord-players might find Hugo Ruf's realization of the keyboard part in the third movement rather thick-textured, for example in bars 5–6; and how does a harpsichord play 'sotto voce'? A harpsichord-player, having regard to the style and chosen interpretation of the movement, and to the response of his own instrument, may wish to thin out some of the chords. Similar considerations apply in greater and lesser degree to the other editions of sonatas referred to in this book, including those listed in Appendix II.

17. A method illustrated by photographs in Scott Reiss's article, 'Pitch Control', and in diagrammatic form by Alan Davis, *Treble Recorder Technique*, 42.

18. It may sometimes be found that breathing out partly through the nose assists in the production of isolated soft high notes.

19. This E′ is more reliable when the recorder is slightly pulled out at the upper joint, but of course this flattens overall pitch, unevenly.

20. In his book *Il flauto dolce ed acerbo* (Celle: Moeck, 1969), Michael Vetter listed almost 300 fingerings for G′ in various types of register.

21. Charles Delusse (Paris, *c*.1761), quoted in Betty Bang Mather and David Lasocki, *The Art of Preluding 1700–1830* (New York: McGinnis and Marx, 1984), 25, associated different types of transverse flute vibrato with different affects. He advocates a form of vibrato produced by shaking the whole instrument; on swelled long notes this expresses 'gravity and fright'. He also describes breath-vibrato, aspirated 'hou hou hou', and finger-vibrato for use on isolated notes.

22. On Telemann's Affettuoso see Ch. 1 n. 36.

23. See p. 130 of Thurston Dart's pioneering book, *The Interpretation of Music* (London: Hutchinson, 1954).

Notes to Chapter 4

1. Julie Anne Sadie has drawn attention to earlier 'sonatas' by Charpentier and others, but these were not conceived for solo and bass—they are 'ensemble sonatas', an instrumental form much cultivated in Couperin's time; see 'Charpentier and the Early French Ensemble Sonata', *EM* 7 (1979), 330–5.

2. These sonatas, like many French pieces with one or more *dessus* parts, and some music outside France, were originally published with the *dessus* in the French violin clef, with G on the bottom line. This causes no great problems to those recorder players who are familiar with reading from the bass clef.

3. But see Anthony, 308. Where a choice was available, instrumental colour was selected to accord with the affect of the piece. Instruments might be doubled (Roger North, 259), or changed from one movement to another.

4. The composer Louis-Antoine Dornel in 1711 also included eight violin 'sonatas' and four flute 'suites' in one publication. On nomenclature see Anthony, 304–5 and Newman, 276, 340, and 366. 'Simphonie', 'concert', 'ordre', and 'partita' all had meanings similar to 'suite' and 'sonata' in varying contexts.

5. See Anthony, 335–7 for an account of the recorder's waning popularity in France in relation to the transverse or German flute. 'Flûtes à bec' are referred to, however, as possible solo instruments for Joseph Bodin de Boismortier's 'Divertissemens de Campagne' in 1734 (though elsewhere Boismortier allows the recorder to play a flute part only 'in case of need'; Anthony, 336), and also, even later than in Lavigne's sonatas of 1739, for Charles Bâton's suites of 1755 (the date given by Helen Neate in her edn. of *Première Suite* for recorder and b. c.—Schott Ed. 10924, though *New Grove* gives 1737–9).

6. Despite the wide use of the word *dessus*, composers of suites did occasionally exhibit a mild preference for a particular instrument. Hotteterre's 1715 pieces are for 'La Flûte-traversiere et autres instruments'. He says the recorder may need to transpose but he also says the pieces could simply by played on the harpsichord. Conversely, Dieupart (Anthony, 256) arranged his harpsichord suites (1701) to suit violin or other melody instruments, including 'flûte de voix' (Suites I to IV) and 'flûte du quatre' (Suites V and VI).

7. The best account of the suite is by David Fuller in the *New Grove*.

8. Quantz, 328: 'what is new among them often seems to be old'; 'they bind themselves all too closely to certain characteristics.'

9. For example, 'Forlane en Rondeau' from Couperin's *Quatrième Concert Royal*, or 'La Timide' from Rameau's *Pièces de Clavecin en Concerts*. Such music is playable on the tenor recorder, and can be simplified into recorder and keyboard form.

10. Two books by Betty Bang Mather are essential reading for recorder players wishing to play French Baroque music well. They are *Interpretation of French Music from 1675 to 1775 for Woodwind and Other Performers* (New York: McGinnis and Marx, 1973) and *Dance Rhythms of the French Baroque*. On dance rhythms there is an interesting article by Patricia Ranum on 'Audible Rhetoric and Mute Rhetoric: The 17th-Century French Sarabande', *EM* 14 (1986), 22–39.

11. Campra's words in the introduction to his first book of cantatas (1708).

12. See Donington, *Interp.* 101–8, from which this table is mainly compiled. See also Quantz, 299. Other words and quotations are drawn from Raguenet (1702), Le Cerf de la Viéville (1725), Frérin (1753), Muffat (1695), and Nemeitz (1727; see Anthony, 335).

13. e.g. the Largo of the C major Flautino Concerto, RV 443.

14. e.g. the pair of Tambourins in *Pièces de Clavecin en Concerts*, No. III.

15. A player with more than one Baroque-style recorder will find that French music sounds best on an instrument with a light and limpid tone. It was the Hotteterres and their contemporaries who redesigned the early Baroque recorder with a narrower, more conical bore, with the elegance and clarity of French music in mind.

16. In *L'Art de Préluder* (1719) Hotteterre uses square brackets rather than slurs to indicate trochaic tonguing 'tu ru'; see Jean-Claude Veilhan, *The Baroque Recorder in 17th- and 18th-Century Performance Practice: Technique, Performing Style, Original Fingering Charts* (Paris: Leduc, 1980), 8.

17. Tongue-strokes 'necessary for perfection of playing' are carefully described in Hotteterre's *Principes* (1707) and elucidated in David Lasocki's edn. The forward position of the French 't' is described by Lasocki in 'The Tongueing Syllables of the French Baroque', *AR* 8 (1967), 81–2 and further developed by Bradford Arthur in 'Hotteterre's "tu–ru" ', *AR*14 (1973), 79–82. See also Ch. 2 n. 19.

18. Of the many accounts of inequality, perhaps the best are those in Donington, *Baroque*, 42–8, le Huray, 46–53, *New Grove* under 'Notes inégales' by David Fuller, and George Houle's *Meter in Music 1600–1800*. Both Fuller and Houle have done some interesting research into inequality in music transcribed for reproduction by 18th-c. mechanical organs and music-boxes. See also Quantz, 123–4.

19. Hotteterre, *Principes*, ed. Lasocki, 60. As Curt Sachs pointed out in his book on *Rhythm and Tempo* (London: Dent, 1953), 195, French-style inequality was already causing confusion as early as the 14th c. Marchetto of Padua (1318) said that if a composer writes four semibreves per breve, the Italians would render them of equal value but the French (mindful of the symbolism of the Trinity, 'perfectio') would render them as two trochaic triplets $(2 + 1) + (2 + 1)$. Marchetto added the letters 'G' or 'Y' to the music to show whether the passage should be read in the 'Gallic' or the 'Ytalian' style.

20. Nor even in the *New Grove*, so 'minor' a composer is he. Yet his sonatas and duets (including 'Les Fleurs') are charming; they have long been in publication, and one sonata movement has been set for a Grade examination. All this reminds us that there are still Baroque composers of attractive music who are receiving too little attention.

21. See Hotteterre, *Principes*, ch. 9.

22. Donington, *Interp.* 448–51. Donington's views were, however, strongly opposed by Frederick Neumann, and the question of vigorous overdotting in French-style overtures is still not completely resolved. The best current (1992) discussion of the subject is in le Huray, 72–7, in relation to J. S. Bach's *Ouvertüre* in D, BWV 1068. The Dieupart example here could certainly be played faster, in two minim beats to the bar, with only slight overdotting to give it crispness.

23. *Interp.* 460, and Appendix (665–70).

Notes to Chapter 5

1. Quantz's tonguing advice is sometimes confusing because he makes certain unstated assumptions about inequality, which, as shown in Ch. 4, affects choice of tonguing consonants. Ganassi's extremely valuable account of tonguing in his time in *Fontegara*, 13–14, also needs elucidation and demonstration on a Renaissance recorder by an experienced teacher to bring out its full significance. Tonguing is the subject of ch. III of *RT* (2nd edn. 1986—do not use the first edn. of 1959, which, like other recorder-tutors of that time, dealt too summarily with tonguing). The most complete historical account is in Italian in Marcello Castellani and Elio Durante, *Del portar della lingua negli instrumenti di fiato* (Florence: S.P.E.S., 1979). The tonguing sections of tutors by Freillon-Poncein (1700), Hotteterre (1707), and Quantz (1752) are amalgamated in Veilhan, *The Baroque Recorder*. Betty Bang Mather and David Lasocki, in various books and articles, have concentrated on French-style tonguing. There is an excellent article by Scott Reiss in *AR* 27 (1986), 144–9, on 'Articulation: The Key to Expressive Playing'—an admirable title. A useful section on wind-instrument tonguing in the early Baroque period is on pp. 202–4 of Timothy J. McGee's book *Medieval and Renaissance Music: A Performer's Guide* (Toronto: University of Toronto Press, 1985). This book also brings out the importance of the strong-weak pairing of double-tonguing. The recognition of strong and weak ('good' or 'bad') notes in Baroque phrasing is extremely important, and is in itself a powerful reason for cultivating historical double-tonguing as a basis for expressive playing of Baroque sonatas.

2. *PB*, Ex. 9, which is designed to achieve contrast *only* by changes in tonguing-strengths, with breath-pressure and note-lengths held absolutely constant, can be made even more demanding by changing the constant dynamic level for the whole exercise from *mf* to *mp* or even *p*. It needs to be tackled after practising the preliminary exercise described in the introduction to this section of the *Practice Book*.

3. Quantz, 73. And note especially what Quantz says about 't' and 'd' (p. 75, para. 12), even before he deals with the interpretational potentialities of double-tonguing: 'It is impossible to define fully in words either the difference between *ti* or *di*, upon which a considerable part of the expression of the passions depends, or all of the different kinds of tongue-strokes. Meanwhile, individual reflection will suffice to convince everyone that, just as there are various shades between black and white, there is more than one intermediate degree between a firm and a gentle tongue-stroke. Hence you can also express *ti* and *di* in diverse ways with the tongue. You simply must try to make the tongue supple enough to be able to tip the notes more firmly at one time, more gently at another, in accordance with their nature. This is accomplished both by the quicker or slower withdrawal of the tongue from the palate, and by the stronger or weaker exhalation of the wind.' Quantz then goes on to point out that in a reverberant hall

tonguing must be 'with greater force and sharpness', and notes shortened to avoid blurring of the sound, especially on repeated notes.

4. It will be seen from Roger North's diagram of the 'plaine' viol note in Pl. 5 that this note achieves its full sonority with a swelling of sound from bow pressure some time after it has been articulated. The note is 'nourished' (Loulié) or 'inflated' (Marin Marais). In a more mannered form, this becomes a *messa di voce*, used by Baroque singers for expressive effect and imitated by instrumentalists; the swelling of the note is more marked and was usually sweetened with vibrato, as in Roger North's second diagram. Recorder-players making use of this form of expressivity need to ensure by carefully controlled shading, or by graded finger-vibrato, that the bulge is not in intonation as well as in dynamic (see Quantz, 165–6). The device can become tiresome to modern audiences, and needs to be used sparingly.

5. Hotteterre (*Principes*, ed. Lasocki, 62) warns against starting 'tremblements' (trills) with 'r'. See Quantz, 73–4 for articulation at appoggiaturas.

6. The flautist de Lusse (1761) advocates very rapid 'Loul loul' for ♪♪♪♪ Vivace repeated semiquavers 'representing tempests', and 'hu hu hu hu' for ('aspiré') (Castellani and Durante, *Del portar*, 149–50). Much earlier, Martin Agricola (*Musica Instrumentalis Deudsch*, 1545) had suggested taking very rapid decorative passages with what he called 'flitter zunge' on 'l': 'tel lel lel lel lel lel lel le' (Castellani and Durante, 82).

7. Players trying out and practising different tonguings will find that wearing ear-plugs emphasizes the sound effect of their tonguings, and this may help them to make a more informed choice of articulation and achieve tonguing accuracy, neatness, and variety.

8. See Bernard Krainis's letter, referring to Staeps, in *AR* 29 (1988), 74–6.

9. It seems likely that, before the early Baroque period, slurring on wind-instruments was regarded as slovenly technique even in very rapid *passaggi* and *tremoli*, although evidence exists from the mid-16th c. that passages were taken slurred in one bow-stroke by string-instruments (Ortiz, 1553; Donington, *Interp.* 477).

10. This whole question is dealt with more fully in my 'A Slur on Slurring?', *Journal of the National Early Music Association* (NEMA), No. 9 (July 1988), 1–6. (The NEMA publication is now called *Leading Notes*.)

11. Beautiful expression in recorder-playing is often achieved by using only one tonguing consonant, such as 'dh', with finely graded articulation from note to note. This is a process which comes naturally to a gifted player in the moulding of phrases, without forethought or analysis. The expressive function of these tonguing gradations may be understood, or even taught, by analysing the exact tongue movement on to the teeth-ridge area, and the strength of this movement, needed for each note, and groups of notes, in the expressive phrasing of, for example, a Telemann 'cantabile', or of the Lœillet movement in Ex. 1.2. Better still, consider the articulation of an actual song, such as Schubert's 'An die Musik', in a recorder arrangement, where expression depends upon the relationship between words and note-lengths, and upon the placing of notes within the music's flow and metre. Attempting to express such music by playing it all on one note illustrates even more clearly the role of tonguing technique in interpretation.

12. It is interesting that Quantz says a Baroque roulade has to be (double-)tongued (p. 85), but Veilhan, in his *Rules of Musical Interpretation in the Baroque Era*, 18, shows how Montéclair (1736) distinguishes between a *tirata* (detached) and a *coulade* (slurred). The Murrill one is very fast indeed and must be slurred. It is then easier to negotiate the F♯'' in this slur. Finger the D' ∅ 12– 4567 (only slightly sharp) and the F♯'' can be got by

rolling back 1 and 2, a slightly flat version of the Method 2 F♯'' fingering shown on p. 157. At such high speed these small inaccuracies of intonation will not be noticed. The G' on the return journey back up this roulade is probably best with the closed fingering – 123 4567. The end of this movement needs very effective timing and total rapport with one's accompanist, especially at the penultimate bar, marked 'Presto', but even more exciting played prestissimo.

13. This sonata probably sounds better with piano than with harpsichord.

Notes to Chapter 6

1. See for example the opening Adagio of Bach's E major flute sonata, which is returned to its non-ornamented form as Ex. 7 in Betty Bang Mather and David Lasocki's book *Free Ornamentation in Woodwind Music 1700–1775* (New York: McGinnis and Marx, 1976).

2. Such as Couperin: 'I declare that my pieces must be performed as I have marked them, and that they will make a certain impression on people of good taste only if everything which I have marked is observed to the letter, without addition or subtraction' (Donington, *Interp.* 191).

3. e.g. in *Trietti metodichi* (1731) for two flutes or violins and basso continuo, quoted in Mather and Lasocki, *Free Ornamentation*, Exx. 12–13, together with examples from Telemann's *Sonate metodiche* (Exx. 9–11).

4. This was exactly the didactic approach to ornamentation in the late Renaissance; see the quotation from Conforto (1593) in *RT* 112.

5. 'Ornamentation for beginners' is also tackled in Kenneth Wollitz, *The Recorder Book* (London: Gollancz, 1982), 71–114, in Davis, *Treble Recorder Technique*, 93–107, in van Hauwe, *Modern Recorder Player*, ii. 38–58, in Betty Bang Mather, 'Developing Baroque Ornamentation Skills', *AR* 29 (1988), 4–6, and in David Lasocki, 'Late Baroque Ornamentation: Philosophy and Guidelines', ibid. 7–10. There is a section 'How to ornament in solos' on pp. 180–4 of McGee, *Medieval and Renaissance Music*, which applies to early 17th-c. Italian sonatas.

6. e.g. in van Hauwe, *Modern Recorder Player*, and in Exx. 104–6 of Helmut Mönkemeyer's *Advanced School of Recorder Playing* (Celle: Moeck, 1967). Van Hauwe emphasizes the speeded-up trill, whereas TBM aims at first establishing neatness and balance in trills in regular semiquavers (see Quantz, 102 and notes, and Donington, *Interp.* 246–7).

7. A singing tutor by G. G. Ferrari, *A Concise Treatise on Italian Singing* (*c.*1820) says: 'Masters differ in their method of teaching the shake; some begin it with the note above that over which the letters *tr* are placed. Others prefer the commencement of it with the note to which the signature is marked. The first mode is certainly the best.' Neumann, *Ornamentation*, however, gives many 17th-c. and some 18th-c. examples where trills start on the main note, and keyboard players were being taught to trill both ways from about 1775 onwards. All this does not, however, invalidate the TBM exercise as a 'good practice' starting-point.

8. Arranged for recorder by 'An eminent Master' (1707), ed. Lasocki (Musica Rara, 1974).

9. This is well brought out in Neumann's monumental *Ornamentation in Baroque and Post-Baroque Music*, where Part III (pp. 47–199) is all devoted to 'One-Note Graces'.

10. Hotteterre, in his *Principes*, gives very full instructions for *flattement* fingerings; see Veilhan, *Rules*, 36, and *RT* 107. 'Close shake' is as described by Playford (1654) and

Christopher Simpson (1659); see Donington, *Interp.* 232–3. Later usage differed; see the discussion in *AR* 31 (1990), 40.

11. C. P. E. Bach, *Versuch*, 150: 'The volume and time value of ornaments must be determined by the affect.' Quantz, 100: 'The little embellishments should be used like seasoning at a meal; if the prevailing sentiment is taken as the guiding principle, propriety will be maintained, and one passion [affect] will never be transformed into another.'

12. The use of vibrato in different Baroque styles of music is described by Neumann, *Ornamentation*, 511–22.

13. See the Lasocki and Legêne article on 'Learning to Ornament Handel's Sonatas through the Composer's Ears'. The third instalment illustrates point 4 on p. 98.

14. Newman, 97–8 lists forty-eight Italian composers of 'sonatas', including many solo/continuo sonatas, published before 1651. If sonata-like pieces under other titles had been included, especially 'canzona', the list would have been much longer. More of this music is being published, often with recorder-players in mind. For example, Linde has edited three such pieces (for descant or tenor recorders) by Quagliati, Selma, and Montalbano (Schott OFB 153), and London Pro Musica publish a series, Chamber Music of the Seventeenth Century. See also Greg Dikmans, 'Florid Italian Instrumental Music circa 1600: An Introduction', *The Recorder* (Melbourne), No. 4 (May 1986), 5–13.

15. Ganassi's and other tutors are listed on p. x of Howard Mayer Brown's *Embellishing 16th-Century Music* (London: Oxford University Press, 1976).

16. See Bianconi, *Music in the Seventeenth Century*, 95.

17. Contemporary performers would have recognized the dynamic requirements of certain musical patterns, especially from their familiarity with expressive madrigals. Some composers marked in *f* and *p* (Gabrieli, Riccio), others marked 'eco' (Cima).

18. *Musica Instrumentalis Deudsch* (1545); Castellani and Durante, *Del portar della lingua*, 80.

19. See Brown, *Embellishing*, 1–11 for 16th-c. 'graces'.

20. Despite Quantz's comment on tongued roulades (see Ch. 5 n. 12), the very rapid passages in ornamented versions of Corelli's sonatas, although derived from earlier Italian florid ornamentation such as this, should be taken slurred, as they certainly would have been in the violin originals.

21. Even this concession still means playing at the speed of sixteen demisemiquavers a second. These passages were intended to be played at the full speed ordained by the sonata's prevailing pulse. Frescobaldi advises 'play resolutely'.

22. Zacconi, in *Prattica di musica* (1622) (quoted by Neumann, *Ornamentation*, 22), warns not to use any embellishments, nor rhythmic alteration, where this would 'spoil the logic of imitation, but let the *fughe*' (i.e. any forms of imitative counterpoint) 'have their due'.

23. Some early Italian sonatas were published only as 'fill-ups' to mainly vocal collections.

24. *Fontegara*, 87–8 and 96. Quantz, two centuries later, though recognizing earlier Baroque practice, says trills 'must take up no more than the interval of a whole tone or semi-tone as is required by the key' (p. 102).

25. The passage in Biagio Marini's *La Foscarina* makes it clear that the type of 'tremolo' he had in mind was not the usual rapid alternation of two notes as shown in Ex. 6.6 but the reiteration of one note, for he marks the violin parts 'Tremolo con L arco [*sic*]'—i.e. with the bow, not by fingering. The rapid repetition of detached notes on a single tone is

proposed as decoration in the 'affetti' section of a Marini trio sonata (Bärenreiter HM 129), a decoration which differs from the vocal *trillo*, where the reiterated notes are not detached (see below, n. 36).

26. See Lasocki, 'Late Baroque Ornamentation'.

27. See Brown, *Embellishing*, on the evolution of stereotypes.

28. See Mather and Lasocki, *The Art of Preluding*. 227 of Hotteterre's preludes for recorder, etc. (1719) are published by Ixyzet (Amsterdam), and 45 of them with 23 others by Freillon-Poncein (1700) by Faber (ed. Bang and Lasocki).

29. The same principle was still applicable two centuries later to the ornamentation of Italian-style music. Quantz (p. 163) emphasizes that in decorating the simple melody of an Adagio 'knowledge of harmony is indispensable'. He comments on the ineptitude of some performers, and suggests 'you must keep a master constantly at hand'. Evidently the ability to extemporize good ornamentation from chord to chord was not acquired easily, even by 18th-c. musicians versed in the conventions of their time.

30. Brown, *Embellishing*, 12–16, embellishes a madrigal melody from Ganassi's tables. The result is like a jazz-singer's rhapsodizing.

31. Bianconi, *Music in the Seventeenth Century*, 95. Cf. the ending of the first movement of Handel's G Minor sonata (Ex. 2.1).

32. Sonata Quarta, bars 17, 20, 28, 32–4, and—especially—97–103. This uninhibited sonata is paired with Sonata Terza in the Moeck edition.

33. The tripla starts (bar 42) in firm 3/2 time; after a cadence, bars 54–9 become an indecisive 3/2, but seem to switch in bar 60 to a 6/4 dance rhythm like a fast volta. In bar 63 the music swings back into the 3/2 of bar 54 before cadencing hugely in bars 66–7.

34. If the usage of this book is accepted in differentiating 'pulse' from 'beat', it must be borne in mind that the communicated *pulse* of a piece of music, which manifests its inner vitality and motion, is often at a slower rate of recurrence than the *beat* used privately by a player, or overtly by a conductor, to keep time. This difference was described on p. 32 in relation to the Larghetto of the Handel G minor sonata. 'Pulse' is the natural swing of the music determined by the shape of its melody and the music's rate of harmonic change; the beat may be the same (as in the Andante of this Handel sonata), but it could be counted shorter to ensure good ensemble or accurate reading of difficult rhythms. Thus waltzes and minuets, often conducted in three beats to a bar, usually have an underlying one-in-a-bar pulse. It is, however, frequently helpful—at first at least—to count beats in one's head (or foot) to sort out any complicated rhythms or to control passages with many fast notes, before achieving a more flexible one-in-a-bar pulse. Similarly, galliards and courantes which have a complex alternating 3 and 2 pulse may need at first to be counted out at 6 beats to the bar. This is also true of the Presto of Herbert Murrill's Sonata (Ex. 5.8). Many Baroque pieces with a ₵ or 4/4 time signature have a pulse of two in a bar, but an andante with a 'walking bass' and a melody decorated with many short notes may have an eight-to-the-bar beat and pulse. Pierre Boulez, in another context, described this dichotomy between beat and pulse as a 'double respiration', so that a piece of music can sound slow and fast at the same time. For pulse, see Donington, *Interp.* 420–4. Donington rightly emphasizes that accentuation within phrases will often not coincide with the underlying pulse or even with the beat. There are therefore three variables for a performer to keep in mind, the first two contributing most to the impetus and swing of the music, the last to its rhythmic subtlety. Good phrasing, and therefore good ornamentation, takes account of them all.

35. See Donington, *Interp.* 424. Handel's C major recorder sonata provides many examples of hemiolas in the second movement, where two bars of 3/8 time are phrased as if they were one bar in 3/4 time (bars 16–17, 31–2, 46–7, 63–4, 87–8, 105–6, 126–7, and 130–1), as well as at section ends in the fifth movement, and three in the Larghetto third movement.

36. Strictly, the reiterated note should not change in pitch, which makes this glorious vocal *gorgia* difficult to perform on the recorder. Trumpet players used a 'ha–ha–ha' chest pulsation. Control by the tongue ('y–y–y') is easier on the recorder but lighter in effect. See Brown, *Embellishing*, 10, and Neumann, *Ornamentation*, 288–9.

37. Some of the description in this paragraph is drawn from Bukofzer, *Music in the Baroque Era*, 52 and 65–6. Record-sleeves can be excellent sources of interpretational commentary, e.g. Anthony Rooley on Decca DSLO 570 (violin sonatas by Biagio Marini, who was possibly a pupil of Fontana): 'sections marked "affetti" require the performers to contribute cadenza-like elaborations to the simple framework provided. The shadow of renaissance "passaggi" can still be discerned, but there is a new energy coursing through the work which forces the performer to step into the role of virtuoso in the Baroque sense.' It is significant that within the short but eloquent 'Affetto' section of his 'Canzona Passaggiata' (1613) Notari marks ten slurs, over varied groups of up to six notes, and that there is only one slur elsewhere in this piece. Neumann, *Ornamentation*, 21–30, quotes the views of Cavalieri and Caccini that ornamentation should be applied to notes in phrases selectively in order to 'muovere l'affetto', to stir the affections, and that long gyrations of continuous *passaggi* only serve to tickle the ear. Perhaps the finest example of affective ornamentation is the scene of Orfeo's appeal to Charon in Act III of Monteverdi's *Orfeo* (1607). *Passaggi*, as opposed to 'affetti', continued to be used in non-'affetti' sections of instrumental music (e.g. Frescobaldi's toccatas). By the middle of the 17th c., passage-work had returned as vocal ornamentation—to great effect later in Handel's operas and oratorios.

38. No contemporary writer, it seems, refers to note-inflection in vocal or instrumental solos. Had it been in any general use it would surely have been referred to by the Florentine Caccini in his detailed account of vocal style in the Foreword to *Le nuove musiche*; an edited version of Playford's 1693 translation is in Oliver Strunk, *Source Readings in Music History: The Baroque Era* (New York: W. W. Norton, 1965), 17–32. Caccini sought after 'novelty . . . to delight and move the affections of the mind' (p. 22). It is not beyond the bounds of possibility that Venetian players of sonatas and canzonas, in searching to capture on their instruments the overwhelmingly expressive effects of the new vocal style, might have found inspiration from the Arabic and oriental music—of which note-inflection is a feature—which must have been heard in that cosmopolitan city.

39. *Early Music for Recorders*, 46.

40. Among the composers involved in the marriage celebrations of Ferdinand I, Grand Duke of Tuscany, in 1589, were Caccini (author of *Le nuove musiche*, 1602), Cavalieri (composer of 'the first oratorio', *Rappresentazione di anima e di corpo*, 1600) and Peri, composer of the first opera (*Euridice*, 1600).

41. Comment by Jeffery Kite-Powell in a review in *AR* 30 (1989), 159.

Notes to Chapter 7

1. In Baroque music, as in Baroque architecture, this is more likely to be a complex,

mathematical, relationship. It is not incompatible with my earlier statement that no two movements of a Baroque sonata should be played at exactly the same tempo.

2. Some triple-time sections are *sesquialtera*, i.e. three beats in the time of two previous (minim) beats instead of three in the time of one as in the fast tripla. *Sesquialtera* can have the effect of broadening out the pulse of the music into a slow one-in-a-bar feeling, especially if the minims of the previous section have regularly been divided into crotchets and quavers.

3. Roger North (1728, p. 260) says that 'during the whole sonnata, the *basso continuo* should not cease one moment'. Georg Muffat asks in his concertos of 1701 for 'no noticeable wait or silence, above all no annoying tuning of the violins', between movements, so that listeners might be kept 'in continuous attention from the beginning to the end' (Strunk, *Source Readings*, 92).

4. The intentions of a composer regarding repeats are not always apparent, especially as early printed music has dots before *and after* a double bar where the previous section is to be repeated (see, for example, the end of the Andante in Ex. 2.1). One then has to rely on the vagaries of the publisher's engraver in putting in or not putting in repeat dots before the next double bar according to what was required. If in doubt, assume a repeat was probably expected. This includes repeating both sections at the second playing of the first of two paired dances (e.g. 'Minuet I') in suites and sonatas, and repeating each time the refrain of a Rondo. But Baroque composers were often quite willing to leave such matters to performers, or to the needs of the occasion.

5. There is no objection to playing a sonata sitting down (though sitting up) if the player feels more comfortable that way, provided he does not find his breathing is adversely affected, and that he is just as visible to achieve rapport both with the other players and with the audience.

6. Walsh arranged six of J.-B. Lœillet's sonatas as treble-recorder duets, the second treble part being largely a straight transposition of the bass line.

7. See James Massy, 'The Flattening Effect of "Pulling Out" the Recorder', *RMM* 6 (June 1978), 34–5.

8. Should recorder-makers be encouraged to provide tuning-holes (normally wax-filled) in head-joints, despite the slight coarsening of tone caused by using them? For tuning-holes see *RT* 63–4 and Adrian Brown's *Manual*, 37.

9. e.g. 'short versions' by the Cambridge Buskers (now 'Classic Buskers') of Tchaikovsky's Violin Concerto and of Stravinsky's *Rite of Spring* on recorder and concertina.

10. For example, the 'Esurientes' in the first (E♭, BWV 243a) version of J. S. Bach's Magnificat is scored with recorders, the second D major version with flutes. The solo violin part of the fourth Brandenburg Concerto was rearranged for harpsichord (BWV 1057), and transposed to F, which happens better to suit present-day recorder-players (see John Martin, 'Echoes from the Past', *The Recorder* (Melbourne) No. 9 (Feb. 1989), 1–3, and John Martin, Fred Morgan, and Malcolm Tattersall, 'Echoes Resounding', ibid., No. 10 (Dec. 1989), 19–24.

11. *Sechs Sonaten für zwei Klaviere und Pedal*, published by Bärenreiter for flute and keyboard.

12. e.g. Telemann in his 1727 flute (or violin) duets (see Ch. 8 n. 27). On Purcell's Chaconne for three violins and continuo (in D) the copyist wrote 'play two notes higher for F(lutes)' i.e. putting it in F, which may be its original version (see Hunt, 51).

13. 'Les Nations' (trio sonatas): Quadro Amsterdam with Frans Brüggen playing flute and recorder.

14. Conversely, how many performances of Vivaldi's *Four Seasons* with 'original instruments' and unimpeachable Baroque stylishness are totally unauthentic because they miss the points in Vivaldi's carefully worked out 'demonstrative sonnets' which include descriptions of the horrors the elements inflict upon man and beast? Summer: 'A merciless season of burning sun'; Winter: 'the rough howling of the cruel storm'; Autumn: when the terrified game 'tries to flee from danger but, worn out, dies'. Awareness of affects is more important than wholly authentic instrumentation, though playing the violin part of these particular concertos on recorder or flute (as in Corrette's arrangements) bowdlerizes them.

15. Those specializing in Renaissance and early Baroque music will want a full set of matching Renaissance-model recorders, including a treble in G, which, however, needs good high notes to cope with the early sonata literature. Playing an instrument with G as its bottom note involves difficulties in reading (see *RT* 127–8 for a method of tackling unfamiliar clefs and transpositions).

16. e.g. the courses at the Istituto Comunale di Musica Antica at Pamparato, Italy.

17. The responsibilities of the editor are described in Denis Stevens's *Musicology* (London: Macdonald, 1980), and in John Caldwell's *Editing Early Music* (Oxford: Oxford University Press, 1985). Many editions of recorder sonatas, especially old ones where piano accompaniment is intended, are less than ideal, and editorial statements and interpretations should never be accepted uncritically. A good edition is one which helps the player to think about the music and arrive at his own interpretation.

18. This is even more expensive if two facsimile copies of a sonata (always printed in solo/figured-bass score—see Ex. 2.1) are required. In playing through music in the 18th c., the bass player(s) (certainly) and the soloist (presumably) read the music on the harpsichord. There is no evidence in collections that purchasers habitually bought two copies of solo sonata publications.

19. One of the least musical (but nicely played) performances of the first movement of Handel's F major recorder sonata was by David Munrow on Argo ZRG 746 ('The Amorous Flute'). He modelled the decoration upon a version on an 18th-c. barrel-organ in the Colt Clavier Collection, a version in keyboard style, and one moreover which ignores the implications of the movement's ostinato-type bass line (see David Lasocki's instructive article, 'A New Look at Handel's Recorder Sonatas', *RMM* 6 (Mar. 1978), 2–9, and his and Eva Legêne's article, 'Learning to Ornament Handel's Sonatas'. Bad taste was as common in the 18th c. as it is now.

20. Raymond Leppard, *Authenticity in Music* (London: Faber, 1988), 73. See also Lasocki, ' "Authenticity" in Performances of Early Music', *RMM* 5 (Dec. 1977), 384–7. Although sometimes contentious, the symposium publication *Authenticity and Early Music* (ed. Nicholas Kenyon; Oxford: Oxford University Press, 1988) is strongly recommended and thought-provoking, such as the implications of a passage from Diderot's *Le Neveu de Rameau* (pp. 79–81), Gary Tomlinson's views on 'Authentic Meaning in Music' (e.g. p. 123), and Richard Taruskin's strictures about 'the composer's intentions' (pp. 145–51).

Notes to Chapter 8

1. This is the date assigned to two 'sonatas' entitled 'Sinfonie' by Alessandro Scarlatti, claimed by his biographer Edward J. Dent as having been written for 'flauto'.

2. Newman, 175. He refers (p. 177) to the 'elegant, unsentimental lyricism of his themes.

The purity and expressive force of his slow movements belie the rather elementary appearance and few markings of his scores.' Hans Maria Kneihs writes interestingly about 'Musical Structure and Interpretation with Reference to Marcello's Sonata in D minor' in *The Recorder* (Melbourne), No. 3 (1985), 15–19.

3. Newman, 184: 'the debut of a superior composer, both in the quality of ideas and the grasp of over-all design'.

4. Francesco Barsanti was born in Lucca but emigrated to London in 1714. Walter Bergmann regarded his six sonatas of 1724 as 'belonging to the best music ever written for the recorder' (Preface to his edn. of Barsanti's Sonata in F (No. 5) Schott).

5. For Bigaglia's sonatas, see articles by Thiemo Wind in *RMM* 8 (June and Dec. 1984), 49–54 and 106–8.

6. Edwin Alton, editor of Schott OFB 1036, says Mancini's sonatas 'reflect something of the new emotive style of the later Neapolitan school' (Pergolesi, Porpora). Eve O'Kelly found some movements 'laboured to the point of banality' (*RMM* 8 (Mar. 1985), 157).

7. The Milanese oboeist-composer Giuseppe Sammartini settled in London in 1728. Richard Platt, who edited six of his recorder sonatas (Faber), says they may have been written before he left Italy. They differ from the Corelli-based English sonatas by being usually in a Vivaldian three-movement form (fast-slow-fast). They have some odd melodic phrases and unexpected harmonies—the nearest any sonatas designated for recorder get to the 'rococo' musical style of the mid-18th c.

8. There is a full account of the Corelli pirating in David Lasocki's editions of two of the 1707 recorder versions, No. 3 (London: Musica Rara, 1974) and No. 4 (New York: Hargail, 1972).

9. The 'Pastor Fido' sonatas are in fact partly arrangements, quite skilfully accomplished, of concertos by Vivaldi and others, with some French material that may have been composed by the publisher, Marchand; see pp. 132–5 of Michael Talbot's *Vivaldi* in 'The Master Musician' Series (London: Dent, paperback edn. 1984). For Vivaldi and the recorder, see articles by David Lasocki in *AR* 9 (1968), 103–7, reprinted in *RMM* 3 (Mar. 1969), 22–7, and by Eleanor Selfridge-Field, 'Vivaldi's Esoteric Instruments', *EM* 6 (1978), 332–8 (for the recorder; see p. 332 and note). The 1986 Ryom catalogue of Vivaldi's instrumental works mentions only one 'flauto' (= recorder) sonata, RV 52, published by Schott (ed. Nagel) in 1973 as OFB 115 together with another 'Vivaldi' sonata from a manuscript in a library in Venice as OFB 116. Both are pleasant works, but not nearly as interesting as several Vivaldi concertos with recorder and small groups of other instruments.

10. e.g. Frescobaldi, Christopher Simpson ('Faronell's Ground'), Marin Marais, Gaspar Sanz (guitar), Lully, Domenico Scarlatti, Vivaldi, Pergolesi, C. P. E. Bach, Cherubini, and, in a derived form, Paganini, thence Brahms and Rachmaninov. Cherubini's use of the tune was in his opera *L'Hôtellerie Portugaise*, which was particularly appropriate as this madness dance probably originated in Portugal, not Spain, and may have been brought there by the Moors.

11. Some editions show an up-beat phrasing before the last crotchet in bars 4 and 8, which weakens the symmetry of the theme. Editions also differ in their numbering of the variations, some counting bar 23, 'allegro', as variation 1.

12. See Ch. 3 n. 3. Purcell's sonatas are trio sonatas for violins, one solo violin sonata, and trumpet pieces. Although, like J. S. Bach, he wrote wonderful music for recorders, he composed no solo sonatas for the instrument.

13. For Roger North's lively descriptions of the richness of English musical life in this period see John Wilson's *Roger North on Music*, especially p. 25 (quoted), and, on Corelli, pp. 358–9. North mentions Cazzati and Vitali as earlier influences on the English sonata (p. 351).

14. Purcell 'to the Reader', 1683 (Newman, 307).

15. From Finger's dedicatory preface to his 1689 sonatas, quoted by Arthur W. Marshall in an article on Finger's chamber music in *The Consort*, 26 (1970), 423–32. See also his article on Finger's recorder music in *RMM* 5 (Sept. 1977), 350–2. He considers Op. 3 No. 2 in C minor to be Finger's finest sonata.

16. Quoted from his preface Nova Music publications of Finger's chamber music, referred to by David Lasocki in his article on 'The Detroit Recorder Manuscript', *AR* 23 (1982), 95–102. This manuscript, from about 1700, contains 20 sonatas and sets of divisions, being 9 by Finger, 7 by Paisible, 2 by William Williams, 1 by Edward Finch, and 1 attributed to Corelli. Lasocki's commentary gives an admirable account of the recorder sonata in late 17th-c. London, and describes the social background of sonata-playing in England at that time.

17. Roger North in 1728 refers to Corelli's music as 'to ye musitians like ye bread of life' (Newman, 43).

18. Thornowitz's Sonata da Camera in F (1721) is the subject of consideration in Freda Dinn's *Early Music for Recorders*, 51–4.

19. This is John Lœillet 'of London', not his cousin J.-B. Lœillet 'of Ghent'. John Lœillet, a wind-player who prospered in London's concert-room musical life and was instrumental in popularizing the transverse flute, wrote six sonatas 'for a Common Flute' and six 'for a German flute' as his Op. 3, as well as trio sonatas with recorder and oboe (Op. 1 and 2). See Hunt, 59.

20. The recorder sonatas (London, *c.*1720) of William Turner have not yet been published in a modern edition, nor have eleven of the twelve in Mercy's two sets (1718 and 1720) despite their quirkiness—including passage-work intended to be in imitation of violin double-stopping.

21. For a general review of English (and Scottish) sonatas, see Newman, 301–38. The *New Grove* and Julie Anne Sadie's *Companion to Baroque Music* are good sources of information on individual composers, though several in this list do not appear there. See also Hunt, ch. 4.

22. It should be said that Paisible's sonatas were probably intended more for the composer's much-admired performances in London music-rooms than for amateur recorder-players, and were rather too difficult to be pounced upon for publication by Walsh; but thirteen survive in manuscript. Lasocki, in his article on the Detroit manuscript, comments interestingly on Paisible's French-style background and says that his Italianate recorder sonatas 'have a bold, even reckless quality about them, as if he had been given the freedom to try out something novel and exciting and was enjoying himself enormously' (p. 100). This movement of Paisible's F major sonata is quoted from a series of English recorder sonatas from around 1700 (ed. Schneider) in the Bärenreiter edition, HM 208, 209, and 237 (with two Paisible sonatas).

23. Schickhardt's compositions were usually published by Estienne Roger, and later by Le Cène, in Amsterdam; see David Lasocki, 'Schickhardt in London', *RMM* 6 (Sept. 1979), 203–5.

24. Excluding recorder appearances in primarily vocal compositions (e.g. Schütz, J. S. Bach, Zelenka), the list of German and Austrian Baroque composers who wrote for

recorders in small instrumental groups includes (in roughly chronological order) Schmelzer, Biber, Fux, Pez; Mattheson, Prowo, and Telemann; Heinichen, Graupner, J. C. Faber, Fasch, and Quantz. To this list might be added J. S. Bach, as his A major flute sonata (BMV 1032) has a possible antecedent version in C for recorder, violin, and continuo (see Michael Marissen's article in *EM* 13 (1985), 384–90).

25. Four in the periodical *Der getreue Musikmeister*, including the superb F minor sonata for bassoon or recorder (Schott also published another F minor Telemann sonata), two masterpieces of the genre in *Essercizii musici* (in D minor—see Ch. 3—and in C), and two recorder or bassoon sonatinas in C minor and A minor, for which the bass part is still missing.

26. e.g. in Cassel. Also in Vienna.

27. This reduces the key signature by three sharps, or adds three flats, which suits the recorder well except if there are high D♯s or E♭s in the original: this causes the odd F♯'' problem with Telemann's flute duets.

28. Both Roman (Newman, 349–50) and de Fesch (ibid. 344–5: 'a kind of Dutch Mendelssohn in his day') worked for a while in London.

29. Many German Baroque composers, however, while usually preserving their independent characteristics, were strongly influenced by French as well as by Italian music, especially in certain princely courts aping Versailles.

30. For example, the pyrotechnics in the Vivace movement ending Telemann's *Der getreue Musikmeister* recorder sonata in C major should be played with a certain deliberation, emphasizing the form and harmonic structure of the movement, not as an unsectionalized cascade of semiquavers.

31. See David Lasocki's articles on Schickhardt in *RMM* 5 (Dec. 1976 and Mar. 1977), 254–7, 287–90.

32. In his preface Schickhardt does, however, suggest transposing those sonatas which are too difficult. As to his music, it is always workmanlike and pleasing, but his inspiration comes less often in the solo sonatas than in compositions with more instruments.

33. In *Critica Musica* (1722), quoted by Walter Bergmann, 'Henry Purcell's Use of the Recorder', *RMM* 1 (Nov. 1965), 333–5.

34. Another fingering that may work is – 1–3 45ᵛ6– with 3 leaking to reduce its clickishness. For partial venting (slide-fingering or leaking) on trill-fingerings, see Eugene Reichenthal's article in *RMM* 5 (June 1976), 193–5.

35. The Zen-On edition of Schickhardt's sonatas in all the keys obligingly provides a pull-out supplement on trill-fingerings, based on those of Hotteterre.

36. ed. Andreas Habert (Amadeus Edition, Winterthur, Switzerland (Schott) BP 406). This sonata features in several recorder recitals on CD.

37. He was, like other members of this family of musicians, a member of Louis XIV's Grande Écurie and Chambre du Roi.

38. This reflects more upon what was expected of composers (limits of good taste) than upon the composers' versatility. Thus Dieupart wrote totally French suites (see Ch. 4 n. 6) while he remained in his native country, but he moved to London in about 1700, and in 1717 published six recorder sonatas in close imitation of Corelli, if anything with traces of an English accent.

39. They occur in bars 7 and 33, but another, perhaps better, phrasing is to take the first of the pair, with a half-trill or mordent to render its +, as the end of the phrase, and to play the second quaver as the up-beat note to the following phrase.

40. Edited for recorder and continuo by Ulrich Thieme with the 'Neuvième Concert' ('The Portrait of Love')—Moeck Ed. 2531, and also in Musica Rara. In Couperin's piece the disjunct semiquavers of the second subject are rather Italian, though, arguably, inequality might apply to some conjunct semiquavers elsewhere in Couperin's Fuguéte.

41. e.g. the Allemande Fuguée and Air Contre Fugué of the second Concert Royal—another Couperin piece playable on tenor recorder and continuo.

42. Recorder-players are by no means unanimous in this view of J.-B. Lœillet. Some would nominate Barsanti as their 'third sonata composer'. Lœillet's sonatas are elegant, melodious, and predictable, managing to combine restraint with liveliness. Barsanti's are more adventurous and elaborate—they are uncompromisingly Italian, but with some signs of *galant* mannerisms. Barsanti's sonatas are more interesting than Lœillet's, but which are the more musically satisfying is a matter of personal taste.

43. Anthony quotes examples from sonatas by Senaillé and Leclair (pp. 332–3).

44. Ed. Carl Dolmetsch (Schott Ed. 10132).

45. Douglas MacMillan's article on 'The Recorder in the Late Eighteenth and Early Nineteenth Centuries' lists seventeen pieces composed for the recorder between 1750 and 1811, when Anton Heberle's 'Sonate brillante' was published in Vienna for 'czakan or flûte douce' (Hunt, 86–7). He also lists twelve recorder tutors from 1750 to 1818. There is a fuller account of the Viennese czakan (a kind of soprano recorder with or without keys) in Hugo Reyne's introduction to his edition of Heberle's 1808 unaccompanied 'Sonate' (Moeck Ed. 1119). Music for csakan and piano by Ernst Krähmer (ed. Piers Adams) is published by Dolce Edition, Brighton. This minuscule repertoire is refreshingly different from any other music written specifically for the recorder.

46. i.e. those composed with violin or flute in London in 1764 (when Mozart was 8), K. 10–15, and the six with flute arranged in 1800 from the violin sonatas K. 296 and K. 376–80.

47. Pugnani wrote most of his sonatas for violin and keyboard without the flute option (see Newman, *The Sonata in the Classic Era* (New York: W. W. Norton, 1963), 241–6). As a violinist Pugnani gave himself a measure of melodic independence, and his sonatas do not therefore work as well as some others of the period as solo keyboard pieces.

48. Thus Pugnani is described by Rangoni in 1790 (*Essai*, quoted by Newman in *The Sonata in the Classic Era*, 232–3): 'This great sonata composer, who derives as much from the magic of his impassioned lyricism as from that of his performance, sacrifices . . . stylistic elegance to the sentiment that consumes him, and often enraptures the spirit with the fancies of the imagination. His music is ruled neither by the art of bowing nor the problem of the hand, [both of] which he subordinates entirely to the communication of the sentiment . . . his modulations are clear, concise and energetic, like the sentences of a philosopher and an orator.'

49. Daniel Heartz, defining 'Empfindsamkeit' in the *New Grove*.

50. Schott's published the Berkeley Sonatina in 1940, but the Leigh had to be deferred to 1944. Both are still in print—OFB 1040 (Berkeley) and 1041 (Leigh).

51. Hunt, 140, part of his first-hand account of the recorder revival in his chs. 7 and 8 (which he intends to up-date in the next edition of his book). The most complete critical account of 20th-c. recorder music is that by Eve O'Kelly, which incorporates a select catalogue of currently available 20th-c. recorder music published for concert performance, i.e. omitting school, etc., recorder music. She comments on the Leigh, Berkeley, and

Reizenstein pieces on pp. 38–40. There are interesting short articles on 20th-c. recorder music by Niall O'Loughlin in *EM* 10 (1982), 36–7, and by Malcolm Hund-Davies in *RMM* 6 (Sept. 1978), 66–8, both referring to these three pieces. The Darnton, Kisch, and Rawsthorne sonatinas were withdrawn from publication by their composers.

52. Sonatina Op. 128, but finer still are several pieces in variation form, including the nostalgic 'Meditazioni sopra *Cœurs Désolés*', Op. 67 for treble recorder and harpsichord (Lengnick). See O'Kelly, 46, and article by Edgar Hunt in *RMM* 8 (June 1986), 296–7.

53. Thirteen compositions with recorder (O'Kelly, 46–8). In common with several other composers who wrote for recorders (ibid. 43–4), Cooke was strongly influenced by Hindemith, whose one recorder work, a trio from 1932, is an extraordinarily powerful piece (ibid. 40–3).

54. Walter Leigh was born in 1906 and was killed in action in Libya in 1942. He is best known for his Concertino for harpsichord and strings.

55. A slighter, single-movement Sonatina in the same vein was written by Christopher Edmunds for descant recorder and piano (Schott).

56. More generally in 20th-c. music, slurs, especially long ones, indicate legato phrasing (see Murrill sonata, Exx. 5.4–7). Thus Staeps, in his preface to his first recorder sonata (in E flat, Universal Ed. 1951), said: 'Phrasing-marks [i.e. 'slurs'] in the recorder part indicate a *legato* in the special sense understood by recorder-players: notes grouped under such a phrasing-mark should be neither slurred nor separated, but evenly tongued. Notes without phrasing-marks are to be played *non-legato*.' In his Sonata in C minor 'In Modo Preclassico' (New York: Galaxy), Staeps suggests 'well-connected legato tonguing. The last note under a slur is always to be somewhat shortened.'

57. See van Hauwe, *Modern Recorder Player*, ii. 89–90, 'How to Survive among Louder Instruments'.

58. It should be noted that older copies of this publication show in the recorder part a high E♯ in the slow movement before the two-bar rest. This should be E♮. It is correct in the score (and in current copies). Composers check the scores of their music, but not always the parts.

59. Lennox Berkeley studied with Nadia Boulanger in Paris, and was a close friend of Ravel and Poulenc.

60. Spiky rhythms can be very effective on the recorder, with its neat and lively articulation. See, for example, the Presto of Ronald Finch's Sonata (Schott), and the last movement of Robin Milford's Sonatina (Oxford University Press).

61. Published by Doblinger (Vienna and Munich), his Op. 76. Robert Schollum (b. 1913) has some sixty-five publications by Doblinger, including four symphonies and eleven sonatas for a variety of wind instruments, two of them for recorder.

62. A sonata for treble recorder, and one for descant recorder, by Bergmann, several by Linde, including a 'Sonatine française' (though Linde excels in approachable avant-garde music—O'Kelly, 60–1), and by Staeps a great variety, including one for flute or recorder, and Sonatas 'In Modo Preclassico' (written for a gifted 12-year-old) and 'Im alten Stil', *Gebrauchsmusik* at its best. For Staeps, see O'Kelly, 48–9.

63. 'The only real sonata the recorder has yet been privileged to receive' (Richard D. C. Noble, 'The Recorder in Twentieth-Century Music—A Personal View', *RMM* 1 (Feb. 1965), 243–4). It is one of three recorder works by this prolific Dutch composer (he wrote forty-one symphonies). See O'Kelly, 44–5.

64. Luciano Berio ('Gesti'), Rob du Bois (see Roderick Arran, 'Muziek voor Altblokfluit—

Rob du Bois', *RMM* 7 (Dec. 1981), 91–4), Louis Andriessen ('Sweet'), and Will Eisma ('Hot Powdery Stones' and 'Wonders are Scarce') have all written avant-garde music, often for Frans Brüggen. Other interesting music in this idiom has been written by Jürg Baur ('Incontri' and 'Mutazioni'), Michael Vetter (the graphic 'Rezitative'; see O'Kelly, 75–7), Gerhard Braun (O'Kelly, 61–3), Konrad Lechner ('Spüren im Sand'), Hans-Martin Linde ('Music for a Bird'), John Casken ('Thymehaze'), and the Polish composer Kazimierz Serocki ('Arrangements' and 'Concerto alla Cadenza'). The Japanese composers include Hirose, Ishi'i ('Black Intention'; O'Kelly, 67–9) and Shinohara ('Fragmente'; O'Kelly, 57–9).

65. A three-movement sonata by Noriyuk Waki, who studied with Genzmer (see Ichiro Tada, 'The Recorder in Japan', *EM* 10 (1982), 38–40). This sonata achieves a good balance between recorder and piano by concentrating on the treble's high notes.

66. Gordon Crosse, in his 'Watermusic'—a suite of three pieces for recorder and piano (Oxford, 1989)—uses tenor, treble, descant, and optional sopranino recorders, with three changes of instrument, all during the course of the final 'Very Fast' Hornpipe (only for drunken sailors).

67. See also *RT* 89–90.

68. If the Berkeley Sonatina is played sitting down, though this somehow does not really look right for a 20th-c. sonata, Method 4 (with tensed lip or chin protection) is a securer way of playing the F$\sharp''$ in bar 20.5 than Method 2, with its risk of flatness and coarse tone at a climactic crotchet. It also makes it practicable to play the (better) flute version at 5 in the first movement. The F$\sharp''$ in the following bar may then be played Ø 1–3 4567X (i.e. adding 5) to give more time to lift the foot of the instrument to play E' onwards with normal fingering. The downward double-tongued semiquaver scale of the flute version in bar 5.1 then constitutes an element of balance with the downward double-tongued semiquaver arpeggio of bar 7.2 in both versions.

69. Eve O'Kelly (p. 119) believes 'It is important for the survival of the instrument that it should avoid being pushed into a ghetto, heard only in all-recorder programmes given before audiences composed almost exclusively of recorder enthusiasts, as happens very often at the moment.' Players of recorder sonatas should take every opportunity to participate in programmes with other instruments, such as Baroque violin or oboe, maybe playing only one recorder sonata within a programme including trio sonatas or other ensemble music, such as 20th-c. quartets with recorder by composers such as Berkeley, Cooke, Mellers, William Mathias, and others listed in the O'Kelly catalogue (pp. 137–68). It is encouraging to note that Eve O'Kelly's choice of about 400 of the best 20th-c. compositions with recorder includes 30 sonatas or sonatinas for recorder and keyboard, 10 of them written in the 70s and 80s; and her list excludes some excellent sonatas that are now out of print and unavailable. Even while this book was being completed, new sonatas by Andrew Challinger, Dennis Bamforth and Carl Rütti were given their first U.K. performances. The recorder sonata is by no means an outmoded form.

Note to Appendix 1

1. Reprinted from *RMM* 8 (Mar. and June 1984), 14–16, 47–8, with slight revisions.

Supplementary Notes

(Publications not in Bibliography, except for first and fourth notes.)

Ch. 3	For a comprehensive account of recorder dynamics see Johannes Fischer, *Die Dynamische Blockflöte*, Moeck ed. 4048 (Celle, 1990), reviewed by Pete Rose in *AR* 32 (1991), 22–3.
p. 86	See Malcolm Tattersall, 'When is a Slur not a Slur', *The Recorder* (Melbourne) No. 11 (June 1990), pp. 13–16.
p. 109	See Stewart Carter, 'The String Tremolo in the 17th Century', *EM* 19 (1991), 43–59.
p. 126	See also Bibliography under Arnold, Hayes, and Ledbetter.
p. 146	Voice-flute players may also explore late Baroque flute sonatas by Pietro Locatelli (Newman, 345–9), Giovanni Battista Sammartini (younger brother of Guiseppe—Newman, *The Sonata in the Classic Era*, 217–27), and Johann Adolf Hasse (Newman, 278–9).
p. 155	Other pieces for recorder and guitar include a sonata by Jean Françaix (Schott, 1984), Linde's 'Musica da Camera' (Schott, 1972) and Alun Hoddinott's 'Italian Suite' (Oxford, 1983).
p. 190 n. 12	See also G. Moens-Haenen, *Das Vibrato in der Musik des Barock* (Graz, 1980).
p. 190 n. 14	In an article in *EM* 19 (1991), 61–7 on 'Instrumentation and Genre in Italian Music, 1600–1670', Eleanor Selfridge-Field makes it clear that early Italian sonatas and canzonas would rarely have been performed on the recorder. But do not let that discourage us.
p. 193 n. 10	. . . and David Lasocki, 'More on Echo Flutes', ibid., No. 13 (July, 1991), 14–16.
p. 6 Ex. 1.1	The trills in bar 4 are best taken as unturned passing trills (see pp. 164–5).
p. 48 Ex. 3.3	A pupil has pointed out an interpretational dilemma in this Grave movement—should the semiquaver groups in bars 7–10 be in up-beat or down-beat phrasing?

Addendum

Dr Carl Dolmetsch very kindly commented on this book, but at too late a stage of production for all his points to be taken into account. Some, however, are referred to below:

1. pp. 44–5. There are various devices by which a harpsichord player may make gradations of volume, but normally a single note once struck cannot get louder (see p. 24).

2. p. 69 — length of appoggiaturas. Some French Baroque writers advocate long appoggiaturas. See Arnold Dolmetsch, *The Interpretation of the Music of the XVII and XVIII Centuries* (London: Novello, 1915, and Dolmetsch Foundation, 1990) 99–100 (Marais) and 165–6 (Hotteterre and Couperin).

3. Carl Dolmetsch and Herbert Murrill gave the first performance of the Murrill Sonata (see pp. 86–93) in 1950, and Murrill preferred the harpsichord to the piano (see p. 189 n. 13!). They agreed that the slurs represented a mixture of real slurs and legato expression indications (p. 86), although Murrill did not want an (unphrased) 'continuous smooth legato'

(p. 88). They slurred the first seven notes of the Largo (p. 87) as 3 notes then 4, not 2+2+3 as suggested in Ex. 5.6. The Presto (Ex. 5.8) was played at lightning speed, and Murrill would not have liked it to be slowed down (see p. 116). Carl Dolmetsch suggested, and Murrill accepted, that trills might be from the upper note, and at Murrill's request wrote the cadenza at the end of the Presto, with an intonationally accurate high F#'' within the slur (p. 188 n. 12). But Murrill (p. 121), Berkeley (p. 157), and Rubbra (p. 158) generally only put in slurs up to this note on account of the recorder's limitations. If one performs these works, standing up of course, with the composers' preferred articulation of the F#''s, this will usually necessitate the use of a bell-key, which would, however, also resolve problems with other high notes such as A'' (p. 122): see chapter on Dolmetsch bell-key fingerings in Carl Dolmetsch's *Advanced Recorder Technique* (Nelson, 1989).

BIBLIOGRAPHY

ANTHONY, JAMES R., *French Baroque Music from Beaujoyeulx to Rameau* (rev. edn., New York: W. W. Norton, 1981).

ARNOLD, FRANCK THOMAS, *The Art of Accompaniment from a Thorough-Bass* (London: Oxford University Press, 1931; repr. New York, Dover, 1965).

ARRAN, RODERICK, 'Muziek voor Altblokfluit—Rob du Bois', *Recorder and Music Magazine*, 7, No. 4 (Dec. 1981), 91–4.

ARTHUR, BRADFORD, 'Hotteterre's "tu-ru" ', *The American Recorder*, 14 (1973), 79–82.

BACH, CARL PHILIP EMMANUEL, *Essay on the True Art of Playing Keyboard Instruments* (1753), tr. and ed. W. J. Mitchell (London: Cassell, 1949).

BERGMANN, WALTER, 'Henry Purcell's Use of the Recorder', *Recorder and Music Magazine*, 1, No. 11 (Nov. 1965), 333–5.

BIANCONI, LORENZO, *Music in the Seventeenth Century* (Cambridge: Cambridge University Press, 1987).

BROWN, ADRIAN, *The Recorder: A Basic Workshop Manual* (Brighton: Dolce Edition, 1989).

BROWN, HOWARD MAYER, *Embellishing 16th-Century Music* (London: Oxford University Press, 1976).

—— and Sadie, Stanley (eds.), *Performance Practice: Music after 1600* (London: Macmillan, 1990).

BUELOW, GEORGE J., and MARX, HANS-JOACHIM, *New Mattheson Studies* (Cambridge: Cambridge University Press, 1983).

BUKOFZER, MANFRED, *Music in the Baroque Era* (New York: W. W. Norton, 1947).

BUTLER, GREGORY G.. 'The Projection of Affect in Baroque Dance Music', *Early Music*, 12 (1984), 201–7.

CALDWELL, JOHN, *Editing Early Music* (Oxford: Oxford University Press, 1985).

CASTELLANI, MARCELLO, and DURANTE, ELIO, *Del portar della lingua negli instrumenti di fiato* (Florence: S.P.E.S., 1979).

CLARK, KENNETH, *Civilisation* (London: BBC, 1969).

CLARK, PAUL, Review of Niels Viggo Bentzon, Sonatina Op. 180, in *Recorder and Music Magazine*, 5, No. 2 (June 1975), 69.

COOMBER, DAVID, 'Rhetoric and Affect in Baroque Music', *The Recorder* (Melbourne), No. 3 (Nov. 1985), 23–7.

DART, THURSTON, *The Interpretation of Music* (London: Hutchinson, 1954).

DAVIS, ALAN, *Treble Recorder Technique* (London: Novello, 1983).

DIKMANS, GREG, 'Florid Italian Instrumental Music circa 1600: An Introduction', *The Recorder* (Melbourne), No. 4 (May 1986), 5–13.

DINN, FREDA, *Early Music for Recorders* (London: Schott, 1974).

DONINGTON, ROBERT, *Baroque Music: Style and Performance* (London: Faber, 1982).

—— *The Interpretation of Early Music* (London: Faber, 1989).

—— *A Performer's Guide to Baroque Music* (London: Faber, 1973).

—— *String Playing in Baroque Music* (London: Faber, 1977).

FISCHER, JOHANNES, *Die Dynamische Blockflöte* Moeck, ed. 4048 (Celle, 1990).

GANASSI, SYLVESTRO, *Fontegara* (Venice, 1535), ed. Hildemarie Peter, tr. Dorothy Swainson (Berlin: Lienau, 1956).

GIRDLESTONE, CUTHBERT, *Jean-Philippe Rameau: His Life and Works* (London, 1957; repr. New York: Dover, 1969).

GOODDEN, ANGELICA, *Actio and Persuasion* (Oxford: Oxford University Press, 1986).

HAYES, GREGORY, 'Your Accompanist and You', *The American Recorder*, 32 (1991), 14–16, 24.

HAYNES, BRUCE, 'The Baroque Recorder: A Comparison with its Modern Counterpart', *The American Recorder*, 10 (1969), 3–8.

HOTTETERRE LE ROMAIN, Jacques, *Principles of the Flute, Recorder & Oboe* (1707), tr. and ed. David Lasocki (London: Barrie and Jenkins, 1968).

HOULE, GEORGE, *Meter in Music 1600–1800: Performance, Perception and Notation* (Bloomington: Indiana University Press, 1987).

—— 'Tongueing and Rhythmic Patterns in Early Music', *The American Recorder*, 6 (1965), 4–13.

HUND-DAVIES, MALCOLM, 'A Review of Historical Styles of Recorder Playing, Part 1', *Recorder and Music Magazine*, 6, No. 3 (Sept. 1978), 66–8.

HUNT, EDGAR, *The Recorder and its Music* (enlarged edn., London: Faber, 1977).

—— 'The Recorder Music of Edmund Rubbra', *Recorder and Music Magazine*, 8, No. 10 (June 1986), 296–7.

HUTCHINGS, ARTHUR, *The Baroque Concerto* (London: Faber and Faber, 1961).

KELLER, HERMANN, *Phrasing and Articulation* (London: Barrie and Rockliff, 1965).

KENYON, NICHOLAS (ed.), *Authenticity and Early Music* (Oxford: Oxford University Press, 1988).

KITE-POWELL, JEFFERY, Review of early seventeenth-century dances in London Pro Musica publications, *The American Recorder*, 30 (1989), 159.

KNEIHS, HANS MARIA, 'Musical Structure and Interpretation with Reference to Marcello's Sonata in D minor' in *The Recorder* (Melbourne), No. 3 (1985), 15–19.

KOTTICK, EDWARD L., *Tone and Intonation on the Recorder* (New York: McGinnis and Marx, 1974).

Lasocki, David, ' "Authenticity" in Performances of Early Music', *Recorder and Music Magazine*, 5, No. 12 (Dec. 1977), 384–7.

—— 'The Detroit Recorder Manuscript', *The American Recorder*, 23 (1982), 95–102.

—— 'Johann Christian Schickhardt', *Recorder and Music Magazine*, 5, No. 8 (Dec. 1976), 254–7; No. 9 (Mar. 1977), 287–90.

—— 'Late Baroque Ornamentation: Philosophy and Guidelines', *The American Recorder*, 29 (1988), 7–10.

—— 'A New Look at Handel's Recorder Sonatas', *Recorder and Music Magazine*, 6, Nos. 1 and 3 (Mar. and Sept. 1978), 2–9, 71–9.

—— 'Quantz and the Passions: Theory and Practice', *Early Music*, 6 (1978), 556–67.

—— 'Schickhardt in London', *Recorder and Music Magazine* 6, No. 7 (Sept. 1979), 203–5.

—— 'The Tongueing Syllables of the French Baroque', *The American Recorder*, 8 (1967), 81–2.

—— 'Vivaldi and the Recorder', *The American Recorder*, 9 (1968), 103–7 (repr. in *Recorder and Music Magazine*, 3, No. 1 (Mar. 1969), 22–7).

—— and Legêne, Eva, 'Learning to Ornament Handel's Sonatas through the Composer's Ears' *The American Recorder*, 30 (1989), 9–14, 102–6, 137–41.

Ledbetter, David, *Continuo Playing According to Handel: His Figured Bass Exercises* (Oxford: Oxford University Press, 1990).

le Huray, Peter, *Authenticity in Performance: Eighteenth-Century Case Studies* (Cambridge: Cambridge University Press, 1990).

Leppard, Raymond, *Authenticity in Music* (London: Faber, 1988).

Lussy, M. Mathis, *Musical Expression* (London: Novello, n.d.).

McClure, Theron, 'Making the Music Speak: Silences of Articulation', *The American Recorder*, 29 (1988), 53–5.

McGee, Timothy J., *Medieval and Renaissance Music: A Performer's Guide* (Toronto: University of Toronto Press, 1985).

MacMillan, Douglas, 'The Recorder in the Late Eighteenth and Early Nineteenth Centuries', *The Consort*, 39 (1983), 489–97.

Marissen, Michael, 'A Trio in C major for Recorder, Violin and Continuo by J. S. Bach?', *Early Music*, 13 (1985), 384–90.

Marshall, Arthur W., 'The Chamber Music of Godfrey Finger', *The Consort*, 26 (1970), 423–32.

—— 'The Recorder Music of Godfrey Finger', *Recorder and Music Magazine*, 5, No. 11 (Sept. 1977), 350–2.

Martin, John, 'Echoes from the Past', *The Recorder* (Melbourne), No. 9 (Feb. 1989), 1–3.

—— , Morgan, Fred, and Tattersall, Malcolm, 'Echoes Resounding' *The Recorder* (Melbourne), No. 10 (Dec. 1989), 19–24.

MASSY, JAMES, 'The Flattening Effect of "Pulling Out" on the Recorder', *Recorder and Music Magazine*, 6, No. 2 (June 1978), 34–5.

MATHER, BETTY BANG, *Dance Rhythms of the French Baroque* (Bloomington: Indiana University Press, 1987).

—— 'Developing Baroque Ornamentation Skills', *The American Recorder*, 29 (1988), 4–6.

—— *Interpretation of French Music from 1675 to 1775 for Woodwind and Other Performers* (New York: McGinnis and Marx, 1973).

—— and Lasocki, David, *The Art of Preluding 1700–1830* (New York: McGinnis and Marx, 1984).

—— —— *Free Ornamentation in Woodwind Music 1700–1775* (New York: McGinnis and Marx, 1976).

MATTHESON, J., *Der vollkommene Capellmeister* (Hamburg, 1739), tr. Ernest C. Harriss (Ann Arbor: UMI Research Press, 1981).

MÖNKEMEYER, HELMUT, *Advanced School of Recorder Playing* (Celle: Moeck, 1967).

NEUMANN, FREDERICK, *Ornamentation in Baroque and Post-Baroque Music, with Special Emphasis on J. S. Bach* (Princeton: Princeton University Press, 1978).

New Grove Dictionary of Music and Musicians, ed. Stanley Sadie, 20 vols. (London: Macmillan, 1980).

NEWMAN, ANTHONY, *Bach and the Baroque: A Performing Guide to Baroque Music with Special Emphasis on the Music of J. S. Bach* (New York: Pendragon Press, 1985).

NEWMAN, WILLIAM S., *The Sonata in the Baroque Era* (4th edn., New York: W. W. Norton, 1983).

—— *The Sonata in the Classic Era* (New York: W. W. Norton, 1963).

NOBLE, RICHARD D. C., 'The Recorder in Twentieth-Century Music—A Personal View', *Recorder and Music Magazine*, 1, No. 8 (Feb. 1965), 243–4.

NORTH, ROGER, *Roger North on Music*, ed. John Wilson (London: Novello, 1959).

O'KELLY, EVE, *The Recorder Today* (Cambridge: Cambridge University Press, 1990).

—— Review of Francesco Mancini's Sonatas VII and XI in *Recorder and Music Magazine*, 8, No. 5 (Mar. 1985), 157.

O'LOUGHLIN, NIALL, 'The Recorder in 20th-Century Music', *Early Music*, 10 (1982), 36–7.

PALISCA, CLAUDE, *Baroque Music* (Englewood Cliffs, NJ: Prentice-Hall, 1968).

QUANTZ, JOHANN JOACHIM, *On Playing the Flute*, tr. Edward R. Reilly (2nd edn., London: Faber and Faber, 1985).

RAMEAU, JEAN-PHILIPPE, *Nouvelles Réflexions de M. Rameau sur sa Démonstration du Principe de l'Harmonie* (1752), ed. Erwin Jacobi, in *Jean-Philippe Rameau: Complete Theoretical Writings*, v (Rome, 1969).

RANUM, PATRICIA, 'Audible Rhetoric and Mute Rhetoric: The 17th-Century French Sarabande', *Early Music*, 14 (1986), 22–39.

REICHENTHAL, EUGENE, 'Partial Venting', *Recorder and Music Magazine*, 5, No. 6 (June 1976), 193–5.

REISS, SCOTT, 'Articulation: The Key to Expressive Playing', *The American Recorder*, 27 (1986), 144–9.

—— 'Pitch Control: Shading and Leaking', *The American Recorder*, 28 (1987), 136–9.

ROWLAND-JONES, ANTHONY, *A Practice Book for the Treble Recorder* (Oxford: Oxford University Press, 1962).

—— *Recorder Technique: Intermediate to Advanced* (2nd edn., Oxford: Oxford University Press, 1986).

—— 'A Slur on Slurring?', *Journal of the National Early Music Association*, No. 9 (July 1988), 1–6.

SACHS, CURT, *Rhythm and Tempo* (London: Dent, 1953).

SADIE, JULIE ANNE, 'Charpentier and the Early French Ensemble Sonata', *Early Music*, 7 (1979), 330–5.

—— (ed.), *Companion to Baroque Music* (London: Dent, 1990).

SCHECK, GUSTAVE, 'The Recorder Sonatas of Telemann', *Recorder and Music Magazine*, 2, No. 8 (Feb. 1968), 236–8.

SELFRIDGE-FIELD, ELEANOR, 'Vivaldi's Esoteric Instruments', *Early Music*, 6 (1978), 332–8.

STEVENS, DENIS, *Musicology* (London: Macdonald, 1980).

STRUNK, OLIVER, *Source Readings in Music History: The Baroque Era* (New York: W. W. Norton, 1965).

TADA, ICHIRO, 'The Recorder in Japan', *Early Music*, 10 (1982), 38–40.

TALBOT, MICHAEL, *Vivaldi* (London: Dent, 1984).

THOMAS, BERNARD, *The Baroque Solo Book* (Brighton: Dolce Edition, 1989).

VAN HAUWE, WALTER, *The Modern Recorder Player*, 2 vols. (London: Schott, 1984–7).

VEILHAN, JEAN-CLAUDE, *The Baroque Recorder in 17th- and 18th-Century Performance Practice: Technique, Performing Style, Original Fingering Charts* (Paris: Leduc, 1980).

—— *The Rules of Musical Interpretation in the Baroque Era*, tr. John Lambert (Paris: Leduc, 1977).

VETTER, MICHAEL, *Il flauto dolce ed acerbo* (Celle: Moeck, 1969).

WAITZMAN, DANIEL, *The Art of Playing the Recorder* (New York: AMS Press, 1978).

WENZINGER, AUGUST, 'Expression and its Interpretation in Baroque Music', *The American Recorder*, 11 (1970), 8–15.

WILSON, MICHAEL, *The National Gallery, London* (London: Orbis, 1977).

WIND, THIEMO, 'Bigaglia's Sonata in A minor—A New Look at its Originality', *Recorder and Music Magazine*, 8, No. 2 (June 1984), 49–54.

—— 'New Facts Concerning Bigaglia's Sonata in A minor', *Recorder and Music Magazine*, 8, No. 4 (Dec. 1984), 106–8.

WOLLITZ, KENNETH, *The Recorder Book* (London: Gollancz, 1982).

INDEX

Entries in italics relate to music examples. The main entries in a list are in bold print. The Notes section (pp. 173–202) is not comprehensively indexed, but notes of special importance or interest are referred to by both page and note-number.

Abel, Carl Friedrich 147
'accens' 63, 98
accenti, see ornaments
'accompanist' 115, 125, 130
  see also bass; continuo; harpsichord;
    piano; *etc.*
acting 6, 45
  see also dramatic music; opera; orator
affects (= 'passions', or mood) 3, **4–5**, 6, 10, **12**,
    13, **30**, 31, 40, **46–7**, 53, **55**, 58, 63, 87, 98,
    108, 110, 124, 126–7, **149**, 160, 173, **174–5**,
    177 n. 43, 185 n. 21
  in relation to articulation 5, 74, 92
  in relation to ornamentation 54, **98**, 101, 107,
    190, 192
  in relation to speed 114, 116, 117
'affetti' 51, 101, 103, **107–11**, 130, 131, 192
Affettuoso 5, *9*, 47, *51*, 111, 176 n. 36
agogic accent 55, 84, 183
Agricola, Martin (*Musica Instrumentalis*
  Deudsch) 18, 104, 188, 190
'Air Contre' (Couperin) 63
'Alberti bass' 149
Alemann, Eduardo 155
Alembert D', Jean le Rond 175
allemande, *see* dance
Alton, Edwin 195
Amalia, Anna 147
American Recorder, The (*AR*) xiii, 97, 175, 176,
    180, 181, 184, 186, 187, 188, 189, 192, 195,
    201
Anthony, James R. (*French Baroque Music*) xiii,
    14, 60, 67, 174, 185, 198
archlute 125
'Ariete' (Lavigne, Sonate IV) 70
'arioso' (section of Fontana, Sonata Terza) *102,
  103*, 108, 111
Arnold, Denis 135
Arnold, Malcolm 119, 150
Arthur, Bradford 186
articulation 6, 11, 14, **15**, 18, 24, 38, 69, **74–85**,
    88–93, 118, 160, 174 n. 12, 180 n. 12
  duration of 38, 40, 66, 75, **77**, 120
  and metre 36, 37, 38
  and room resonance 45, 187 n. 3
  strength of 38, 40, *68*, **75–6**, 81

  see also tonguing
assimilation (of rhythms) 39
Aubert, Jacques 63
audience (communication of music) 2, **3–4**, 5, 6,
    14, 16, 18, 42, 45, 50, 100, 115, **117**, **124–5**,
    127, 128, 129, 134, 138, 160, 161, 200
  see also orator; rhetoric
authenticity 22, 79, 82, 86, **127–9**, 161, 173,
    194 n. 20
autograph manuscript (of Handel sonatas) xii, 30,
    33, 112, 181 n. 24
avant-garde music and techniques 24, 50, 75, 119,
    156, 173, 181, 199 n. 64

Babell, William 179
Bach, Carl Philipp Emanuel 47, 126, 127, 147,
    149, 175, 177, 182, 190, 195
Bach, Johann Christian 147
Bach, Johann Sebastian 5, 6, 61, 72, 94, 113, 174,
    176, 177, 183, 187, 189
  music for or suited to recorders 16, 20, 85, 127,
    128, 193, 196
Badings, Henk 155, 199 n. 63
Baglioni, Giovanni (the Muse Euterpe) ii, vii
Bamforth, Dennis 200
Bärenreiter (publishers) vii, 145, 171, 191, 193,
    196
barlines (bars) 14, 31, 34, 36, 37, 86, 112
Baroque bow 76, 78, 125, 134
'Baroque era' 112, 173 n. 1
Barsanti, Francesco 135, 184, 195 n. 4, 198 n. 42
Bartlett, Clifford vii, viii
Bassano, Giovanni 14
bass (continuo bass) **xii**, 7, 9, 10, 13–14, 67, 107,
    114, 117, 118, **125–6**, 130, 131, 132, *136–7*,
    138
  in Fontana, Sonata Terza *102*, 108, 111–12
  in Handel, sonatas in Dm. and Gm. *26–9*, 30,
    32, 33, 34, 35, 37, 38, 39, 72, 84, 178 n. 52
  in Lavigne, sonate 'La Persan' 67, 68
  in Telemann, sonata in Dm. 47, *48*, 52, *51*, 58,
    122
basse danse, see dance
bassoon 125, 130, 131, 139, 197
bass recorder 30, 79, 80, 125, 157
bass viol 125